Praise for
Tolkien: A Biography

"White's approach is to render his subject as clearly as possible. . . . [He] also traces neatly Tolkien's key influences from Icelandic myths to Beowulf, and makes a fair attempt to reveal the author's labored writing process."   —*The Times* (London)

"Michael White is an industrious and enthusiastic author of some twenty books, including biographies of Stephen Hawking and Leonardo da Vinci. [He] . . . makes a good point with the inclusion of Tolkien as one of that disparate group who instinctively tapped Jung's "collective unconscious" with regard to popular culture. Like Steven Spielberg, the Beatles, and Picasso, Tolkien, who had no patience with modern technology and forms of entertainment, somehow had the recipe for something people would love."   —*The Irish Times*

"White does a good job in explaining the sources, both linguistic and literary, for *The Lord of the Rings.* The relationship with C.S. Lewis is handled well, particularly the simmering rivalry between the outwardly clubbable men."   —*Scotland on Sunday*

"Fans of Middle-earth should find this book enhances their enjoyment and understanding of Tolkien's fantasy world."
—Good Book Guide

"[White] has clearly done his research into Tolkien's Birmingham childhood, his time in the trenches, and then his career as an Oxford don, as well as his friendship with C.S. Lewis."
—*London Observer*

"If you wondered what is really behind those hobbits, those battle scenes, the seemingly everlasting friendship and quest, wonder no more."   —*The Courier-Mail* (Queensland, Australia)

continued . . .

"White's Tolkien is a quick, vivacious figure, laughter-loving and prey to the most petty of human foibles. It is small wonder that the greatest inventor of worlds should also have invented himself." —*Independent on Sunday* (London)

"Immensely readable." —*Irish Independent*

"White brings a fan's passion to the subject. . . . [His] work does touch on a few points that make the ears stand up. . . . Those looking for an introduction to Tolkien's life and the themes that inform his work will find much of interest." —*Sunday Age* (Melbourne)

"This new biography . . . will undoubtedly find a wide, receptive audience. . . . And while [White's] approach is sympathetic, he does expose some of the warts in Tolkien's life." —*Sydney Morning Herald*

"White provides a readable summary . . . of Tolkien's life." —*Canberra Times* (Australia)

"White's biography is packed with everything. . . . He is particularly good on the troubled relationship with C.S. Lewis, whom Tolkien managed to convert to Christianity but not Catholicism. Here White fulfills his promise, made in the book's introduction, to get away from sanitized accounts of the author's life." —*The Weekend Australian*

"Vivid and accessible." —*The Independent* (London)

"White knows a lot about Tolkien and his works, and his judgment of these will probably satisfy fans, for whom the book is principally written." —*The Daily Telegraph* (London)

Tolkien

A Biography

MICHAEL WHITE

Previously published as
Critical Lives: J.R.R. Tolkien

NEW AMERICAN LIBRARY

New American Library
Published by New American Library, a division of
Penguin Group (USA) Inc., 375 Hudson Street,
New York, New York 10014, U.S.A.
Penguin Books Ltd, 80 Strand,
London WC2R 0RL, England
Penguin Books Australia Ltd, 250 Camberwell Road,
Camberwell, Victoria 3124, Australia
Penguin Books Canada Ltd, 10 Alcorn Avenue,
Toronto, Ontario, Canada M4V 3B2
Penguin Books (N.Z.) Ltd, Cnr Rosedale and Airborne Roads,
Albany, Auckland 1310, New Zealand

Penguin Books Ltd, Registered Offices:
80 Strand, London WC2R 0RL, England

Published by New American Library, a division of Penguin Group (USA) Inc.
Previously published in an Alpha Books edition as *Critical Lives: J.R.R. Tolkien.*

First New American Library Printing, November 2003
10   9   8   7   6   5   4   3   2   1

For Jennifer and Peter

Contents

Acknowledgements

Many people have had a hand in making this book happen. I would especially like to thank my agent Russ Galen for handling often tricky negotiations and my editors both sides of the Atlantic, Alan Samson and Tim Whiting at Little, Brown in London and Gary Goldstein at Alpha in New York. Invaluable assistance has come from Jude Fisher, from Peter Schneider who offered information about the value of literature and from Josephina Miruvin who was always enthusiastic and gave me some great internet contacts.

My thanks go also to Michael Crichton, for without his help an entirely different author would have written this book.

Finally, heartfelt gratitude goes to my wife Lisa for offering important objective insights about Tolkien I would not otherwise have figured out.

Michael White, September 2002

Introduction

On the scale of things I came quite late to Tolkien's work. I was seventeen when a school friend gave me their dog-eared copy of *The Lord of the Rings* and told me I really should read it. But, although I was slow to join the ranks of devotees, I made up for it quickly by reading Tolkien's most famous book eight times in a row. I was so obsessed by this tale of heroism, tragedy and ageless adventure, that as soon as I finished the final chapter, I was compelled to begin Chapter One again.

Soon, I was collecting every scrap of information I could find about Tolkien. I read *The Hobbit* of course and tackled Tolkien's translation of *Beowulf*, his *Farmer Giles of Ham*, *Leaf By Niggle* and other, less well-known works. Then, in 1977, a year after I had been introduced to *The Lord of the Rings*, news of the long-awaited publication of *The Silmarillion* reached me. On the day of publication, I was queuing at the local bookshop at 8 a.m. ready to pick up my pre-ordered copy, and an hour later, as I headed for the bus-stop and the ride home, I was reading of elves and men and was bumping into commuters hurrying off to work.

Around this time, I had become involved in music. I was learning to play the guitar and getting into bands at school and in my first year at university. In complete contrast to the ethos of the time (punk was just happening), I formed groups with names like Palantir and started writing songs about Galadriel that had middle-eights in Elvish. I shudder at the memory. But actually, from a distant perspective, it is clear to me that, immature as it undoubtedly was, my devotion to Tolkien had sprung from something exceptionally powerful. There must have been something irresistibly attractive about Middle-earth to cause such a profound effect.

It was only later that I discovered how many millions of other people had gone the same way and become huge Tolkien fans; some had even formed bands and sung songs about Middle-earth. Indeed, I was introduced to *The Lord of the Rings* by a girlfriend, and during my first year at university, having a copy of the book under your arm in the common room was considered a great way to pick up girls. And I know at least one person who studied Icelandic to degree level after being inspired by Tolkien and his work. But inevitably perhaps, there was also a growing body of those who disliked Tolkien simply because so many were devoted to the man's work. Theirs was an anti-fashion reaction and it is easy to understand. Whenever anyone gets obsessed with a subject they become boring and often irritating to those outside the frame. Tolkien doesn't appeal to everyone and some of those who genuinely felt nothing for *The Lord of the Rings* had to react with scorn and cynicism.

During the year I discovered Tolkien, one of my best friends at school decided that he would reject the overtures of *The Lord of the Rings* and kick out against what he saw as the 'insidious cult of Middle-earth'. He did not once try to read the book but instead studied avidly an (admittedly very funny) National Lampoon spoof called *Bored of the Rings*. He even ignored me when I asked him how he could possibly find a spoof funny if he had not troubled himself to read the original.

Needless to say, after a while I calmed down. Gradually I let fade the Tolkien influence and began writing songs about love, sex and death and more importantly, I began to read more widely. But I never left Tolkien behind entirely, I always had a soft spot for *The Lord of the Rings* and remembered the story with fondness. In my early twenties, I moved to Oxford, and within a few years I had forged a career as a writer. I heard about Tolkien's life in the city and how he, C.S. Lewis and the other Inklings met at a pub called the Eagle and Child and I would often take myself off there for a beer in the hope that some sort of inspiration might seep out from the walls. And so, when I was approached to write this biography, I felt an immediate attraction to the task.

However, before the ink was dry on the publishers' contract, I recognised that returning to my youthful obsession brought with it potential hazards, for I would have to read *The Lord of the Rings* again almost twenty-five years after that last of eight times. Part of me relished the thought, but at the same time, I was filled with anxiety – would I like the book now, a quarter of a century on?

When I had completed the last chapter for the eighth time back in 1977, I was about to go to university, I was listening to Yes albums and I had hair down to my shoulders. Now, here I was, middle-aged with a wife and three children, I had read a thousand books since those far off days and I now listened to Yes only very occasionally. Could I still identify with Aragorn?

Would I still hanker for more information about Gandalf and the other Istari? Would I even care what happened to Frodo and Sam? On many occasions, I had re-read old favourites only to find they no longer held the slightest attraction. Would *The Lord of the Rings* go the same way? Would I turn into my cynical school friend and prefer *Bored of the Rings*?

I bought a new copy of *The Lord of the Rings* and took it home. For days it sat on the dining-room table, unopened. It was transferred to the bedroom and then the bathroom and still the spine remained uncreased. I began researching this book and learning anew about Tolkien's life and times, and finally, after weeks of prevarication, I managed to open the cover of his greatest work.

Naturally, I was enthralled once more. Little of the magic had gone and indeed I began to find new aspects to the story, new insights that only came to me now, things that had passed me by or had been of little interest to my younger self. I was delighted by this and not a little relieved, for how could I have written about Tolkien if I no longer appreciated his work?

Yet now, now that I've immersed myself in the world of Middle-earth once more and feel invigorated by the experience, I see that my anxieties were actually ill-founded. I believe there are those who love Tolkien's world and will remain life-long fans, and there are those who will never appreciate it.

Today, my anti-Tolkien friend is as middle-aged as me and he still scoffs at my fascination with *The Lord of the Rings*. He has not read the book (now of course, Waterstone's 'Book of the 20th Century'), and he has absolutely no intention of ever reading it. But then, as the saying goes, 'Tolkien is Hobbit-forming.'

During the preliminary research for this book I was encouraged to discover that my search engine of choice threw up some

450,000 websites connected with Tolkien or *The Lord of the Rings*, and that many of these sites are amazingly professional and entertaining. But, upon reading some of the 'official' material linked to Tolkien it has struck me how much of it is ridiculously subjective, almost devotional.

I consider myself a long-standing fan, but I am dismayed by the over-protective stance of 'official' or 'authorised' material about Professor Tolkien. The published letters relate almost nothing of his private life. Veils of mystery are spread over anything personal, such as his relationship with his wife, Edith and his friendship with C.S. Lewis and some of his fellow Inklings. No authorised description ever questions Tolkien's inner drives or tries to identify the man's personal demons. Worse still, the accepted wisdom concerning Tolkien's emotions, his motivations and his opinions are rarely investigated. Tolkien was, as this book shows, a good man, a moral and upright, trustworthy and very intelligent man, but he was not in line for canonisation.

I have seen such deifying before. During the research for my biography of Sir Isaac Newton, *Isaac Newton: The Last Sorcerer*, I found his disciples had, for their own reasons, kept concealed for centuries material that, when unearthed, revealed the fuller human being behind the school textbooks. Another of my subjects, Stephen Hawking, is still painted by some of his associates as being someone beyond the normal human ken. In both cases, a search beneath the surface revealed for me a world of colour and vitality.

In writing this book, I did not set out in search of monsters and I found only the expected, fictitious ones. But, creative people are rarely anodyne despite the best efforts of their protectors to make them appear so. I would like to think true fans search for a little more than monochrome images of their heroes. And as a Tolkien fan, I hope I've here provided, if not Technicolor, then at least a little pastel shading to give a more colourful image of the creator of Middle-earth, the most popular author in history.

CHAPTER I

Childhood

Professor John Ronald Reuel Tolkien is pedalling fast and he can feel the sweat under his collar. It's a warm, early summer afternoon soon after the end of college term and the traffic along The High is light. By midday he has seen a post-graduate student and addressed the problems she had interpreting an Anglo-Saxon text, bought fresh ink and paper in a shop on Turl Street, returned a book to the college library and found the copy of a poem he was writing for *The Oxford Magazine* which he had lost among the papers in his college room a week earlier. He normally makes sure to be home for lunch with the family, but today he had to attend a faculty meeting and this meant he was obliged to lunch in college. Now he is returning home to begin ploughing through a daunting pile of School Certificate exam papers that has been on his desk since the beginning of the week.

As he passes Carfax Tower in the centre of Oxford the clock

strikes three and he begins to peddle still faster; at best, he calculates, he may have just two hours in his study before he has to
cycle back into town again for another meeting, this time in the
Senior Common Room at Merton College over a late tea, and as
he rides he calculates that he might at best manage to mark
three exam papers.[1]

Up the Banbury Road he cycles, and turning right and then
left, he emerges onto Northmoor Road where at Number 20,
the Tolkien family have lived since early that year, 1930. As
Tolkien swings his leg over the saddle and balances on one side
of the still moving bike, he glides through the side gate and
along the path. He greets his wife, Edith, by poking his head
around the kitchen door and smiling. But then he sees that his
baby daughter, five-month-old Priscilla is awake and gurgling
merrily in her mother's arms. He walks over and pecks his wife
on the cheek and tickles Priscilla under the chin before heading
back to the door and striding along the corridor to his study at
the south side of the house.

Tolkien's study is a cosy room lined with bookshelves that
create a tunnel as you enter the room before they fan out to each
side. The professor's desk is positioned so he has a view south-
ward toward a neighbour's garden directly ahead of him, and to
his right is another large window that faces the road across an
expanse of well-manicured lawn. On his desk, Tolkien has a
writing pad and a collection of pens in a container, and to each
side, papers are piled. On the left are examination papers to be
read (a tall pile) and to the right, papers already read (a significantly smaller stack).

Tolkien makes himself comfortable at the desk, pulls his pipe
from the pocket of his jacket, stuffs it full with fresh tobacco
and lights the pipe with exaggerated care. Sucking on the pipe,

he leans over to pluck the top paper from the pile on his left, brings it in front of him and starts to read.

Marking School Certificate exam papers, the work of sixteen-year-olds, is tedious and almost always boring, but it helps pay the bills and with a wife and four children to support, Tolkien needs to augment his professor's salary. Soulless as the work usually is, Tolkien takes pride in reading each piece of work carefully and pays attention to every detail. And so, for the next half hour he concentrates upon a single manuscript. Occasionally he scribbles a comment in the margin and once in a while he places a small tick at the end of a paragraph. He slowly turns the pages and all around is peace and silence broken only by the visit of a bird to the window ledge and a light breeze brushing leaves upon the study window.

After a while, Tolkien is satisfied he has judged the exam paper fairly and places it on the right-hand pile before plucking another from the pile to his left. For a further few minutes he reads the opening pages of this new paper and then, turning the page, he is surprised to see before him a blank sheet of paper. Pausing just for a moment and feeling as though he had been rewarded for his day's labours – one fewer page to mark – he leans back in his chair and looks around the room. Suddenly, his eye is drawn to the carpet close to one of the desk legs. He notices a tiny hole in the fabric and stares at it for long moments, day-dreaming. Then, he turns back to the paper in front of him and begins to write: 'In a hole in the ground there lived a hobbit' . . .

Although Tolkien had no idea why he wrote this and even less awareness of how much this outpouring from his subconscious would mean for him, his family, and the future of English literature, he knew that with that single sentence he had written something interesting, so interesting in fact that he was then inspired to, as he later put it, 'find out what hobbits are like'.

And in that moment, from a single sentence, generated perhaps by boredom, a sentence that maybe had been trying to find expression for a long time, came the impetus that would lead to the writing of *The Hobbit* and *The Lord of the Rings*. Along with *The Silmarillion* and a vast collection of miscellaneous notes on the mythology of Middle-earth, his work would, in the fullness of time, become globally famous, give pleasure and offer inspiration to millions and play a crucial role in creating an entire literary genre, that of fantasy fiction. Within a few years of that fateful afternoon, many thousands would know a great deal about hobbits and by the 1960s, hobbits and the world in which they lived would become as familiar as any Hollywood star or Royal figurehead. For many, Middle-earth is considered more than a fantasy realm. From what could have been a mere one-off line scribbled on a scrap of paper in the study of an obscure professor's study, Tolkien's writings took on a life of their own, they blossomed into heroic tales, self-contained, self-consistent and utterly absorbing; a mythology for the modern mind.

J.R.R. Tolkien's family background was, in many ways, completely unremarkable, almost plain. His father, Arthur Tolkien, was a bank clerk who worked at Lloyds bank in Birmingham. Arthur's father, John had been a piano manufacturer and sheet-music seller, but by the time Arthur Tolkien had come of age, Tolkien pianos had stopped selling, the business was liquidated and John Tolkien was made bankrupt.

Arthur was acutely aware of the dangers of self-employment, which in part accounts for his decision to opt for a safe job with the local bank. But promotion within the Birmingham branch of

Lloyds was to prove slow, and in spite of his enthusiasm, Arthur knew the only chance of preferment would come from filling dead men's shoes. So when, late in 1888, the offer of a position overseas came up, he did not have to think too long or too hard about whether or not to take it.

The job was in the outpost of Bloemfontein in South Africa working for the Bank of Africa. This, Arthur knew, offered huge potential for a young man with ambition. The Orange Free State of which Bloemfontein was the capital was becoming an important mining region with new gold and diamond discoveries encouraging investment from European and American venture capitalists. The only problem for Arthur was that a year before he set sail for the Cape, he had fallen in love and proposed to a rather pretty eighteen-year-old woman named Mabel Suffield, and making this career move would mean leaving her behind.

Mabel's family, the Suffields, did not entirely approve of young Arthur and hoped for something better for their daughter. However, this was an opinion based upon snobbery rather than anything to do with the character of Arthur Tolkien. The Suffields considered the Tolkiens to be little more than impoverished immigrants (although they could trace back their English ancestry several centuries before looking further still to distant family roots in Saxony), but they had their own social inadequacies. Mabel's father was the son of a draper who had managed his own shop but his business had crumbled and he was as bankrupt as Tolkien. By the time Arthur and Mabel met, John Suffield was working as a travelling salesman for a disinfectant company called Jeyes.

Little of this influenced Arthur or Mabel, except that Mr Suffield prohibited his daughter from marrying her sweetheart for at least two years after young Tolkien proposed to her, which meant that when Arthur took the posting abroad, Mabel was obliged to wait for news from her fiancé and hope that soon his prospects would allow her to travel out there to join him so they could be wed.

Arthur did not disappoint. By 1890, he had been made manager of the Bloemfontein branch of the Bank of Africa and was set for the fast track. Feeling suitably settled, he wrote to Mabel Suffield to ask her to join him so they could marry. Mabel was now twenty-one and the couple had kept their relationship blossoming past the two-year condition Suffield had imposed, so, ignoring any misgivings of her family, in March 1891, Mabel bought herself a ticket for the steamer *Roslin Castle* and was soon on her way to the Cape.

Today, Bloemfontein, set in the heart of the Orange Free State, is a rather nondescript city, but towards the end of the nineteenth century when Arthur Tolkien first arrived there, it was little more than a ramshackle collection of a few hundred buildings. Strong winds blow in from the desert and sweep through the town. Now, most residents can shelter in air-conditioned malls and homes; in the 1890s there were few creature comforts and life was little better for the white settlers than it is now for the black Africans who live in a shanty town that girdles the modern city centre of Bloemfontein.

The couple were married in Cape Town Cathedral on 16 April 1891 and they spent a brief honeymoon at a hotel in nearby Sea Point. But when the excitement and the novelty had passed, Mabel quickly realised that life in this place was not going to be easy.

She was soon desperately lonely and found it hard to make friends amongst the other settlers in the town. Most of the population were Afrikaans, descendants of Dutch settlers and they did not mix readily with the English population. The Tolkiens met other ex-pats from Britain, Mabel played hostess, but she found the town lacking in almost every respect. There was a tennis court, a few shops and a small park; it was a far cry from the bustle of Birmingham and the constant excitement of big city life. She also hated the climate, the scorching hot and humid summers and the freezing winters.

But she had no choice but to try to adapt. Arthur was work-ing flat-out to make his mark in the Bank of Africa and was rarely at home. He seemed to be enjoying himself, which only exacerbated the situation. Arthur had his friends at work and was constantly busy, so there was not much time for him to ponder the less attractive aspects of life in Bloemfontein. He appears to have spared little thought on Mabel's unhappiness and saw it as a passing depression she would get over soon enough.

Mabel did try to make the most of things and was clearly devoted to her husband. Sometimes she managed to drag him away from the bank and they would go off on long walks together or play tennis at the town's single club. At other times the two of them simply sat and read to each other at home.

And if Mabel was merely bored then all that soon changed when she discovered she was pregnant with their first child. They were both delighted, but Mabel was also concerned that the town could not provide adequate health care for her and a new-born baby. She hinted that it might be best for them to take a break and return to England to have the baby, but Arthur con-stantly argued that he could not afford the time, and so Mabel decided that, on balance, she would rather stay and take her chances in Bloemfontein than face the long journey home and childbirth without a husband there to support her.

Their son was born on 3 January 1892. They called him John, but there was some debate over the boy's full name. Arthur insisted they keep up the tradition of 'Reuel', a middle name that had been given to several of the Tolkien boys over the generations, whereas Mabel preferred Ronald. Eventually they agreed upon both, so the baby was christened in Bloemfontein Cathedral on 31 January 1892 with the names John Ronald Reuel Tolkien. However, he was never called John by anyone. His parents, and later his wife, called him Ronald. At school he was often referred to by his friends as John Ronald, and at university he was called 'Tollers', a rather gauche epithet typical of the time. To his colleagues, he was called J.R.R.T. or more formally Professor Tolkien. To the world, he became known as J.R.R. Tolkien, or most usually just plain Tolkien.

His earliest days, the start of his childhood in South Africa, was every bit as exotic as one would expect and a world away from what he would have experienced if those years had been spent in Birmingham. A few family tales have survived and were remembered into adulthood by Tolkien then related to his own children. There was the time the neighbour's monkey escaped and leapt the fence to enter the family's garden where it proceeded to rip asunder three of the boy's pinafores hanging on the washing line. On another occasion, one of the servants, a house-boy named Isaak decided to take baby Ronald to show him off to his family who were living on the outskirts of the town. Amazingly, the Tolkiens did not sack him on the spot.

It was certainly a dangerous environment in which to raise a child. The weather went from extreme to extreme and the baby's first South African summer was a trial for Mabel. The flies were incessant, the heat unrelenting. The garden harboured deadly snakes and dangerous insects aplenty and when the baby was little over a year old he was bitten by a tarantula. His life was saved only by the quick wits and skill of his nanny who located the bite and sucked out the venom.[2]

Life improved greatly for Mabel soon after the baby was born. Arthur was still deeply entrenched at the bank, but in the spring of 1892, Mabel's sister and brother-in-law, May and Walter Incledon, arrived in Bloemfontein. Walter had business interests in South Africa and decided to spend some time surveying the gold mines of the area. Mabel now had plenty of company and some help with the baby, but even so, she was becoming homesick and more and more resentful of Arthur spending his entire time away from the family. Things were further complicated when she discovered she was pregnant again.

Hilary Tolkien was born on 17 February 1894, and not a moment too soon for Mabel who had had to endure a particularly brutal summer heavily pregnant. Not surprisingly, soon after the birth she hit a new low. Her sister and brother-in-law had returned to Europe and she had to face the prospect of raising two very young children in this hostile environment and with little help from her husband. She was lucky that Hilary turned out to be a healthy child, but Ronald was constantly ill with childhood complaints – a bad chest that was made worse by the heat and dust in the summer and the chill wind in winter, and later, a succession of skin complaints and eye infections. By November 1894, Mabel was desperate for a change of scene and some fresher air and took the boys to Cape Town for a much needed holiday. Arthur, who (if he could only have admitted it) also needed a break, was adamant he could not allow himself time off for even a short vacation. He stayed in Bloemfontein for yet another punishing summer.

Upon their return, it was clear Mabel had now set her heart on the family having an extended break away from the dust and the wind. She tried hard to persuade Arthur to take time to visit his family in England. He had been away from home for almost six years, he deserved a sabbatical at least. But he would hear none of it, claiming that an extended leave could endanger his position within the bank. Instead, it was agreed that Mabel and the boys would return to England without him and spend the South African summer there. If all went well he could join them later.

So, in April 1895, Mabel, Ronald and Hilary sailed from Cape Town aboard the SS *Guelph*. Three weeks later, they docked at Southampton where they were met by Mabel's youngest sister, Emily Jane who was introduced to the boys as Aunt Jane. They travelled to Birmingham by train and a room was found for them in the tiny Suffield home in the King's Heath district of the city.

It was extremely cramped. Mabel and the boys shared a bed, and five other adults lived in the house; Mabel's parents, her sister, their younger brother, William, and a lodger, a young, blond insurance clerk named Edwin Neave who, when he wasn't flirting with Jane, entertained Ronald by playing the banjo and singing music-hall songs. But compared with the Orange Free State, life was comfortable; the weather was mild, the wind did not howl through the rafters so hard it seemed the house would fall down, there were no tarantulas in the garden nor snakes in the grass. Mabel missed her husband, but then he had chosen not to join them. For Mabel, the welfare of the boys came first.

As one would expect, Arthur missed his family. He wrote frequently and expressed his sadness at their separation but still he maintained he could not leave his position, even for a few months, and he seems to have been quite obsessed with the notion that others might usurp him, damaging his career irreparably.

Meanwhile the whole region of South Africa was facing political chaos. Led by Paul Kruger, the Boers were threatening rebellion against the British, and from their base in the Transvaal the Boers had set themselves up as a formidable guerrilla force. By 1895, as Arthur Tolkien was managing the finances of wealthy Europeans in Bloemfontein, Kruger's fighters formed a military alliance between the Transvaal and the Orange Free State that would, within a few short years, push the British into all-out war in South Africa. It was not a comfortable time for British citizens living in new commercial centres like Bloemfontein and in some respects Arthur was relieved his family were far away, safe in Britain.

But then suddenly, in November 1895, there was more bad news. Arthur wrote to Mabel to say he was ill with rheumatic fever. This was a very serious disease and Mabel pleaded with Arthur to take time off work and to join the family in England. But he refused steadfastly, now claiming he could not face the cold of the English winter.

Summer came to Bloemfontein and with it Arthur Tolkien's condition degenerated rapidly. Hearing this news, Mabel decided she must return with the boys to South Africa. So, late in January 1896, arrangements were made for her return voyage; the liner was booked and the date set. On 14 February 1896, Ronald, then just turned four dictated a letter to his father that was then written out for him. In it he told his father how much he was missing him and how he was looking forward to seeing him again after so long away.

The letter was never sent, for the next day news arrived at the Suffield home that Arthur had died after a severe haemorrhage. Mabel, grief-stricken, packed immediately, placed the boys in the care of her parents and caught the first liner to the Cape. By the time she reached Bloemfontein, her husband of under five years had been buried in the local cemetery.

And so, at the age of four, Tolkien's life was to enter a new stage. Gone was the wilderness of Bloemfontein to be replaced by the industrial sprawl of Birmingham, England's second city, one of the powerhouses of the British Empire. Gone was the distant horizon, the red sun low over the distant hills; gone were games under a shade in the sweltering dusty heat of a January afternoon. Instead, young Ronald's new world was dominated by terraced houses and brick chimneys, concrete backyards and the smoke of the local factories.

In spite of the fact that Arthur had worked long hours, ruined his health through his labours and died convinced he was unable to spare time for his family, he left his wife and two young sons with precious little with which to build a new life without him. His capital had been invested in Bonanza Mines but the dividend provided Mabel the sum of only thirty shillings a week, which in 1896 was barely sufficient to eke out a modest existence for the three of them. Mabel's brother-in-law, Walter Incledon, provided the boys with a small allowance, but neither the Suffields nor Arthur's parents had the resources to help financially. By the time of Arthur's death, Mabel and the young brothers had been living in the tiny Suffield home for over nine months and the cramped conditions were to nobody's liking; a cheap rented place would have to be found as soon as possible.

By the summer Mabel had found the family a tiny semi-detached cottage, Number 5 Gracewell, in the hamlet of Sarehole, a mile and a half outside the city, to the south. Today, Sarehole is a suburb of Birmingham, concreted over and densely populated, but when the Tolkiens set up home there it was still a peaceful and tranquil spot far from the hubbub and noise of the city, surrounded by fields and woods. The cottage was a pretty, brick building at the end of a small terrace, and Ronald felt at home there immediately.

As an old man he could still recall in some detail his memories of his time living with his brother and mother in this country idyll. The house was small but comfortable and the elderly neighbours were friendly and supportive. Hilary was only two and a half at the time of the move, but before too long he was playing with his older brother in the fields around the house and the pair went on long, adventurous walks. Sometimes they would trek to the nearest village, Hall Green, and gradually they made friends with the children who lived there.

The boys shared an unusually strong bond. Without a father figure the only male company they had was each other and not surprisingly, both of them also became exceptionally close to their mother. Those pre-school days were filled with invented games and flights of the imagination. The boys fantasised that a local farmer was an evil wizard, and they turned the conservative and peaceful English countryside into a theme park of the mind in which good and evil wizards struggled for control of the land. Throughout the long summer days they went on crusades and journeys into strange lands (the local woods) to protect the innocent against the baddies. At other times, they picked blackberries in a place they christened the Dell. Most interesting as a later reference point in Tolkien's work, there was a mill close to Gracewell. It was run by a father and son, both of whom seemed to have been particularly unsociable. The older miller had a long black beard but was relatively passive whilst his son, whom the boys christened the White Ogre (because he was always covered in flour) appears to have been genuinely frightening and extremely unfriendly. Almost half a century later, these childhood figures were to take on new life as the unctuous miller, Sandyman and his unpleasant son, Ted.

For Ronald, fantasies about ogres and dragons became better defined when he began to read. His mother encouraged him and introduced him to many of the great childrens' books of the day, evocative tales such as the newly published *Treasure Island*, *Alice in Wonderland* and traditional stories such as *The Pied Piper*. But most important to the seven-year-old Ronald was a book called the *Red Fairy Book* by Andrew Lang. Lang, a Scottish academic who collected, adapted and wrote his own fairy tales became very successful with his anthologies. Ronald adored them and read with relish story after story just so long as it mentioned dragons and sea serpents, mythical adventures and the deeds of noble knights.

Tolkien quickly became an avid reader and before long Mabel became aware of his enthusiasm and what seemed a natural ability with language. She had undertaken the preliminary education of both boys and when Ronald was seven she began to teach him French and the rudiments of Latin which he took to immediately. Around this time, Mabel, who was a capable, self-taught pianist, also tried to interest the boys in music. Hilary was keen, but Ronald showed little aptitude for playing the piano.

It is a strange fact that although Tolkien wrote a great deal of poetry and what could be called lyrics, words he placed in the mouths of his elves and hobbit characters, throughout his life, he had almost no interest in music. He rarely attended concerts; his future wife, Edith, was an accomplished pianist, but he listened to her play only occasionally, and he found jazz, jive, and later, pop music, offensive and irritating. Music seems to have been a blank area in his artistic tastes.[3]

For Tolkien, this was a happy time. He loved Sarehole and his imagination had been fired up by the discovery of books. It was a period he would cherish in memory and savour for the rest of his life. As a man, this all-too-brief interlude shone out as the most peaceful and dreamlike time. Almost nothing remained in memory of his time in South Africa; his father, a man whom he had known only fleetingly, now became a mere shadow and then faded still further. For Tolkien, his childhood *was* this time in Sarehole with his brother and beloved mother; it seemed nothing of any significance had preceded it.

And then it all changed again. The wonder years of Sarehole could not last forever, and by the end of 1900, just as Ronald was approaching his ninth birthday, Mabel was forced to move them all back to Birmingham.

There were many reasons for the move. Mabel wanted the boys to attend a school in the city rather than the country. In 1899, Ronald had taken the entrance examination for the prestigious King Edward's, his father's old school. He had failed on his first attempt, but upon retaking the exam the following year, he had passed and was subsequently offered a place to begin there in September 1900. However, the school was four miles from Sarehole and Mabel could not afford the train fare, so each day Ronald had to walk most of the eight-mile round-trip. Clearly, it was impractical for the family to stay in the country no matter how much a move would pain the boys.

But there was another reason for the move and one that was perhaps even more compelling for Mabel. In 1899, she had discovered Catholicism and had begun the process of converting to Rome, and the nearest Catholic church was in central Birmingham.

Until the untimely death of her husband, Mabel seems to have been completely orthodox in her religious leanings, but it is easy to see why she found solace within the Roman Church. After all, Ronald and Hilary had each other, but Mabel had few friends, and although she had remained close to her family, especially her sister Jane, she had not known her husband's family well. John Tolkien, Ronald's paternal grandfather, had died within six months of his son's death and Mabel had little in common with her mother-in-law, Mary Tolkien.

Beyond this, Mabel Tolkien appears to have shown absolutely no interest in remarrying. The opportunity to find romance was, of course, slim. Living in the countryside with her two young sons, almost penniless and approaching thirty, she was not the most eligible of women. There was also the fact that she wanted to bring her boys up as she saw fit, and being an independent, strong-minded character, she would not have found it easy to simply take on a new relationship in order to provide a father-figure for her sons.

Yet, even Mabel could not have realised the full consequences of her decision, for her conversion meant facing the utter rejection of her family. Mabel's father, John Suffield, had been brought up a strict Methodist and had in later years become a Unitarian. He loathed the Catholic Church with all his being and Mabel's adoption of Rome infuriated him so much he refused to have anything more to do with her. Things were then made worse when Mabel's brother-in-law, Walter Incledon, who had spent some time with the Tolkiens in Bloemfontein, decided he too could not accept Mabel's decision.

Walter had grown relatively wealthy from a succession of wise investments and had risen to become a pillar of the Anglican community in Birmingham. Mabel's news not only offended him personally, far worse, it had the potential to embarrass him socially, and as a consequence, the small allowance he had been providing his sister-in-law and nephews since Arthur's death was abruptly withdrawn. From just about managing, Mabel was now facing financial disaster.

Of course, such antipathy only drove her further into Papal arms. From 1900, she rarely spoke to her father or her brother-in-law and her relationship with Mary Tolkien (another anti-papist) went from being nondescript to almost non-existent. Now her only contact with either family came via her sister and brother.

Personal relationships could be dealt with, but what was to be done about money? Mabel could not work because she could rely on no one to look after Ronald and Hilary, so she simply had to try to make ends meet, to find a cheaper home and to survive on the dividends and interest from Arthur's meagre investments. Their new home in the Mosley district of Birmingham remained in Tolkien's memory long into adulthood, a place he described as 'dreadful'. It was poky and dark, its small windows covered in dirty lace curtains.

Within months, they had moved again because the property turned out to be on the condemned list, ready for demolition. The next house lay close to King's Heath Station, only a few short streets from the Suffields'. But of course, Mabel was unwelcome there and the boys could visit their grandparents only when escorted by Aunt Jane. For the boys, this place came with the attraction of a railway line at the foot of the garden where the locomotives made their last stop at King's Heath before reaching Birmingham's main station, New Street. For Mabel it was a better home because it was situated close to St Dunstan's, a Catholic church she and the boys began attending toward the end of 1901.

It had been a monumental year both for the Tolkiens and for the world at large. The Boer War that had begun two years earlier seemed no nearer resolution and England was still getting used to Queen Victoria's death the previous January and the succession of her ageing playboy son, Edward VII. Understandably, Mabel felt exhausted by all that had happened to her since leaving Bloemfontein and she needed to find some form of stability, some source of inner peace.

Unfortunately the Church of St Dunstan's provided neither. But then, early in 1902, Mabel stumbled upon the Birmingham Oratory in the suburb of Edgbaston, where a community of priests had lived for more than fifty years. The establishment had been founded in 1849 by the most famous churchman of his day, John Henry Newman, who had been a Church of England Minister before converting to Catholicism in 1844. He had stayed for a while in Rome, where he had been received into the Church and had based his own church in Birmingham upon the model of the Congregation of the Oratory in the Vatican. What attracted Mabel was that the resident fathers conducted the sort of services she liked. There was also the great bonus of a nearby Catholic school, St Philip's, and best of all, a small house at a manageable rent had become vacant next door to the school and very close to the church. This house was 26 Oliver Road, and in January 1902, it became Tolkien's fifth Birmingham home.

In many ways this was a very positive move for the Tolkiens and, for a time at least, Mabel was happier than she had been for years. At the Oratorian house she found a little of the support she needed and she made a particularly important friend in one of the priests, a man named Father Francis Xavier Morgan.

Father Francis began to visit Mabel soon after the family moved to Oliver Road and he became their family priest and a close friend of the Tolkiens. He was half-Welsh and half-Anglo-Spanish on his mother's side. Stocky and dark-haired, he was a veritable bundle of energy. His voice boomed and invariably his laugh could be heard resonating throughout the house within minutes of his arrival at the front door. Hilary and Ronald soon grew to love and respect Father Francis and Mabel trusted him implicitly.

But although he could offer Mabel spiritual guidance, Father Francis could do little to alleviate the practical difficulties she faced. Money problems were constant and Oliver Road was in a deprived district. The nearby streets were unsafe after dark and so the boys were usually confined to the house during the long winter months when it grew dark by five.

St Philip's School also turned out to be less than desirable. It was a typical state-run school in a poor district of a British city at the turn of the century. Fifty or more children were crammed into a classroom where they were taught basic grammar and mathematics by uninterested teachers with inadequate training. Academic standards were very low at St Philip's and pupils attending the school were expected to pass through the system having gained little before being packed off to local factories, shops and warehouses.

Fortunately for Ronald and Hilary, Mabel did not let her attachment to the Roman Church blind her to the academic needs of her sons. Within a few months of starting them at St Philip's, she removed them again and began to teach them at home while simultaneously re-establishing contact with King Edward's with a view to getting both boys back there with scholarships.

In 1903, they heard that Ronald had been accepted back at King Edward's School and that his fees would be paid by a scholarship; but Hilary had failed at the same sitting of the entrance exam. Mabel abrogated responsibility for both Ronald's success and Hilary's failure. Ronald, she realised, had much academic promise and a disciplined mind, but his younger sibling was far too dreamy and other-worldly and would therefore have to continue his tuition at home in the hope that he might yet pass at a second attempt.

So, in the autumn, Ronald, now aged eleven, returned to his old school having missed almost two academic years. Fortunately, his mother had taught him well during his absence and he found he could cope readily with the work expected of him. By this time his interest in languages was blossoming and, for his age, he was becoming a very capable linguist. King Edward's provided the best encouragement for him. As well as the standard curriculum languages, French and German, by the age of eleven, Ronald had begun Greek, and through a lively teacher and enthusiast of medieval literature named George Brewerton, he was soon introduced to Chaucer and the well-spring of Middle English.[4] By the end of the year, Mabel could report in a letter to her mother-in-law, Mary Tolkien, that Ronald, recently Confirmed at the Oratory, was doing well and that he was reading books usually given to fifteen-year-olds.

But after the joy of Ronald's Confirmation and First Communion, the beginning of 1904 brought the first hint of further upset. Mabel was feeling exhausted, and it was quickly realised that her fatigue was not simply a result of trying to look after Ronald and Hilary, nor was it solely due to the stress of living in little better than a slum; she had diabetes.

In 1904, there was no effective treatment for diabetes and medical science was then ignorant of the role of insulin. Mabel grew steadily worse and was taken to hospital in April.

At first, no one was sure what to do with the boys. The house in Oliver Road was emptied and the tenancy terminated. Mabel was kept in hospital, but the doctors could do nothing for her but hope that she would recover a little strength. Nobody in the family was able to look after both Tolkien brothers, so they were split up for a while. Hilary was packed off to his grand-parents' house a few streets away and Ronald was taken in by Aunt Jane who had married the Suffields' lodger, the banjo-playing insurance clerk, Edwin Neave. They now lived in Hove near Brighton on the south coast, so Ronald had to leave King Edward's early that academic year and do his best to keep up with his studies by reading recommended texts and practising his language work in notebooks.

By June, against the odds, Mabel had improved enough for her to leave hospital, and with the help of Father Francis the boys were reunited with their mother while she convalesced. The priest had managed to find the family two rooms (a bed-room and a sitting-room) in a tiny cottage owned by the Oratory and rented to the local postman. The cottage lay in the grounds of the Oratory House which was used by ill and elderly members of the Birmingham church, bought for this purpose by the founder, John Henry Newman, half a century earlier. For a small fee, the local postman's wife, Mrs Till, took care of the family and cooked meals for them.

The summer of 1904 was to shine out in Tolkien's memory as perhaps the most idyllic time of his entire childhood, an unsullied image of life in the English countryside, which almost certainly provided the inspiration for the fictional Shire of Middle-earth. He was not really aware how ill his mother was and if he thought about it at all he would have assumed she was on the mend. Ronald had pined for Sarehole since the day they had been forced to leave their cosy little cottage almost four years earlier and their new temporary home in the tiny village of Rednal in the heart of the Worcestershire countryside, far from the smoke and grime of Birmingham, felt like a return to a lost paradise. Each sunny day, and there were many that long summer, Ronald and Hilary went off on long walks in the woods, where they forded the nearby streams, climbed trees, sketched and flew kites.

That summer, the boys grew much closer to Father Francis. He visited them often and joined them on many a long ramble. During those visits he would smoke a pipe, and as an adult, Tolkien claimed that it was from watching the Father so evidently enjoying drawing on a long cherrywood pipe on the veranda of the Oratory House at Rednal that had inspired him to start smoking a pipe himself.

Sadly, the idyll could not last. In September, Ronald had to return to school (while Hilary continued to be taught at home). The walk to the station took half an hour each morning and each evening, and as the autumn closed in, Ronald was met at the station by Hilary bearing a lamp to help them pick their way back to Rednal through the descending grey of evening.

Neither of the boys had realised how ill their mother had become. Mabel's diabetes continued to worsen, and on 14 November she collapsed in front of Ronald and Hilary in the sitting-room of the cottage at Rednal. Shocked and terrified, the boys watched, powerless to help, as their mother slid rapidly into a coma. Six days later, with the boys downstairs comforted by the kindly Mrs Till, Mabel Tolkien died, aged thirty-four. Only Father Francis and Mabel's sister, May Incledon, stood beside her bed as she slipped away.

Chapter 2

Two Women

Tolkien never entirely forgave his relatives for sending his mother to an early grave. He was convinced their rejection of her conversion to the Catholic Church had worsened her illness, and he greatly resented the lack of support she was then given.

Some of this we can certainly put down to natural bitterness over the loss of his mother, but he did also have sound reasons for feeling this way. Mabel was undoubtedly depressed and deeply upset by the reaction to her adoption of Catholicism and this could have sparked off her illness. For Tolkien, the resentment did not subside with the passing of time. In a letter to his son Michael written in 1941, thirty-seven years after his mother's death, he expressed the view that his mother, whom he remembered as being beautiful and intelligent, had suffered much in her life and had become ill because of the persecution she had been subjected to when she had adopted Catholicism. She had, he was sure, died young because of her pain.

Mabel Tolkien's death also had a profound effect upon the development of Ronald's maturing character and his own approach to religion. As an old man, Tolkien claimed that he had been inspired by Catholicism before his mother's death and in another letter to Michael Tolkien written in 1963, he commented: 'I fell in love with the Blessed Sacrament from the beginning – and by the mercy of God never have fallen out again.'[1]

This may well be true, but there is little doubt that Tolkien also associated his mother with Catholicism and he saw her as something of a martyr both to her faith and to the welfare of her sons. For Ronald at the age of twelve, the link between the two, mother and faith, was profound. From that time on he was a devout Catholic, if not evangelical then certainly proselytising, and as we shall see, this religious devotion steered his life and career, but it also informed the roots of his mythology and often guided his pen.

Mabel Tolkien's premature death affected her son in other ways. Ronald had always been a gregarious and extrovert lad and to all outward appearances this aspect of his personality never entirely faded. As an adult, he could talk to anyone about almost anything, but from November 1904, there was a new dark thread running through his personality. He had lived in poverty, he had been moved from one uncomfortable house to another, he had seen and half-comprehended the hostility of his grandparents towards his beloved mother, and he had, in distant memory, suffered the loss of his father. These things had made him adaptable and versatile of spirit, but for him, the seemingly senseless death of his young mother triggered a deep-rooted feeling that ultimately all man-made things are futile, all human endeavour, mere vanity.

This attitude would sometimes overwhelm him, pushing him into dark, depressed periods during which he could hardly bring himself to work. When consumed by such pessimism, he even found it difficult to relate to others around him, including his close friends and family. In one such wretched mood he told a friend: 'What a dreadful, fear-darkened, sorrow-laden world we live in.'[2]

For Tolkien's relatives, the first few days following Mabel's funeral was a time of confusion over what to do with Ronald and Hilary. Shortly before her death, Mabel had appointed Father Francis as the boys' guardian, but they could not live at the Oratory, and although the idea of boarding school was mooted, it was quickly rejected because there was insufficient money available to pay the fees. Ronald was at King Edward's thanks to a scholarship, but this would not stretch to include his board, and Hilary had only just passed the entrance exam and been accepted as a day boy.

The problem was solved when Aunt Beatrice on the Suffield side of the family agreed the boys could stay with her in her house in Stirling Street in the Edgbaston district of Birmingham. Beatrice had married Mabel's younger brother William, but he had died just a few months before his sister, leaving Beatrice alone in a relatively spacious house with spare bedrooms. She was a rather severe woman who showed little emotion to anyone and was still deep in mourning. She gave the boys a large room in her house and offered meals for them, but showed not the slightest interest in them or what they did. Ronald was horrified when one day he came into the kitchen at Stirling Street and found Beatrice poking the ashes of what had been his mother's letters and personal papers. His aunt had borne no malice, it was simply a reflection of her rather arid personality. She had quite simply assumed the boys would not want to keep such things and decided to get rid of them.

At first, Ronald was thoroughly miserable in Stirling Street. He was once more back in the grimy heart of Birmingham, close to where he had lived with his mother before the temporary idyll of Rednal. From his bedroom all he could see was roof after roof, chimney after chimney without even the thrill of the locomotives under the window. Beatrice hardly spoke to the boys and the house was dark and dreary especially during the long winter months immediately after Mabel's death. That first Christmas without his mother was by far the worst Ronald had known or would ever know.

But there was another side to the boys' lives; they had grown to rely upon the Church and their relationship with Father Francis. Indeed, they spent more time at the Oratory than they did in Stirling Street. Each morning, as soon as they were up, Hilary and Ronald would race each other along the street, past their old school, St Philip's, and the decrepit house they once shared with their mother in Oliver Road and on to the gates of the Oratory where they would serve mass for Father Francis and have breakfast with him. Then, it was either a brisk walk, or occasionally, a horse-bus ride to school. When the final bell rang at four o'clock, the brothers would meet outside the school gates and run back to the Oratory to have tea and spend the early evening with their guardian.

Such a warm relationship with Father Francis melded Ronald to the Catholic Church and reinforced a need in him to follow his mother's devotion to Rome, and neither the Tolkiens nor the Suffields attempted to confuse the boys by forcing them away from the Church and the path their mother had prepared for them. Walter Incledon and Mabel's sister May took the brothers on holiday with their two young girls, Mary and Marjorie, and Hilary and Ronald were always welcomed at the home of their grandparents.

Ronald also loved school and this provided him with another important distraction. He was popular both with the other pupils and the teachers and showed a broad interest in academic subjects as well as sport. He especially enjoyed rugby. At the end of 1905, Tolkien came top of his year and had made a close friend in a boy one year younger than him named Christopher Wiseman.

Christopher Wiseman shared many of Ronald's interests. He was academically precocious and even though he was a year younger than Tolkien he had achieved second place in the school ratings in 1905, thus prompting a friendly rivalry between the boys that continued until they left King Edward's. He and Wiseman shared a great love for languages and their origins. George Brewerton, who had introduced Ronald to the joys of Middle English a few years early, now felt that both his very bright pupils were ready for Anglo-Saxon and it was thanks to him the pair first grew acquainted with pre-Chaucerian literature and in particular the high drama of a great classic of the Old English cannon, *Beowulf*.

During the long summer vacations when there was little pressure to revise for exams as there always was at Easter, Ronald and Hilary would spend most of the time at the Oratory, but Father Francis also managed to get them out of Birmingham for a short holiday once a year. Their most usual destination was the town of Lyme Regis in Dorset. They stayed at the homely Three Cups Hotel in Broad Street and walked for miles along the great swath of beach that led away from the hotel, stopping to explore rock pools and to take a quick dip in the chilly waters.

Father Francis was more than a family friend who had been charged with the duties of guardianship, he had become a surrogate father to the boys and a special bond between them had developed. He loved them as his own sons and was a good listener who treated Ronald and Hilary with respect, so they could talk to him more freely than most boys could with their natural fathers.[3] Because of this, Father Francis quickly learned that neither of the boys was happy in the oppressive home of Aunt Beatrice.

Fortunately, he knew of an alternative. Friends of the priests at the Oratory, Mr Faulkner, a local wine merchant and his voluble wife (who threw weekly musical evenings for the entertainment of the Oratory fathers) owned a substantial house in Duchess Road in an altogether better district than Edgbaston where Aunt Beatrice lived. The Faulkners rented out rooms and Father Francis had heard that one large room on the second floor had recently become vacant. So, in February 1908, Ronald and Hilary packed their things, said their goodbyes to Aunt Beatrice and moved home once again.

This was all good news for Ronald. The house in Duchess Road was nothing much to look at; it was covered in creepers and was over-furnished, but it was clean and light of atmosphere compared to the morbidity of Stirling Street. The Faulkners were an entertaining and sociable pair and the house was usually filled with chatter and music. Mrs Faulkner was a keen musician, a social climber and something of a snob perhaps, but she was also merry and lively and she liked the Tolkien boys.

But apart from the friendly atmosphere, in a material sense the Faulkners' home provided a greatly improved lifestyle and it was by far the most comfortable residence in which the boys had ever lived; the Faulkners even had a live-in maid named Annie.

Certainly, Ronald still yearned for the country and the wide open fields of Sarehole or Rednal, but he was as happy as he could have hoped to be in Duchess Road. And, within a day of arriving with their suitcases and bags and having arranged things in their room on the second floor, Ronald and Hilary went down to dinner and discovered there was another lodger in the house. On the first floor immediately beneath their bedroom lived a young and very pretty girl named Edith Bratt. She was petite, had grey eyes and wore her hair in a fashionable short bob. She was nineteen, almost three years older than Ronald, and to him she possessed an alluring maturity.

Edith had much in common with Ronald. Her mother, Francis Bratt, had died five years earlier and she had not known her father because she was illegitimate. Late in 1888, Francis had gone away to Gloucestershire to have her baby, who was born on 21 January 1889, but she had returned to the Handsworth district of Birmingham to bring up her daughter in the face of gossip and the reproving attitudes of her relatives. The Bratts were quite well to do and Edith had been brought up in a more comfortable environment than the Tolkien brothers. She was sent to a girls' boarding school and from a young age she had shown a flair for music. Indeed, by the time she was ten she had become such an accomplished pianist it was hoped she might have a chance to enter a music academy. But with her mother's untimely death in 1903, all such plans evaporated. Edith inherited some land in Birmingham and this provided her with enough of an income to support herself. In the Faulkner home, she had access to the family piano and her playing was welcomed so long as she stuck to popular tunes and light classics, for Mrs Faulkner could not stand hearing her practise scales.

With such unhappy childhoods, it was no surprise then that Edith and Ronald should hit it off. In a way, they saw themselves and each other as victims, survivors of misfortune, and this bonded them immediately. Tolkien often expressed the view to his own children that he and their mother had, in some way, saved one another from the hardships of their respective childhoods.

At first they simply flirted playfully at the Faulkners' home. Ronald's room was directly above Edith's and they could communicate by leaning out of their windows when the rest of the house was asleep, and they devised a private call to attract each other's attention. Later they began to meet outside the house, cycling off alone and meeting up in teashops in Birmingham or going for long rides into the surrounding countryside. By a stream or under the shade of an oak they would sit and tell one another of their hopes and dreams, their plans for the future, and gradually, during the long hot summer of 1909, they began to fall in love.

For a short while, their relationship went without censure. Certainly Hilary never spoke of it, neither did Helen Faulkner, nor Annie, the Faulkners' maid, but word of the couple's clandestine, unchaperoned meetings did eventually get out via a certain Mrs Church, who was the owner of one of the teashops Ronald and Edith had frequented. She spotted them one Saturday and mentioned it to the caretaker of the Oratory. Very soon, Father Francis learned that Ronald was seeing a young woman and he immediately intervened.

This was a bad time for Ronald to be distracted by love. He was supposed to be studying hard for his Oxbridge entrance exams at King Edward's and these presented enough of a challenge without Edith's charms to take him away from his books.

Father Francis knew this and was extremely concerned. He immediately sent for Ronald and lectured him on the need to concentrate upon work. Taking a hard line, he forbade the boy from seeing or speaking to Edith again. When Ronald protested that he and the girl were in love, Father Francis insisted their relationship must end immediately and that if they still felt the same way when Ronald came of age three years into the future, then he could of course resume the relationship at that time. But in the interim, Father Francis's wishes were to be obeyed and Ronald had to return to concentrating fully upon preparing for the Oxbridge exam. Straight away, arrangements were made for Ronald to be taken away from the Faulkner home and it was decided that Edith should be sent to live with relatives in Cheltenham.

Ronald immediately knew he must obey his guardian. He respected and loved Father Francis who had been the only real father figure in his life. He also knew that Father Francis was right to be concerned for his academic future. This was what Ronald's intellectual self could accept, but he was also an emotional boy and the prospect of being wrenched from the girl he loved for three long years upset him deeply.

In the middle of this turmoil, during the late summer of 1909, Ronald was required to travel to Oxford to sit the entrance exam. He took the train, sat miserably in the university examination halls, and did his best. Later that day, before catching the train back to Birmingham, Tolkien joined a small group gathered around the notice board in the reception area of the examination halls and learned that he had failed to obtain an award, the all-important scholarship to the university.

For a while, during the journey back to the grime and the

heartache of his life in Birmingham, Tolkien must have believed his life was over. He had lost the girl he loved and failed to pass muster academically – he knew he would have another chance to sit the exam the following year but his failure was another great blow. That Christmas was almost as miserable as the one of 1904, and Tolkien wallowed in self-pity and bemoaned his fate in a diary he began on New Year's Day 1910.

And with the New Year came little hope of a brighter future. The brothers were moved to new lodgings a few streets from the Faulkners' residence and Ronald learned that Edith was to be sent to Cheltenham very soon. He decided he could not bear to stay apart from Edith for so long without at least the chance of saying goodbye properly. Breaking his promise to Father Francis, he arranged to meet Edith so they could spend one last afternoon together in the countryside. They met far from Birmingham in a tea shop they had not visited before. Ronald took Edith to a jeweller's shop and bought her a wrist watch for her twenty-first birthday, and Edith bought him a pen for his eighteenth. That afternoon they promised each other they would be true, that they would meet again three years on and pick up where they had left off.

But somehow, word of this meeting reached Father Francis and Ronald was called back to the Oratory to face the music. This time the priest was furious and deeply hurt that Ronald had ignored his wishes. Tolkien tried to explain that he had simply wanted to say goodbye, but his guardian was impervious to anything the young man said and declared that not only was Ronald forbidden to see or speak to Edith until his twenty-first birthday, he added the rather cruel caveat that henceforth there would be no form of communication between them at all, not even a letter.

Ronald was shattered by this and slid into a rather pathetic state of mind. In his diary he wrote endlessly of his woes and took to standing on street corners close to Duchess Road in the hope that he would see his beloved Edith walk by or cycle past. He prayed he would catch a glimpse of her 'by accident' and for a while he seemed unable to think of anything but Edith.

But even Ronald's occasional opportunistic sightings of his beloved were brought to a stop. Somehow, Father Francis once more learned that Ronald had been seeing the girl. Perhaps he had received exaggerated reports, but this time his anger boiled over and he threatened to cut short Tolkien's academic career by refusing financial help through college.

Ronald had been banned from any form of communication with his love, but Edith had not. She wrote to Ronald one final time before their parting and reiterated her feelings for him. Inspired by this, on the day Edith was due to set out for the station to take the Cheltenham train, Ronald again found himself wandering the streets hoping to catch sight of Edith as she cycled past. And against the odds, he did just that, catching a fleeting glimpse of the girl he would not see again for three years as she cycled along the street on her way to the station and a new life in Cheltenham.

It soon became clear to Ronald that the only thing he could do now was to throw himself into work. If Edith kept her promise, he would see her immediately after his twenty-first birthday, for he knew he would remain true to her. If he hoped to make anything of his life, to succeed in a career and to finally be the victor in this matter, he would have to play by the rules.

As painful as this period was, it also helped to mould Tolkien; it was character-building stuff. Absorbing himself with his studies he excelled academically and King Edward's now became the focus of his life. Any hard feelings toward Father Francis soon passed – he understood that his guardian had his best interests at heart – but his casual, childhood days at the Oratory were now replaced with serious intellectual pursuits and a close circle of friends among the senior boys at the school. He also became more interested in sport, and although he was slight of build he became captain of the rugby team. He enjoyed the game but during the first term he suffered a broken nose and a badly-bitten tongue.[4]

He founded a club at King Edward's that met most days in the library after class or sometimes over tea in a shop called Barrow's Stores in Corporation Street in the centre of Birmingham. The group called itself the Tea Club and it con-sisted of four boys who had been given the title of Librarian, a special class of prefect. Later, a couple of the group decided they should change their name to the Barrovian Society (after Barrow's Stores), but when this caused an argument it was finally agreed they should combine the two and so they became known as the Tea Club, Barrovian Society or T.C., B.S., a name that stuck.

They were the brightest boys in the year, those who would soon be gracing the halls of Oxbridge colleges. The club included Christopher Wiseman, the headmaster's son Robert Gilson, and a younger boy, Geoffrey Bache Smith, known among them simply as GBS. Each afternoon when they met in the library they made tea with a kettle and stove they had smuggled in and each of them brought along cakes or sandwiches. Over tea they would discuss their mutual obsessions – ancient lan-guages and mythology. They read from *Beowulf* and *Sir Gawain and the Green Knight*, talked about classical music and current affairs and passed on any new discoveries they had made in the world of books, art and 'high culture'. In many ways, this little gathering formed the template for the Inklings, the famous group of intellectuals centred around Tolkien, C.S. Lewis and other Oxford dons. It was a gathering of like-minded young men with common interests, a shared intellectual curiosity and high principles.

In December 1910, Tolkien returned to Oxford for a second and final attempt at the entrance exam. This time he felt far more confident and with some justification. He had prepared well and was altogether a better scholar and more experienced in dealing with the sort of questions he knew he would be asked. And, at the gathering around the notice board later that day his hopes and his confidence were vindicated. He had succeeded in obtaining an Open Classical Exhibition to Exeter College to begin the following October.

An exhibition was a slightly less prestigious award than the scholarship (which he had hoped for and secretly believed he should have been awarded), but he wasn't going to allow this to mar his achievement. The exhibition paid £60 per year (rather than the annual £100 that came with a scholarship), and with a small bursary from King Edward's for getting into Oxford plus a generous allowance from Father Francis, he could just about manage to make ends meet for the duration of his course, so long as he was frugal and modest in his tastes. He was so excited he broke his promise to Father Francis and sent a telegram to Edith telling her of his news and she sent him her anonymous congratulations.

Returning to King Edward's for his final two terms, he felt better than he had done for a long time. Edith was certainly never far from his mind, but by throwing himself into his work he had succeeded in surmounting one of the great hurdles in his life. He now had only two years to wait for Edith and by that time he would be some way through his second year as an Oxford undergraduate.

CHAPTER 3

Oxford

Birmingham is only some fifty miles from Oxford, but this belies the enormous gulf between the two cities. And, as if to emphasise the fact that he had moved on, Tolkien arrived in Oxford in grand style – as a passenger in a friend's car – a rare novelty in those days. It was a scorching day, and for a while Tolkien and his friend, Dickie Reynolds, could find no other students until they realised everyone was out punting on the river.

In 1911, life at Oxford University was dominated by the British class system. It was a place where the serious-minded went to learn and to forge careers through the power of their intellect and determination but it was also a playground for the sons (and very rarely, daughters) of the aristocracy, young people who knew they could sail through and walk away with a Third before taking up a position in the City, the army or heading up a division of their father's corporation. The middle-class (and the extremely rare) working-class undergraduates survived on scholarships and exhibitions. Most of them worked hard but had fun with their own kind and they almost never mixed with the upper-class students who were principally drawn to the colleges of Christ Church, Magdalen and Oriel. It was all very *Brideshead Revisited* for the wealthy, but equally, some of the glamour rubbed off on the poorer students; how could it not? Although there was little interaction between the classes, the middle-class, state-school boys did many of the same things as their wealthier peers: they learned to drink and smoke, they discovered the joys of dining in their rooms late into the night with close friends. Some stumbled upon such exotica as opium and cocaine and a few were even introduced to sex.

Tolkien was typical of the lower-middle-class student at Oxford, and for him, more powerful than any inspiration to learn or to broaden his intellectual horizons was the realisation that student life gave him the opportunity to experience much more than the Oratory or the chaste pleasures of the T.C., B.S. could offer. But of course, he had been brought up as a conventional youth, conservative and respectful of authority in whatever guise and the realisation of astonishing freedom dawned only gradually.

He began to smoke a pipe and to drink beer. He spent more time with his friends than studying and he spent too much money on entertaining himself and these new friends. In common with almost all his contemporaries, when his 'battel' or college account was slipped under the door of his room each Saturday, it invariably delivered worse news than he had anticipated, so that by the end of his first year he had run up debts that were quite typical, but (to him) worrying.

But there were also more cerebral distractions to occupy him.

He joined debating societies, the college Essay Society and the Dialectical Society. These felt like gatherings of the T.C., B.S. in the library of King Edward's School and Tolkien was in his element.

Most of Tolkien's time was spent in an entirely male domain. This was, in part, governed by the social mores of the time. Unmarried men and women were allowed to mix only when chaperoned, and the relatively few women then studying at Oxford attended separate lectures in their own ladies' colleges such as Lady Margaret Hall and St Hilda's. This all seemed entirely natural to Tolkien and his friends, and in many ways they were extending their female-free adolescence, enjoying the company of other men. Admittedly, Tolkien had found Edith, and, alone in his empty college room overlooking Turl Street, he still pined for her when the excitement of an evening's debating and drinking was over. But the young men who had come from schools across the country and graduated from their own T.C., B.S.-type gatherings wanted each other's company, and, in their minds, women would have simply ruined the dynamic for them.

For Tolkien at least, there was no hint of homosexuality about any of this. Indeed, later in life, he claimed he hadn't known what it was until he was recruited into the army. This entirely male world was more akin to the camaraderie of boys playing Cowboys and Indians or pirates. By the age of eighteen they could no longer wield wooden swords or put on feathered headgear (at least not without the excuse of being drunk) so, instead, they pitted their wits, competed on intellectual turf and experienced the heady whiff of elitist, undergraduate games. While the majority of their contemporaries across the nation were toiling in factories and offices, theirs was an enchanted existence with little responsibility. For better or worse it moulded the intellectual, political and military custodians of Britain's future, just as it had for generations.

Then, of course, there was work. And once again, Tolkien was lucky to be taught by an inspired teacher. Dr Joe Wright was far removed from the stereotype of the Oxford don. He had been born in a small Yorkshire town and at the age of six he had been sent to work in the local woollen mill. He had completely missed any formal education, but by the time he was fifteen he had begun to realise an entire world lay just beyond his reach — the world of words, language and writing. He taught himself to read and write and started at night-school where he studied French and German before moving on quickly to Latin. By the age of eighteen, he had left the mill and set up his own night-school in a spare bedroom in his mother's house. Having earned a little money, he then set out to travel Europe and found his way to Heidelberg where he took a degree and then a doctorate. Along the way he had mastered Russian, Old Norse, Old Saxon, Old English and many other languages both contemporary and ancient. Returning to England, Joe Wright set up home in Oxford and was eventually appointed to the position of Deputy Professor of Comparative Philology, a post for which no one could have been better qualified. In 1892 (the year of Tolkien's birth) Wright had written *A Primer of the Gothic Language* which Ronald had been given by his teacher at King Edward's.

Wright was a stern teacher and he drove Tolkien hard, but at the same time Tolkien was a keen and extremely able linguist and Wright soon came to realise his student possessed a pure and deep love for language, a natural empathy for the ebb and flow of words and sounds. At school, Tolkien had delved deep into Latin and Greek and, encouraged by good and enthusiast teachers, he had learned a little of ancient languages such as Ancient

Finnish and Norse. Professor Wright took Tolkien deep into this arcane wilderness and showed him how languages from very different cultures and separated chronologically contained intrinsic connections, undercurrents and themes.

So Tolkien's first year as an undergraduate swept past him almost as a blur. During that time he was probably happier than he had been since early childhood and he managed to establish a delicate balance between the pleasures and the pressures of student life. For sure, he had accrued debts, but this was almost so standard that to have done otherwise might have been considered eccentric. He had almost ignored religion during that year and had attended church only very occasionally, but he had lost none of his faith and love for the Catholic Church, and in Joe Wright, he had found an inspiring teacher. Life would have been entirely rounded, his contentment and sense of well-being complete, but for one thing – Edith.

Fun and work at Oxford had afforded Tolkien a distraction from the heartache of being forcibly separated from Edith, but his feelings for her had not diminished in the slightest and throughout his first year and into his second at Oxford, he had counted off the days until his twenty-first birthday. Finally, the moment arrived. On the night before his birthday, late on 2 January 1913, he composed the letter to Edith he had long dreamed of writing. In it, he told her again of his feelings and expressed his desire that they might be reunited after so long apart.

The following morning, his birthday, he posted his letter and waited patiently for Edith's reply. But when it came only a few days later, his hopes and dreams were temporarily shattered, for it contained the worst possible news; Edith had recently become engaged.

Edith's fiancé was a young man named George Field who was the brother of an old school friend of Edith's, Molly Field, who lived in Cheltenham. But, although this news could have ended things for Edith and Ronald, in her letter to Tolkien, she had hinted that she was not actually in love with George but had simply come to the conclusion that Ronald would not be there for her. Afraid of being left on the shelf she had started a relationship with one of the only eligible young men in her social circle.

But Tolkien had always been there for her and he had no intention of letting Edith slip away now, not after waiting so long. By 8 January, he was on a train to Cheltenham to resolve the matter. Edith was there on the platform waiting for him. They talked and talked long into the evening, and when Edith was convinced that Tolkien did indeed still love her she promised she would break off her engagement and accept him.

At first, poor George Field was mortified, for he had been in love with Edith even if his feelings had not been fully reciprocated, but Edith had made up her mind. She ignored the tittle-tattle of neighbours and the mutterings of the older members of her social set in Cheltenham and began to look forward to a future with the young man to whom she had pledged her troth three years earlier.

But both Edith and Ronald had difficult hurdles to surmount that winter. During January and February of 1913, Tolkien had to work flat-out in preparation for his Honour Moderations at Oxford, the first of two sets of examinations that would lead to a degree in Classics. He had not worked consistently through his first year, which meant he had to cram into a couple of months what he should have spent a year doing. With the distraction of his reunion with Edith and journeys to and from Cheltenham, he was struggling to find time to revise. At the end of February, he took the exams and was secretly unsurprised when he achieved only a Second Class.

Tolkien's masters at Exeter were disappointed with him. Although achieving a First was extremely difficult, it was their view that anyone bright enough to be given an award to attend Oxford and dedicated enough (presumably because they were so grateful they had got into the university at all) should fly through the year with a First. However, there was something uncommon about Tolkien's papers. Although he had secured only a Second overall, he had written an almost faultless paper in his special subject, Comparative Philology, the course taught by Joe Wright. The examiners had not only given him a First for this paper but had made a particular note of the outstanding quality of Tolkien's work. As a result, the Fellows, headed by the Rector of Exeter, Dr Farnell recommended that he change course, from Classics to English Language and Literature.

For Tolkien, this made perfect sense. He had never shown great interest in what constituted a major part of the Classics course – the study of Greek and Roman literature. For him, the ancient mythologies of the German peoples and the legends written in ancient Norse (or Icelandic) were infinitely more attractive, somehow more honest. The English Language and Literature course was by no means perfect but it suited Tolkien far better than Classics. It was a relatively new course at Oxford and, as its name implied, it was divided into two distinct aspects. In one part, students studied the structure and development of language from ancient to modern times, and in the other, they were expected to read and analyse literary works dating from a period after the fourteenth century.

Tolkien's interests lay almost exclusively with language. He had never shown great concern for 'modern' literature. He considered Shakespeare over-rated and he disliked many of the Bard's plays. He had little time for Dryden or Milton and he loathed 'modern' writers, authors of the eighteenth and nineteenth century whose works had become part of the canon and an essential component of the Oxford Language and Literature course.

Fortunately, Tolkien was assigned another very talented and versatile teacher, Kenneth Sisam, a New Zealander who was only four years older than Tolkien. Based upon first impressions, Sisam seemed an extremely dry and introverted individual, but he turned out to be an exceptional communicator of his subject and a man Tolkien quickly came to admire. Embarking upon this new course, Tolkien ploughed through the obligatory texts but savoured the side of the course dealing with language and the cross-fertilisation of culture and philology. It proved to be a great improvement upon the academic path he had been following, it suited his temperament, his deeply held interests, and it became a major factor in steering him towards a career as a philologist.

Meanwhile, Edith Bratt was soon presented with a problem that was for her every bit as daunting as Tolkien's troubles with examination papers. For several reasons, the couple had not yet made their engagement official. First, there was the fact that Tolkien was anxious about telling his former guardian, Father Francis Morgan, of their reunion. Of course, Father Francis no longer had any power over Tolkien, but old habits die hard and Ronald was probably overly concerned about what the priest might think. Second, Tolkien had not yet told any of his friends about Edith. None of his fellow members of the T.C., B.S, nor his new friends at university had any inkling of her existence.

But the most profound reason for the delay came from the fact that they had yet to arrange for Edith to join the Catholic Church.

In Tolkien's mind, there was no question Edith would convert to Rome. He loathed the Church of England, To him it represented the evil that had taken his mother away. It is perhaps strange that although deep inside he resented the way his family had treated his mother, Tolkien seemed to show little outward sign of his anger towards those he blamed. He maintained cordial relationships with Walter Incledon and he visited his Tolkien grandmother and Suffield grandparents until their deaths. But he did openly despise the institution of which they were a part, the Church of England.

Edith was not a devout churchgoer, but converting to Catholicism did present difficulties for her. First, and most importantly, she had no real taste for the Roman Church. She had been brought up in the Church of England and Catholic practices were entirely alien to her. Throughout her life she made it plain she did not like confessional and felt little of the spiritual relief devout Catholics like Tolkien claim to feel from baring their soul and having their sins absolved. Furthermore, she disliked the severity of the faith, she hated attending early mass and when, later in life, she developed poor health, she resolutely refused to fast or to follow her husband to mass at 6 a.m.

However, Edith had also to face more mundane but nevertheless painful difficulties in order to comply with Ronald's wishes. Her landlord in Cheltenham was her 'Uncle' Jessop, the head of the family with whom she had lodged since 1910, and another armchair Protestant who hated Rome. Edith knew that if she was to take classes to convert to Catholicism she would be asked to leave the Jessop home without ceremony. Furthermore, although Edith had little interest in religion, her meagre social life in Cheltenham was closely linked with the local parish church.

Yet, Edith knew that if she and Tolkien were to marry, there was nothing to be done but to bow to her fiancé's wishes. Quite simply, for Ronald, Edith's conversion was mandatory. He undoubtedly knew Edith was not keen but chose to see it as a test of her love for him. In his mind, it was quite unthinkable that the woman he was to marry would not follow the same faith as Mabel Tolkien had.

It was an unfortunate way to begin the renewal of their relationship, a poor start to what they hoped would be a long future together. Edith certainly resented the fact that (as she naturally perceived it) she had been forced into Catholicism. She tolerated the process, for that was the way most women of her class would have reacted in 1913. She also genuinely loved Ronald; he had good prospects and he certainly loved her. He was also affectionate, and in most ways, no less considerate than any other man she had met. Edith wanted desperately to marry him, to start a family and to lead a normal life; her spinster existence in the rather over-genteel and dull city of Cheltenham did not suit her and she had turned twenty-four; the years were speeding by.

Weighing it all up, it was perhaps a small price to pay. And so, in the spring of 1913, Edith informed 'Uncle' Jessop of her decision, and as she had predicted, he demanded she leave his house just as soon as she could find alternative accommodation.

Knowing in advance what Jessop's reaction would be, Edith had made preparations to find a new home, a move to the nearby city of Warwick with one of her cousins, a middle-aged woman with a deformed back called Jennie Grove. They soon found temporary rooms there and later moved to a small house close by. Edith began instruction with the local priest, a Father Murphy, who, to make things worse, turned out to have little interest in his task.

Tolkien visited Edith and her housemate in Warwick after the academic year had ended in June and by the end of the summer, the couple were able to take their first Benediction together. Tolkien was overjoyed by this and was delighted that finally both of them could participate in the same service. He wrote of it gushingly in his diary, but Edith's memories of the occasion went unrecorded.

There is no doubt that Edith and Ronald's relationship had been bolstered by the fact that throughout their early times together everyone around them seemed intent upon breaking them up, and although they seemed to share as much love as any other young couple about to marry, they also irritated each other and fought often. There is also the fact that they had been apart for a long time and their relationship before their enforced split had been so very short; they hardly knew each other. Worse still, during the interim, they had each changed and had travelled far along very different paths. After losing Edith, Tolkien had found solace in male company, first with his school friends in the T.C., B.S and then with his cronies at Oxford. He had tasted the freedom of the independent bachelor life, but most importantly, he had found academia.

In some ways Tolkien had been rather slow to find his vocation. He had been a bright schoolboy, but when he and Edith had lived in Duchess Road, there had been only the vaguest hint that he was heading toward life as an academic. He had only blossomed intellectually after Edith and he had separated, and it might be argued that their separation allowed fuller expression of this aspect of his character.

Edith had never been the slightest bit academic. As a child, she had shown exceptional musical talent but this had been allowed to go to waste. Unlike her future husband, no one had encouraged Edith, no one had taken the time or the trouble to allow her talent to develop as much as it should have done, and by the time she and Ronald were reunited, any hopes she may have once had of becoming a professional musician, or even a music teacher, had long since vanished.

Aside from this, Edith and Ronald's personalities did not always mix well. She was an independent and lively young woman who had had her energies stifled by everyone around her. As a child, she, like Tolkien, had had her fair share of bad luck. She had been orphaned and moved from one home to another, never able to claim a proper family of her own. She constantly suppressed her bitterness, but it would burst out occasionally, and often, when Ronald visited the little house in Warwick, the couple had fierce rows usually sparked off by something trivial.

Tolkien also found it difficult to express his love for Edith other than in sentimental and slightly patronising ways, addressing her in letters as 'little one' and describing her home in Warwick as her 'little house'. Also, as a young man he was over-protective towards her. His rather immature vision of modern, practical romance was a product of inexperience but he was also greatly influenced in his thinking by what he had read. The writer Charles Moseley has pointed out that like many people, Tolkien was, in part, directed by a literary image of romance:

> Of course, nobody is unaffected by what he reads. If you spend days reading books and poems from a world where women are honoured, put on a pedestal – worshipped, even – where the chief male virtues are courage, and

honesty, and honour, and generosity, you will in the end
come to think in those terms (and may suffer no harm).[1]

All well and good, but, for a woman who had for so long been
totally self-reliant and independent of spirit, this must have
proved galling. Quite naturally, Edith felt confused. Her fiancé
was capable of forcing her to adopt his faith, he showed little
interest in her musical talent and rarely tried to share with her
anything of his academic life. But at the same time, he smoth-
ered her with his patronising and immature displays of
affection.

Perhaps because of these arguments, and to allow each of
them time for a little reflection, in the summer of 1913, Tolkien
took himself off to Europe on a working holiday. He had taken
a job looking after two Mexican boys and together they began a
tour of France. In Paris, the small party met up with a third
youth and two aunts and Tolkien was expected to give them all
a cultural tour of the city.

It seemed a simple enough task, but it soon turned out to be
such a disaster he would have been better off staying in
Warwick, even if it had meant arguing with Edith. The first sign
of trouble came when, to his great embarrassment, Ronald dis-
covered that although he had mastered comparative philology
and could write intricate essays on obscure and arcane aspects of
Norse or Anglo-Saxon, he could hardly speak a word of
Spanish, and even his French was proving wholly inadequate.
This meant he could not make himself understood by his
Mexican charges who spoke no English.

On top of this, he quickly discovered he had a profound distaste for French food and found the nationals he met, especially
in Paris, uncouth and impolite. To make things worse, the

Mexicans he was supposed to be teaching were far from interested in French culture, insisting instead that they visit what
Tolkien considered vulgar tourist spots. Persuaded to take his
charges to Brittany for a few days, Tolkien thought he could at
least console himself with the prospect of the beautiful landscape and the fine food of the region. Instead, the party ended
up at Dinard on the coast, a seaside town not unlike a smaller
version of Blackpool – for Tolkien just about as vulgar as it
could get.

But things grew worse still. While Tolkien was walking along
a side-street in the town with one of the boys and the elder of
the two Mexican aunts, a car careered out of control and
ploughed into them. It hit the old woman who sustained serious
internal injuries and she died a few hours later.

It was a disastrous end to a disastrous trip and Tolkien was
relieved when he finally managed to make arrangements for the
dead aunt to be returned home and was then able to hand over
responsibility to her bereaved family. Stepping aboard the boat
for Dover, he vowed he would never take on such a job again.

With such a summer behind him, Tolkien was relieved when
his third year at Oxford began in the autumn of 1913. Of
course, his volatile relationship with Edith still troubled him but
there were now plenty of things to distract him. Indeed, he
immersed himself in the Oxford student scene more than he
ever had before. He began to adopt what were, for him, rather
extravagant tastes. With the money he had earned during his ill-
fated excursion in France he bought new, rather voguish
furniture for his room, he adorned his walls with fashionable
Japanese prints and bought himself a wardrobe of new clothes.
When the weather was mild he went punting on the Cherwell
and played tennis regularly. He was elected President of the

Debating Society, and with a small group of friends he formed a new club which they called Chequers, the principal activities of which involved dining in each other's rooms, eating fine foods and drinking copious quantities of expensive wine and brandy.

Meanwhile, Edith was leading a very different existence in Warwick. The city was beautiful, if not in the same league as Oxford, and with its own highly respected university filled with young people, it was certainly more lively than Cheltenham, but Edith had almost no social life there. Her housemate Jennie was the embodiment of every spinster's nightmare. Although Edith often found letters from Ronald a further irritation because they detailed what a merry time he was having, they were at least from a man who loved her and whom she would shortly be marrying. Jennie was a 'professional spinster'. Ironically, although life was dull and tedious for Edith, one look at poor old Jennie with her hunchback and the years heavy upon her brought home to Edith the fact that in spite of Ronald's annoying habits, she had much to be thankful for. Perhaps it was this as much as her love for Ronald that kept her going through this period.

At this time, Tolkien seems to have found a rhythm to his life that would sustain him into old age. He took delight in the pleasures of university life, but he was also producing some very good work. In spite of late nights over the brandy decanter and lazy afternoons watching willow branches from the floor of a punt, that year he won the Skeat Prize for English awarded by Exeter college, and he was now well on his way to obtaining a First Class Honours Degree.

Early in 1914, Edith was received into the Roman Catholic Church. The date for the ceremony was 8 January, chosen by the couple to mark the first anniversary of their reunion. A few weeks later they were officially engaged, their betrothal blessed by Father Murphy, the priest who had instructed Edith. Both ceremonies were conducted in Edith's local church in Warwick. It was a rather drab, ugly building, but for both Ronald and Edith, the surroundings did not matter too much. By this time they had each grown to accept that their relationship was never going to be ideal, but also that none ever was. They were very different people with vastly different perspectives and interests. They had been apart so long it had perhaps taken a disproportionate time to realise these things and to find a way in which they could live together happily, to be compatible.

When Tolkien returned to Oxford for Hilary Term, he must have felt happier than he ever had done. Amazingly, he had still not told his Oxford friends nor indeed his old school pals of his relationship with Edith. Now it felt like the right moment to break the news. He wrote to each of the other members of the T.C., B.S. who promptly sent their congratulations. As a man betrothed to the woman he had wanted since his eighteenth year, he could now look to the future with renewed hope and confidence. To Tolkien, the world seemed bright that spring, no cloud lay on the horizon. Like almost everyone else at the time, neither he nor Edith, nor any of their friends could know that before the year was out, Britain would be at war and the lives of millions of young people, young people just like Ronald Tolkien and Edith Bratt, would be racing to untimely ends.

CHAPTER 4

Marriage and War

There could have been few places in England more dramatically affected by the declaration of war than the city of Oxford. During the late spring and early summer of 1914, as the sunny weather arrived, the city was packed with young men from the university along with their sweethearts. The punts were full, the pop of champagne bottles resonated loudly as examinations ended and the summer ball season began. And then, as it does every year, the city emptied. The wealthy students returned to their country houses or boarded steamers destined for foreign parts. Meanwhile, those who, like Tolkien, were at the university thanks to scholarships and exhibitions, took trains to their modest family homes in cities across the country or began holiday jobs to earn a few pounds to help with the social whirl set to begin again a few months later, in October.

But October 1914 was like no other in the history of the university, for politics and deep-rooted racial hatred were about to send the continent of Europe into the abyss. On 28 June 1914, the heir to the Austro-Hungarian throne, Archduke Franz Ferdinand and his wife were murdered by a Serb terrorist in Sarajevo, an act that sparked off utter turmoil. The Austrian government immediately accused the Serbian leadership of complicity in the murders, and within a month, Austria-Hungary had declared war on Serbia.

Europe, a continent in which some score or more of states had only just managed to maintain a modicum of stability for a generation, experienced a 'political domino effect' on a grand scale. Austria's long-time enemy, Russia, mobilised against them; this caused Germany to declare war against Russia. Russia's ally, France, then began to mobilise her forces and so Germany declared war against France. Britain, bound by the Entente Cordial to side with France, was thus propelled into the burgeoning conflict, and on 4 August, she declared war against Germany and Serbia.

By the autumn of 1914, when Oxford students would normally have been enjoying their first college High Table and getting in a few sets of tennis before the weather became inclement, instead found themselves in training camps. Here, they were made ready for the battlefields of France where thousands of professional soldiers had already been killed as part of the British Expeditionary Force.

At the start of the war, Britain did not have a conscripted army, but the war incited passions with remarkable speed so that by the autumn, hundreds of thousands of young men had volunteered. But Tolkien was not one of them. He was determined to finish his degree first and had opted to return to Oxford, deferring military service until the following summer. Arriving at a deserted Oxford station during the first week of October, he was shocked to find the colleges almost totally empty, the university all but closed. His only friend there from pre-war days was Colin Cullis with whom he had begun the Chequers club the previous year. Cullis had been rejected by the army as unfit for military service.

At first, Tolkien found life in the deserted university almost intolerable, and during his first few days back he wrote to Edith telling her of his boredom and discomfort. But then he and Cullis decided they would leave the sullen, empty college halls to room together in St John's Street not far from Exeter. At the same time, Tolkien joined the Officer's Training Corps so he could learn drill in the University Parks and prepare for eventual enlistment. He was surprised to find he actually enjoyed it.

As the academic year passed, news from the war grew progressively worse. In the jingoistic mood of autumn 1914 there had been talk of the war being 'over by Christmas', but as 1914 turned into 1915 and the months fell away, the conflict reached an uneasy stalemate. Each side positioned hundreds of thousands of soldiers in trenches that ran for miles across the farmland of Northern France. A few hundred yards of no-man's land separated the armies, and each offensive and counter-offensive changed the position of the front line by no more than a fraction of a mile. By the spring of 1915, supplies of ammunition could not keep up with demand and the fighting was forced to slow for a while. But this was only a temporary lull. Already, during the first year of the war, the struggle had cost the lives of over a million men on the Western Front alone and everyone knew that as soon as the armouries were replenished, the shelling would immediately begin again to claim millions more.

With Oxford empty, Tolkien could concentrate more fully on

work than he had ever done before. While Edith passed each dull day with the added misery of having to cope with war restrictions, Tolkien was working solidly, and in June 1915, he took his final examination in English Language and Literature. A few days later, he learned that he had passed with a First.

But there was little time to celebrate, and because of his responsibilities to the Training Corp, and with the war making travel difficult, he didn't even get to Warwick to share his triumph with Edith before taking up his deferred commission as a second lieutenant in the Lancashire Fusiliers, the same regiment as one of his T.C., B.S friends, G.B. Smith.

Even then, the war and its horrors still seemed very far away. The closest battlefields of the Western Front were little more than a hundred miles from Oxford, and families were already grieving for their young men cut down at Mons and Ypres, but for those like Tolkien who had been cloistered in academic centres or had just begun training, there was little physical evidence of the conflict.

In these days of global news coverage and almost instant access to breaking stories anywhere, it is hard to imagine how little news reached home and how slow it was getting there. Without radio or TV, and with newspapers covering the war in minute detail but long after the events had unfolded, it seemed remote. Even the dead were buried close to the Front, no body bags arrived home draped with flags.

There were restrictions on petrol, travel was less free than one was used to and food prices had soared, but the civilians who lived through this war suffered few of the hardships that became a major feature of the Second World War. There was almost no bombing of British cities during the First World War, and the only soldiers seen by civilians were the enthusiastic recruits boarding ship at Portsmouth, Southampton or Dover and the bandaged, burned and maimed returning to English hospitals.[1]

In the barracks of the training camp, little was expected of Tolkien other than to idle away his time until he was posted to France. He drilled and exercised, he grew a moustache and he did more drill. Lectures were given on the role of the officer, the methods of warfare, the minutiae of weapons maintenance and map-reading. From the relative luxury of Oxford where he had dined regularly in college, had access to the best libraries in the world, and had enjoyed common rooms with leather armchairs and good port, he was now thrust into an altogether rougher world. In the training camp, he rubbed shoulders with professional soldiers and raw recruits, young men taken from the farms and the factories, men he was to command and lead into battle. Gone was the ready chance to engage in intellectual discourse, to debate and ruminate. Here, for Tolkien, the food was almost inedible, he slept on a narrow bunk and shared a latrine covered with a leaky corrugated roof, but, worst of all, this life was interminably boring.

There were some distractions. He bought a motorbike with a friend and when it was his turn to use it, he finally managed to get to see Edith in Warwick. This visit and the occasions when Ronald could get a few days away from the training camp were oases of happiness for both of them. They were getting on much better now, perhaps the resentments Edith had felt were subsumed by the privations of war, the constant anxiety that their life together could soon be torn asunder, everything lost.

During this time, Tolkien also began to make some of his earliest notes on the mythology that would dominate his thinking for most of his life. During those days of limbo between the gown and the gun, the first seeds of what would become *The Silmarillion* were taking root in his mind.

After six months of basic training, Tolkien opted to take special instruction to become a signaller. In the days before the advent of radio, signallers relied upon Morse code and semaphore, and Tolkien learned how to use a field telephone that operated by the use of long wires strung out across the trenches.

At Christmas, Tolkien managed to spend some time with Edith, and during this break, they began to talk about setting a date for their wedding. It seemed likely that at some point soon, most probably early in the New Year, Ronald would be posted abroad. They each knew that during the first eighteen months of the war, the average life expectancy of a soldier had been as little as a few weeks. Anytime now, the so called 'Big Push' was expected, and casualties would be high. It was a frightening time to live through.

After a brief debate, they set the date for Wednesday, 22 March 1916. In typical fashion, Tolkien only informed his guardian, Father Francis Morgan, a few weeks before the day, because he believed he would in some way disapprove. But his anxieties were unfounded and Father Francis was delighted for them. He sent his warmest congratulations and offered to conduct the service at the Oratory in Birmingham, but because Ronald had held back from breaking his news, arrangements had already been made for Edith's local priest, Father Murphy, to marry them in the ugly modern Catholic church in the centre of Warwick.

They had waited a long time for this day, and for them, as for many thousands of couples across Europe, they could have no real assurance of a future together. This horrible war had already destroyed the lives of so many and it would shatter the hopes and dreams of many, many more before it was over. Life had suddenly become even more fragile than they had known it to be as children, and each of them could do little but place their trust in God.

About this time, Tolkien was made a full lieutenant and had his photograph taken wearing his army uniform. He looks typical of his class and time. His hair is short and slicked back, there is a neat parting to the left and his uniform is immaculate. He has a moustache and his features are strong, a straight brow, a long, fine nose and prominent cheekbones. He is not classically good-looking but exudes intelligence, integrity and determination: Tolkien has the face of a man one could trust, but the anxiety of the time is also there, his is a face filled with uncertainty. A few weeks later, he was at last posted to the Front.

Tolkien's transport ship docked at Calais on 6 June and he then travelled by road to the British Army base camp in a little town called Étaples. Here, he was to spend the next three weeks never knowing when or where he would be sent into battle; this was a new, alien rhythm that involved doing little but sitting around drinking copious quantities of tea, smoking a pipe, talking, reading and, well, waiting.

It was at once tedious and stressful. The tedium was exaggerated by lack of resources; there were few books or newspapers and a simple walk was out of the question thanks to the constant threat of snipers and mines. Tolkien did not get on especially well with the other officers in his company. Many of them were professional soldiers with whom he had very little in common and who viewed men like him as amateurs, college boys stuffed into fighting men's uniforms. Tolkien preferred the company of the N.C.O.s and the infantrymen, the privates who made up the majority of the army, but the rules forbade officers forming friendships with the common soldier because such familiarity was perceived as having the potential to weaken discipline.

The tedium was one thing, but each day their situation grew steadily more stressful. From the moment Tolkien had received his orders and left English waters, he felt under threat, a target. He had of course heard stories from the Front, who hadn't? There was a constant exchange of men between the base camp and the battle lines and a steady stream of injured and sick soldiers passed through on their way back home. Every soldier had a tale to tell, each could offer unique but consistently harrowing reports of the horrors taking place only a few miles away. But stress also came from lack of any detailed official news, the dearth of any hard information about proposed battle plans. This, combined with the featureless waiting, caused the greatest pain.

But then, suddenly, the monotony was broken. Orders came through that the 11th Battalion, to which Tolkien had just recently been transferred, was moving out, heading north-east-wards, to the front line. It seemed the long-awaited 'Big Push', the Allied counter-offensive, was at last really happening.

Immediately, the pace changed. A troop train took them to Amiens, the capital of the Somme department of Picardy in Northern France, some 75 miles north of Paris. From the train, this land seemed deserted, the villages had been pounded by both the Allies and the German Army. It had been raining for weeks and the fields were awash, the odd chateaux or cottage glimpsed through the misted-up carriage windows was invariably smashed up, shutters hung limp from windows, once grand brass gates lay amongst piles of wet, desolate rubble.

Aboard the train, the soldiers played cards and smoked, the

carriage was dense with the fug of Woodbines and pipe tobacco. Kit was strung out on luggage shelves and filled the aisles. N.C.O.s polished their boots and greased their bayonets. Others wrote home to sweethearts and mothers. Not far off, they could already hear the booming of the howitzers and mortars. For almost all of them it was to be their last train ride.

It kept raining throughout their stay in Amiens, and didn't let up as the battalion began the exhausting march to the village of Rubempré ten miles closer to the lines. The roar and thunder of the guns grew louder all the time. Occasionally, a stray shell screeched overhead, and the ever-present danger of mines and snipers' bullets kept them vigilant.

They stayed in Rubempré for thirty-six hours. The place was all but deserted, the single road that ran between the ramshackle and blasted houses was pitted and made almost impassable for vehicles and horses. The battalion slept in barns and burned-out shells of buildings, make-shift roofs propped up on posts kept out the worst of the rain.

Then they were moving again towards the Front and the nearby village of Bouzincourt where they joined a more estab-lished army camp. This was as close to the front line as they would get before going into battle and large numbers of British troops were gathered there and camped close-by. Bouzincourt was hardly recognisable as a village now, shells and rumbling armour, mines and mortars had more or less flattened the place. The army had built some huts in which a few officers, including Tolkien, were billeted. Others had to make do with ripped, wet mattresses in deserted homes, houses once treasured by villagers now long-dead or scattered by violence. Most slept as best they could in fields or by the roadside.

The 'Big Push' had been a favourite topic of conversation

amongst both the soldiers and the civilians back home, but it was a campaign that had seen delay after delay. Some four months earlier, during late-February 1916, the Germans under the command of General von Falkenhayn had sprung a surprise offensive on the Allies at Verdun on the Meuse River in north-eastern France, and this had put back plans for a counter-offensive. During that four months, there had been extremely heavy losses on both sides, but by 1 July 1916, General Haig had decided to concentrate an army of over half a million men supported by a smaller French force in one location to open the counter-offensive, and, it was hoped, drive the German armies out of France.

It was called the Battle of the Somme. On its first day 19,000 British soldiers were mown down by German machine guns and 60,000 infantrymen were injured. Most of the dead and wounded lay only a few feet from the trenches they had occupied in preparation. It was the biggest single-day loss in the history of the British army and most of the blame for the disaster was justifiably placed upon the shoulders of Haig who had fooled himself into believing the German guns had been taken out by several days of heavy artillery bombardment preceding the advance. In fact, a large proportion of the German guns had gone untouched by Allied shelling. Among the 19,000 dead that day was one of Tolkien's closest friends and fellow member of the T.C., B.S., Rob Gilson who had served in the Suffolk Regiment.

Tolkien did not know of the death of his friend for more than two weeks. His battalion had been kept in reserve as the first wave of troops (of which Gilson had been a part) had gone over the top to face the bullets and the grenades. But then, five days after the start of the battle, it was the turn of the 11th

Battalion to move in. Even then, Tolkien was kept at Bouzincourt; he was an officer in 'B' Company, and 'A' Company were the first to take the road to the Front.

Tolkien knew that two of his friends had been fighting in the trenches not far from his camp as recent letters had informed him that Rob Gilson and G.B. Smith had been posted in nearby encampments. He suspected they had already seen battle but could get no word. Then, the very day 'A' Company left Bouzincourt, Smith arrived in the village as part of a Company that had been granted a few days rest.

They talked and shared cups of tea just as they had in the musty library at King Edward's, Birmingham. They exchanged reminiscences and joked about the antics of their absent friends. But this place was the very antithesis of the genteel surroundings of their youth. Freshly scrubbed schoolboys had become mud-splattered men, books had made way for guns, and they both knew they stood in the eye of the storm.

Three days after leaving the camp, 'A' Company returned. Many had died and one hundred men (over one third of their number) had been injured. On Friday, a week after these men had set out for the Front, it was the turn of Tolkien's 'B' Company. That night, under cover of darkness, they shouldered their packs, put on their helmets and marched out of the village along the muddy track that ran a mile from their huts to the trenches.

> *Bent double, like old beggars under sacks,*
> *Knock-kneed, coughing like hags, we cursed through sludge,*
> *Till on the haunting flares we turned our backs*
> *And towards our distant rest began to trudge.*
> *Men marched asleep. Many had lost their boots*

But limped on, blood-shod. All went lame; all blind;
Drunk with fatigue; deaf even to the hoots
Of disappointed shells that dropped behind.[2]

This is how Wilfred Owen began one of his most famous descriptions of the trenches of the First World War. Little more need be written. Faced with the onslaught of such pain and futility adjectives crumble on the page, everyday language fails.[3]

Tolkien's company were sent to attack the village of Ovillers held by a large German force. Many of his companions were killed during the first hours of the attack, their bodies shattered and racked by machinegun bullets. Tolkien fought alongside his soldiers for forty-eight hours straight and he was amazingly lucky not to sustain more than cuts and scratches. He then rested for a few hours and returned to the fray for another twelve-hour stretch before his company was returned to Bouzincourt.

Back at camp, more exhausted than he had ever imagined possible, Tolkien found a small collection of letters that had arrived soon after he and his men had departed. One was from G.B. Smith imparting the news he and his friends had dreaded hearing since the Battle of the Somme had begun. Their school friend, Rob Gilson, was dead.

Tolkien was crushed by the news. In the distemper of battle, he had seen men die before his eyes, smelled their blood on him; and he had killed, but he had not lost someone close, no one so integral to his own life. It was as though a part of his past had been cauterised. In the midst of death and destruction there had been pain piled upon pain; now there was a new sadness to add to the collection.

Still numb from this news, Tolkien returned again and again to the trenches and each time, he returned quite uninjured. But more than ever, he was now aware of his own mortality. Until Gilson's death, Tolkien had convinced himself that he and his friends were in some way immune from death, that their bond, their mutual love, would protect and sustain them. Such an idea is surprisingly common among soldiers who are forced to face the possibility of death every day, it is seen by some as a protective delusion, a way to deal with danger, horror and seemingly interminable misery.

Throughout that dreadful summer of 1916, the Battle of the Somme raged and Tolkien found himself constantly in the thick of it. He met up with Smith once more in August and they talked sadly of their dead friend and the other founder member of the T.C., B.S., Christopher Wiseman, who was then serving as an officer in the Royal Navy. Now, the two men were war-hardened, bitter and angry. They tried to break down their melancholy with levity but it was only half a success. It was to be their last meeting.

And so, on, on through September and on through October the armies raged, and even as the first bite of winter came and strong winds and icy rain swept across the shrunken and sullied fields, the guns never ceased. The trenches became more mud-clogged than ever; sometimes the slurry ran waist deep, and always it was foul-smelling, infested with rats, diseased.

Little surprise then that in the Somme and elsewhere throughout the war, more men fell sick with fevers and mysterious illnesses than were wounded in battle. The common name given to a collection of severe fever symptoms was 'trench fever', a bacterial infection (called pyrexia by the field doctors) spread by lice, and in November 1916, after five months in France,

Tolkien became a medical statistic, another soldier downed by the disease.

He was in a village called Beauval at the time, and after suffering a raging fever for two days, he was transported to a hospital at Le Touquet on the French coast. A week later, with his symptoms not improved at all, it was decided he should be returned to England. On 9 November 1916, Tolkien found himself in a city with which he was very familiar, Birmingham.

Edith came to visit straight away and among the doctors there seems to have been some concern over the severity of his illness. He was kept in hospital for six weeks, but there was nothing that could be done for him. Trench fever was a serious illness and many soldiers died from it, particularly if they were also weakened by injury. In an age long before antibiotics and with little understanding of the mechanism via which the disease operated, the best medical science could do was to keep patients under observation and well-fed.

Immediately after their wedding, Edith had moved to a village called Great Haywood in Staffordshire close to the training camp in which Tolkien had been stationed in preparation for France. She had again taken up lodgings with her cousin Jennie in a neat little house in the heart of the picturesque village and had been living there throughout 1916. By the third week of December, the doctors in Birmingham decided Tolkien was well enough to travel, and he went with Edith by train to convalesce at the house in Great Haywood.

This was a wonderfully relaxing time for Tolkien. Although the terrible experiences of the trenches were still fresh and painful and there remained the constant thought that he would soon have to return to France, he and Edith made the most of what they suspected might be a mere interlude. They tried their best to force the war from their minds, but of course it was difficult. It was cold, and war restrictions made life especially uncomfortable; there was insufficient fuel and meals were frugal. Worst of all, news from the war always seemed bad. Just before leaving Birmingham, Tolkien had heard that Smith had been killed from shrapnel wounds that had turned gangrenous. Now, of the original four members of the T.C., B.S., only Tolkien and Christopher Wiseman had survived the first two years of the war.

The ever-shifting matrix of politics and military struggle could only offer confusion. In November, Woodrow Wilson had retained the U.S. presidency, and on 7 December, as Tolkien was regaining his strength in Birmingham, David Lloyd George had become Prime Minister. British and American ties were becoming stronger than ever and there was talk that one day soon the United States would add its weight to the fight against the Kaiser. But, beyond any analysis, there was the emotional reaction to the war, the senselessness of it all, the futility and the irrepressible feeling that the future might prove still worse than the present. These impressions were strong in the minds of many across Europe that Christmas, and felt keenly in the house in Great Haywood.

In an attempt to dispel the dark shadows, Edith played piano and Tolkien drew her. They went for short walks wrapped up warm against the biting wind, and they sat by the fire talking as they had only rarely had the chance to do before. Edith fell pregnant that month and this news brought delight and trepidation. What sort of world could they offer the child that was starting to grow in Edith's womb? It was a thought shared by many that chill season.

During January, Tolkien seemed to be making a sound recovery but by the end of the following month he had relapsed. He was ill again for three weeks, and again recovered well enough to travel, this time to a posting at a camp in Yorkshire, where the authorities hoped he would be able to re-train for the war.

Ronald travelled north alone and Edith and Jennie followed shortly after. The women found rooms in Hornsea, a rather sorry, windswept place on the coast. The town was dreary enough during happier times, but now it was almost totally deserted and thoroughly depressing, overcast with a grey and freezing mantel of late-winter cloud.

But then, soon after arriving at the training camp, Tolkien was again taken ill. This time, his symptoms were more severe than at any point since his return to England and he was admitted to a sanatorium close by, in Harrogate. Here, his health improved again and a few weeks later, he returned once more to camp.

And so it went on throughout the spring and summer of 1917. Bouts of illness, sometimes severe, other times less so were punctuated by brief periods of better health. This cycle caused immense difficulties for Edith as well as her husband. By the late summer of 1917, she was heavily pregnant, the hot weather was uncomfortable for her and the lodging in Hornsea was a very poor substitute for the comfortable little homes she had shared with Jennie since before the war. Unsurprisingly, she was growing depressed and anxious, so that by September it was decided she should return to Cheltenham to wait out the final weeks of the pregnancy.

On 16 November, the couple's first child, a boy they named John Francis Reuel was born. Edith had the baby in a nursing home in Cheltenham with cousin Jennie at her side. Tolkien was unable to get leave to visit for almost a week, but as soon as Edith felt fit enough to travel, she and their new-born son took the train north and they moved into yet another temporary home, this time in the small village of Roos near the latest army camp to which Tolkien had been posted.

In England, there were now genuine hopes the war was entering its final phase and that the Allies would soon be victorious. And there were good reasons for a little optimism, for the pattern of the war had changed dramatically during recent months. That spring, America had declared war on Germany and a swelling stream of troops, ammunition and armaments had been arriving in Europe. The Royal Navy, which had been fighting the Germans around the coasts of Europe and in the Atlantic for three and a half years, were now joined by American ships. Together they were assuaging the threat of German submarines that had been wreaking havoc on merchant shipping and severely disrupting supplies of food and munitions crossing the Atlantic.

The involvement of the United States marked a decisive shift in the course of the war and offered England fresh hope the Allies would break down the German forces. But there were still great uncertainties about Russia and the Eastern Front. In October and November 1917, the Bolsheviks, led by Trotsky and Lenin, stormed Moscow and seized power. Russia was in turmoil, the country had lost several million men in the fight against Germany, and in a move dubbed 'the peace offensive', the new leaders called for an end to the conflict.

Roos was another haven for Edith and Ronald, another droplet of happiness and calm amid chaos, and for the first time, they could allow themselves to hope that Ronald would not have to return to the Front. But this idyll was short-lived. Tolkien was not called to fight in France again, but in March, he was posted to a camp some seventy miles south, in Penkridge, Staffordshire, so, once again, Edith, baby John and Jennie Grove were on the move with him. Then, no sooner had they unpacked than the army decided Tolkien should return to Yorkshire.

This was too much for Edith, and she flatly refused to make another move. Instead, she stayed in Penkridge and Ronald was obliged to travel alone to Hull, where he promptly fell ill again and was admitted to yet another hospital.

By now, Edith was close to exhaustion and emotionally distraught. Tolkien had been ill, on and off, for over eighteen months and although Edith could count herself lucky to have a husband who had survived the war, she had moved home half a dozen times since her husband's return from the trenches. Her exasperation is understandable and it is clear from letters written to her husband during this period that she was now past caring to disguise her frustration. In one, she pointed out, with little trace of humour, that Ronald had been in bed so much during the two years since returning from the war that he should never again feel tired.

But now the worst was over. The Allies continued to take heavy casualties during the final year of the war (Wilfred Owen lost his life a week before the German surrender, killed by machine-gun fire while leading his men across the Sambre Canal), but by late-1917, the tide of the conflict had turned.[4] On 11 November 1918, the Allied Supreme Commander, Marshal Ferdinand Foch, accepted the German surrender from a government official, Herr Matthias Erzberger, in a railway carriage HQ on a siding at Compiègne in France. The next day, Tolkien wrote to his commander asking for a posting in Oxford so that he might continue his education until he was demobbed.

CHAPTER 5

Fantastic Worlds

Every fan of J.R.R. Tolkien's work knows that the cycle of books that recount the dealings of Middle-earth are unique. The past half century has seen the publication of many thousands of fantasies that owe much to Tolkien, but none have offered the reader the sense of completeness and integration that comes from *The Hobbit, The Lord of the Rings, The Silmarillion* and *Unfinished Tales.* And there is a very good reason for this uniqueness. Unlike any other author in modern times, when he was not meeting his academic commitments, Tolkien devoted almost his entire adult life, some sixty years, to this single creation. In some respects, his internal world, that of Middle-earth, became more real to him than his external life.

But how did this vast project, this conjuring of a total alternative reality, begin? What were the influences that sparked the creation? And what kept Tolkien immersed and absorbed for so long?

These are complex questions and some aspects of them are difficult to explain, but we may at least try to follow Tolkien's thinking and to search out roots and catalysts.

First, we should look at the nature of Tolkien's early childhood. We have already seen how he loved the countryside of England and this of course had a major impact upon the way he visualised much of his fictional world. Like most children, Tolkien fantasised and played games in which imaginary monsters and fearful beasts roamed the land. Unusually though, these images seemed to have stayed very clear in his mind, so that when he came to write he was drawn to this distant imaginative landscape. When he could no longer play out a role with his younger brother Hilary, he began to create fictional characters through whom he could play vicariously. This is what all fiction writers do. But it is significant that Tolkien's imaginary world took root when he was very young and offered an extremely complex alternative reality based upon the almost fairy-story world of early childhood. As an adult, Tolkien was able to take this simple vision and transform it into something that continues to grip the imagination of readers and to conjure up for them a totally absorbing and believable mythology.

And the desire to produce a mythology lies at the very heart of Tolkien's creation of Middle-earth. Tolkien began working on the early material that later became part of his great saga during the final years of the First World War and he wanted to write what he described as a 'mythology for England'. From his study of ancient languages and the cultures that used those languages, he came to the conclusion that, unlike Iceland, Scandinavia or Central Europe, England had no significant set of written legends that formed a complete mythology. Ancient English literature could offer only fragments, echoes of

Arthurian tales, snatches and glimpses of a long lost time. As we've seen, Tolkien cared little for Shakespeare, whom some consider a recorder of myth and legend, and much of Chaucer too offered Tolkien little inspiration. England had nothing on the scale of the Icelandic mythology, the *Prose Edda* described by the thirteenth-century historian, Snorri Sturluson, the epic poem *Beowulf* or the mythological tales of the Finnish epic, *Kalevala*.[1] It was up to him, he reasoned, to put this to rights.

Tolkien was not the first to suggest this. In *Howards End* (published in 1910), E.M. Forster wrote:

> Why has not England a great mythology? Our folklore
> has never advanced beyond daintiness, and the greater
> melodies about our countryside have all issued through
> the pipes of Greece. Deep and true as the native
> imagination can be, it seems to have failed here. It has
> stopped with the witches and the fairies.[2]

But who better than Tolkien to write such a thing? He was the perfect person to create a mythology of Middle-earth because the author of such a work needed to combine an active and disciplined imagination with an understanding of language. People are often surprised to learn that Tolkien was a full-time academic and wrote fiction largely at night and in snatched moments; certainly many of his fellow dons were startled by what Tolkien had done when his books became famous. But it was in fact because of these twinned skills that Tolkien could produce a fantasy culture that was both hermetic and self-consistent. For as Tolkien learned as a young boy, language is more than mere words.

The study of a language is really the study of a culture. It is striking that although Tolkien was a professor of Anglo-Saxon and knew intimately the rules of language as well as the structure and detail of perhaps a dozen different languages, his spoken French and Spanish were little better than average. This is because Tolkien's interest lay with the relationship between language and culture. The study of a poem like *Beowulf* – a fascination of Tolkien's since his school days at King Edward's – provides whole chunks of information about the way the Nordic people of the seventh century lived and the way they thought. In fact, the *Prose Edda* and *Beowulf* tell us as much about the Nordic people as any collection of archaeological finds ever could.

So from his study of ancient languages Tolkien began to appreciate the concept of myth, that it acted as a document of culture. Realising this, he could then start to build his own mythology to describe a fictional culture, an entire fictional universe in fact, the roots of which lay in the languages of the peoples of his fantasy realm. For Tolkien, language, and in particular the languages of the Elves, provided the seed from which his epic derived.

But of course, a fascination for and a thorough immersion in language was not the only quality Tolkien needed. Three other factors were equally important. First, he needed the sort of imagination that could mould language and move characters through the fictional realm he had devised. Second, he needed the discipline to keep writing, and third, he needed a reason to do it.

It's fair to say that the second and third reasons here are linked for without a powerful initial impetus and an inner need to create this fiction (to 'sub-create', as Tolkien called it), it is hard to imagine anyone working long into the night, week after week, month after month, year upon year.

What were Tolkien's drives? What compelled him to create Middle-earth and why did it take the form it did?

Tolkien's desire to create a 'mythology for England' had its roots in the fact that there was nothing in the national literary canon that, as a patriot, he could call his own but it also has much to do with the fact that producing such an epic was something he *could* do, something he was *trained* to do. And it was this happy thought that occurred to him just as he returned to England sick with trench fever.

However, we must look further back to find the original source of inspiration, back one stage to the schoolboy fellowship of the T.C., B.S. Each of the young men in this group who sat earnestly over their cups of tea in the library of King Edward's School had a powerful sense of destiny. Each possessed a sharply defined confidence in their own intellectual prowess. Although as boys they had not yet found their vocations and still spent much of their time merely flirting with ideas, they each believed they would do something important, something significant with their lives.

The last time they had all met was during the Christmas vacation of 1914, at the home of Christopher Wiseman's parents who had recently moved to a rather grand house close to Wandsworth Common. Under the shadow of war, the four members, Wiseman, Tolkien, G.B. Smith and Rob Gilson, all Oxbridge men, called up, or like Tolkien, in preparation for military duties, had spent, what for them was the ideal weekend, sitting and talking and simply enjoying intellectual banter. Of course, much of the talk was about the war: how could it not have been? But they had plenty of other shared interests; they read to each other, they discussed literature, art and politics, just as they had when they were in school uniform. But now, each had begun to find a path, a direction, and it was during that weekend that Tolkien had come to realise that he wanted to write. He had no clear idea then exactly where this would take him, but he believed that he should begin to write poetry, and being totally uninterested in modern verse and understanding the significance of the epic poem, it was inevitable he would find himself moving towards this ancient form.

But then there was war, and there was death. Within a year, two of the four, Gilson and Smith, were dead, and for the survivors, Wiseman and Tolkien, the shock of mortality was profound. In a letter written by Smith only a few days before he too was fatally wounded, he described how the loss of Rob Gilson had shaken him to the very core of his being but that it could not break up their fellowship. The survivors, Smith believed, those who walked away from the war alive and whole, must represent all of them and carry the flame of the T.C., B.S., to say what the dead had been stopped from saying, to create, to produce something of which they would have all been proud.

This letter affected Tolkien profoundly, and when Smith died, it added still greater poignancy to his words. Within days, Tolkien had begun to formulate some of the earliest elements of what was to become his own epic, his mythology for England, for the T.C., B.S., for Gilson and Smith.

If this then shows how Tolkien was propelled into sub-creation, what is there to help us understand the direction Tolkien then followed? He was of course a linguist and a student of ancient culture and mythology, so this was certain to offer him a lead, but why had he turned to ancient mythology and ancient language in the first place?

To answer this question we need to turn the clock back further still, to a time before the T.C., B.S., to an earlier and more profound love – Mabel Tolkien.

A constant, powerful force throughout Tolkien's life was his love for his mother, and an overwhelming belief in the fact that she had died young because she had been rejected for her Catholicism. This conviction reinforced Tolkien's own faith and led to religion becoming perhaps the most important aspect of his own life.

But it is surely more than a coincidence that Tolkien became interested in language and ancient mythology at almost exactly the same time he lost his mother. Could it be then that a part of Tolkien's subconscious mind felt resentful of Catholicism, resentful of the fact that the Church had taken his mother from him? Could not this aspect of his inner self have sought out a non-Christian realm, a radical, heathen alternative, a place where there was no Orthodox faith?

One of the most striking aspects of Tolkien's mythology is that, like the ancient traditions upon which it is based, it describes a world devoid of Christianity. Middle-earth is a world that has, in Christian parlance, 'fallen', but it has not been redeemed.[3] In other words, it's the world of Tolkien's early childhood, a time and a place before his mother found the Church; Sarehole perhaps, or Bloemfontein, a world in which his mother is young and healthy, a world in which they are together. In his subconscious mind, each night Tolkien opened his manuscript, each night he slid the paper into his typewriter or began an illustration with ink and water colour, he was returning to a happier, purer time, he was returning to his mother's arms.

And who can blame him? What more powerful drive could there be? This supposition takes away none of the magic, nor does it denigrate his marvellous achievement. The death of his mother and the reasons for it gave Tolkien a subconscious impetus, something he almost certainly never realised consciously, but of course this would not, in itself, have given us Middle-earth. Tolkien may have found the inner strength to work on alone in his study writing late into the night because he was metaphorically returning to his early childhood, but he still had to mould an entire mythology, produce believable characters and plots, and then to structure a vast array of material into an eminently readable form.

This feat is even more astonishing when we consider that Tolkien was really writing in a vacuum. Aside from the fact that he was working without any support from a publisher and with no reason to believe his books would ever be read by more than a few close friends, we have to remember that there was almost no precedent for what he was attempting to do.

In terms of global popularity, the genre of fantasy is today one of the most important, but when Tolkien began to write, 'fantastic fiction' (or 'romantic epic literature' as it was called by some) lay at the very margins and was often bundled in with seminal works of science fiction.

Yet fantasy has a long and distinguished pedigree of its own. There are many and varied arguments about who was the first writer in the genre just as there is still some debate about what constitutes fantasy and how it is distinguished from science fiction. The Greek, Lucien of Samosata, who lived during the second century AD, may arguably have been the first; his 'Lucianic Satires' are probably the oldest surviving examples of fantasy and acted as templates for many later works. Later, during the fifteenth century, the English intellectual and statesman Thomas More revived the style of Lucien and composed his classic *Utopia* which was imitated by many including the Italian heretic Tommaso Campanella who was persecuted and tortured by the Inquisition for what he wrote in his book *The City of the Sun*.

Slightly left-of-field from these efforts is one of the most famous fantasies, Jonathan Swift's *Gulliver's Travels*, published in 1726, in which our hero travels to lands far from the reality of the author's own rather genteel life. Swift's talent was quite unique, and because of the complexity of his most famous tale it had many imitators but few successful ones. But the eighteenth and nineteenth centuries produced a growing wealth of significant fictions that could be classed as fantasy, including *A Journey to the World Underground* by Ludwig Holberg, *Micromégas* by no less a figure than Voltaire, and of course, Mary Shelley's *Frankenstein*.

Another writer who greatly influenced future fantasy writers was Walter Scott, a few of whose novels written early in the nineteenth century blended historical realism with fantasy. Today, Scott is best known for his chivalric tales, especially *Ivanhoe* published in 1819, and his Waverley Novels: *Guy Mannering* (1815), *Tähdistälukija – The Antiquary* (1816) and *The Black Dwarf* published in the same year. He was an accomplished scholar and researched his novels with meticulous care. Elements of Scott's writing can still be seen in the fantasy fiction of the twenty-first century, much of which is set within an 'alternative mediaeval landscape'.

A century later, at the advent of the technological age, science fiction and some rare fantasy fiction began to grab the interest of the reading public. The works of Jules Verne and H.G. Wells are perhaps the best examples of the genre from that time, but their books, most notably Verne's *Twenty Thousand*

Leagues Under the Sea (1870) and Wells's *Time Machine* (1895) were quite distinct from fantasy or romantic fiction because they dealt with *possible* worlds, recognisable 'reality' in which scientific and technological innovation played a pivotal role in the plot. Fantasy diverged from science fiction around this time because, instead of working with futuristic scientific ideas, writers in the genre chose instead to set their stories within alternative worlds that could be as far removed from 'reality' as they wished.

One of the most important fantasy writers at the turn of the nineteenth century was the Irish peer, Lord Dunsany. Born Edward John Moreton Drax Plunkett, the eighteenth Baron Dunsany, in 1878, he was educated at Eton, became a close friend of fellow Irishman W.B. Yeats and wrote some seventy books during a career spanning half a century. Like Tolkien, Dunsany was an academic and held the position of Byron Professor of English Literature at Athens University, writing fiction in his spare time. His first book, published in 1905, was a collection of short fantasy stories called *The Gods of Pegana* and he went on to write others including *The Sword of Welleran*. He coined the term 'beyond the fields we know' to describe the genre in which he wrote, the depiction of worlds in which almost anything could happen and the regular rules of our earthly realm did not necessarily apply.

Tolkien certainly read many of Dunsany's books and stories but recorded little concerning his feelings for them. He was excited by them as a youth, but later he came to regard them as superficial and conceived with insufficient attention to detail. His most particular gripe related to Dunsany's choice of names. Tolkien took great pains to make sure all his names were derived using sound linguistic rules and he was critical of the fact that Dunsany simply conjured them up without applying any expertise.

However, it is clear that some aspects of Dunsany's stories lodged in Tolkien's memory. An example comes from his *The Hoard of the Gibbelins*, in which Dunsany describes Gibbelins (goblins or orcs) who eat 'as is well known, nothing less good than man'. Elsewhere, in *The Distressing Tale of Thangobrind the Jeweller*, his hero has a gruesome encounter with Hlo-hlo, the spider idol and in one of Dunsany's most successful stories, *The King of Elfland's Daughter*, Alveric of the Vale of Erl goes beyond the fields we know and returns with the daughter of the King of Elfland.

But a greater influence than Dunsany, and one Tolkien was only too happy to acknowledge as such, was William Morris. Morris was born in 1834. His parents were wealthy Evangelists who indulged their son so much he became something of a loner. When he was seven he became fascinated with medievalism and all things linked with chivalry, knights errant and heroic deeds. This interest was cultivated by Morris's great love for the writings of Walter Scott and in particular the Waverley series of novels. This interest grew into something of an obsession, and when he was nine Morris's doting father even presented him with a pony and a tiny suit of armour, so that young William could live out his fantasies in the depths of Epping Forest, close to the family home.

Morris was academic and highly creative. He was interested in art, books and history, and as he grew older, he began to divert his fascinations from role-playing to sub-creation. He did well at school and went on to study at Exeter College, Oxford, going up in 1853, fifty-eight years before Tolkien. His original intention was to study for the Church, but he was soon smitten by the artist life. When his father died, William inherited an annual income of £900 which was more than enough to live on without the need for a conventional job.

Influenced by Chaucer, Keats and Tennyson, Morris's own fiction is drenched in mediaeval imagery but blended with an alternative world entirely of his own creation. He became a leading figure in what was known as the Pre-Raphaelite Movement of artists and was close to Dante Gabriel Rossetti, Edward Burne-Jones and Algernon Charles Swinburne. His first published work was a poem entitled *The Earthly Paradise* which he began in 1861. Then during the late 1860s, Morris became deeply interested in Icelandic mythology and went on to publish a translation from the Icelandic of two ancient tales, *The Saga of Gunnlaug Worm-tongue* and *The Story of Grettir the Strong.*

By the middle of the 1870s, Morris was blending his life-long devotion to medievalism and the English chivalric tradition with his understanding of ancient myth to create his epic *Sigurd the Volsung and the Fall of the Niblungs.* These were followed by his most famous narratives, *The House of the Wolfings* (1888) and *The Wood Beyond the World* (1894). Two years later, he had published *The Well at the World's End* which, at over 1,000 pages, was, until Tolkien's *The Lord of the Rings*, the longest work of Fantasy ever published. It also bears some of the marks of heroic fiction that would be integrated into Tolkien's own epic saga. Morris's elaborate story is set in a world very much like the north-west of England during the Middle Ages, but significantly, like Middle-earth, it is a world immersed in magic and quite untouched by any form of Christianity.

These later series of books were extremely important to Tolkien, who only really discovered Morris at the beginning of his third year at Exeter in 1913. When, that autumn, he won the

Skeat Prize for English, part of the five pounds prize money went on buying a handsome, leather-bound copy of *The House of the Wolfings*.

There can be no doubt that Morris pointed the way for Tolkien and his elegant style (which only occasionally slipped into being ornate rather than elegant). As this short excerpt from *The Wood Beyond the World* illustrates, his writing had a similar 'feel' to some of Tolkien's own more poetic writing, especially certain passages in *The Silmarillion*:

> He saw there a tall ship, which he had scarce noted before, a ship all-boun, which had her boats out, and men sitting to the oars thereof ready to tow her outwards when the hawser should be cast off, and by seeming her mariners were but abiding for some one or other to come aboard. So Walter stood idly watching the said ship, and as he looked, lo! folk passing him toward the gangway. These were three; first came a dwarf, dark-brown of hue and hideous, with long arms and ears exceeding great and dog-teeth that stuck out like the fangs of a wild beast. He was clad in a rich coat of yellow silk, and bare in his hand a crooked bow, and was girt with a broad sax. After him came a maiden, young by seeming, of scarce twenty summers; fair of face as a flower; grey-eyed, brown-haired, with lips full and red, slim and gentle of body. Simple was her array, of a short and strait green gown, so that on her right ankle was clear to see an iron ring. Last of the three was a lady, tall and stately, so radiant of visage and glorious of raiment . . .'[4]

There were other popular writers of the time who did much

to establish the Fantasy genre. Henry Rider Haggard, best remembered for his stunning novel, *King Solomon's Mines*, and Edgar Rice Burroughs who blended fantasy and science fiction, were becoming popular early in the twentieth century. Another was James Branch Cabell, whose most famous book, *The Biography of the Life of Manuel*, was set in an alternative United States. Like Morris, Cabell created a world in which magic and a mythical tradition replaced conventional religion. His books caused outrage and one of them, *Jurgen: A Comedy of Justice*, was banned for many years.

A most significant close contemporary of Tolkien's and a man who was embarking upon his own wide-ranging fantasy fiction at almost the same time was the English writer, Eric Rucker Eddison. In 1922, he published a novel entitled *The Worm Ouroboros* in which the central character, a man named Lessingham, is transported to an alternative world called Mercurius where he is drawn into an epic struggle by trying to mediate in a conflict between warring tribes.

Tolkien claimed he did not read Eddison's work until the 1940s and he rather brusquely dismissed any suggestion that *The Worm Ouroboros* acted as a literary influence. There is no reason to believe otherwise. There are few parallels between say *The Lord of the Rings* and any of Eddison's fiction except for the fact of setting – the common denominator of almost all fantasy – the creation of a self-consistent, alternative reality. However, it is interesting to note that, like Morris and Tolkien, Eddison was fascinated with Nordic mythology. In 1926, he had published a Viking novel, *Styrbiorn the Strong*, and like Morris before him, he went on to translate an ancient Icelandic epic tale, *Egil's Saga Skallagrimssonar*.

Tolkien met Eddison many times in Oxford because he was

invited by C.S. Lewis to attend meetings of the Inklings whenever he was in the city. However, according to Tolkien's recollections, Eddison was a rather unpleasant and aggressive character who thought Tolkien's writing 'soft'. Tolkien though expressed the opinion that Eddison was probably the best fantasy writer of his generation.

So these then were the precursors to Tolkien's own early literary efforts. He was a great fan of Morris, he had read and liked Walter Scott and Dunsany. He may have read Swift and dipped into protean science fiction from writers such as Verne and Wells. He was steeped in the mythical tradition of the Nordic peoples and Germanic legends, intimate with *Beowulf* as well as the fragmentary backdrop of the Old and Middle English traditions. He was familiar with Chaucer, quite uninterested in Shakespeare, unmoved by the writers of the 'modern era' (from George Eliot to T.S. Eliot via Dickens) and his own literary imagination was driven primarily by the creation of languages and from this the sub-creation of cultures, legends of distant peoples and mythical creatures.

It all began in 1914. Tolkien had dabbled with verse before his final meeting with the other members of the T.C., B.S. His earliest known effort is called 'The Voyage of Earendel the Evening Star', in which he refers to a mariner, Earendel and first mentions Westerland, what became, in *The Silmarillion*, the land of the immortals that lies in the distant West. Tolkien's poem draws much of its atmosphere and imagery from a set of Anglo-Saxon religious poems called the *Christ of Cynewulf* in which an angel named Earendel takes a leading role. This cycle was one of the works Tolkien had to study the previous year, as part of his degree course, and 'The Voyage of Earendel the Evening Star' marks the beginning of the close inter-relationship between Tolkien's own imaginary universe and the one peopled by the writers of Nordic mythology.

Tolkien was pleased with this effort and straight away began to think of expanding the theme of the poem into a broader legend and perhaps a series of linked tales. During the rest of 1914 and into the early part of the following year, Tolkien wrote a collection of poems. At first, he found it difficult to link these with the themes inherent in 'The Voyage of Earendel the Evening Star', and instead, he explored a variety of imaginary settings. He wrote 'Sea Chant of an Elder Day', a slightly over-the-top effort in which he tried his hand at realism along the lines of Wordsworth. It was not a great success and his closest friend, Christopher Wiseman, advised him to try to reign in his language, to learn to control expression. Next, Tolkien turned to a love poem about Edith. Because he had taken Wiseman's advice and written in a plainer, simpler style, this was more successful. He then wrote a poem called 'The Man in the Moon Came Down Too Soon', which was published many years later in the collection, *The Adventures of Tom Bombadil*, and by early in 1915, he felt confident enough to write something for Edith, a light, humorous ditty called 'Goblin Feet'.

Yet Tolkien's most interesting and original work remained the slow, quiet efforts he was putting into broadening the hint of a tale enclosed in 'The Voyage of Earendel the Evening Star'. By this time, he had been working on what he called his 'nonsense fairy language' for several years and it had now grown into the basis of an authentic and versatile language system that would eventually form the two Elven languages, Quenya (or High Elven) and Sindarin, spoken by other elvish groups of Middle-earth. It was when he realised that he could combine his images of an Elven people with the germ of a broader idea emerging from 'The Voyage of Earendel the Evening Star' that the pieces began to fall into place and the mythology of Middle-earth and the three ages of the world really began to take shape.

By the spring of 1915, as he was working for his final examinations at Oxford, Tolkien began the 'Lay of Earendel' about the earthly voyages of Earendel the star-mariner who travels to the land of Valinor. There, he finds two trees, one bearing golden fruit, the other silver. This poem bears only a passing relationship to Tolkien's later narrative work that would lead to his famous books and it is perhaps akin to a poem an Elvish prince might sing in Rivendell or a background tale to an episode in *The Silmarillion*. Crucially, however, it set Tolkien upon the right course and opened up an entire universe of possibilities.

The year 1916 began with joy when Tolkien and Edith finally married, but then Ronald's fortunes began to wane. Frustration followed, when he received his first rejection letter from the publishers Sidgwick and Jackson to whom he had sent a short collection of his poetic efforts. Then followed a dramatic change of gear in Tolkien's life. Academia was stripped away and replaced with military training and the rigours of war. With it, in the trenches of the Somme, he experienced desperation and fear. The year that had begun with so much promise and optimism ended with death all around, with sickness, and with little hope for the future.

Tolkien never spoke of writing more of his mythology during lulls in the fighting nor during the long, boring anxious waits between missions, but a part of his mind was never far from planning and imagining. The war, and in particular, the death of two of his closest friends served to focus Tolkien's imagination and to spur him onto serious efforts after he had returned to England. But there can be little doubt that what he experienced during the Battle of the Somme greatly influenced his later writing.

In a later chapter, we will consider specific aspects of how Tolkien's wartime experiences made an impact upon his plots and characters. But, as much as these details were crucial to his literary success, after his part in the war was over, the blood and the pain and the barbarity of trench warfare informed his work with a new and most important steeliness. Tolkien, in his own idiosyncratic fashion, began to imagine a universe in which dark powers strove with those of light, ultimate evil versus ultimate good. And so, convalescing in England with visions of hell and heroism still fresh in his mind, Tolkien's real work began.

The setting in which this work started could not have been more different from the mud and squalor of the Somme. Great Haywood, the idyllic English village in which Edith had been living since early in 1916 and where Tolkien was sent to rest and try to regain his health, provided a quiet and peaceful backdrop.

As we saw in the last chapter, this was a time during which Tolkien and Edith grew closer than they had ever been. It was perhaps the only time in their lives when they did not have to share their emotions with anyone else, they were without work commitments and it was just before their first child was born. Little wonder then that at the core of what became *The Silmarillion* is a blend of romance, heroism and tragedy, for these were the dominant forces within Tolkien's mind late in 1916; the romantic spur was Edith, the elements of heroism and tragedy were derived from the war.

Tolkien bought himself an inexpensive notebook and wrote on the front 'The Book of Lost Tales'. Immediately, he began to fill it with fragments of stories, poems, sketches and more detailed passages of his own sub-creation, his own mythology. The first full-length tale (which eventually became one of the later episodes in *The Silmarillion*) was 'The Fall of Gondolin' which depicts a terrible battle in which our hero, Earendel, the mariner, helps the elves and men of Gondolin fight the ultimate evil being, Morgoth.[5]

Fresh memories of the trenches support this tale from beginning to end; this is heroism and tragedy coming to the surface, and with this first whole, complete narrative Tolkien was able to move on to shape the entire epic. Working steadily through 1917 and 1918, the full, over-arching drama began to unfold.

'The Book of Lost Tales', or *The Silmarillion*, is, of course, modelled upon the traditional 'legend form', a tale of good and evil, pitted one against the other. The drama really begins in the First Age when an Elven craftsman, the Noldor, Fëanor creates three great jewels, the eponymous Silmarils. These jewels contain light from the Two Trees of Valinor that illuminate the immortal lands and are beloved by all the Elves and the Valar (demi-Gods who work for The One and guide the world). Indeed they are so beautiful, one of the Valar, the renegade Morgoth (a pagan Lucifer perhaps) so covets them, he steals them, flees to Middle-earth, and for good measure, poisons the Two Trees as a parting gesture of malice.

The Elves are so enraged by this act that they pursue Morgoth intent upon retrieving their precious Silmarils, and he begins a series of wars, a cycle of legends and tales involving a vast cast of characters, unions of men and elves who struggle for centuries to retrieve Fëanor's beautiful creations.

The Silmarillion is, at its heart, a deeply sorrowful story. The Elves (the Noldor) can never really win the war of which the fall of Gondolin is but a small part. Ultimately, after much pain and loss, they call upon the Valar to help them. The Valar eventually take pity upon the Noldor and come themselves to Middle-earth. A titanic battle ensues, the Valar crush Morgoth and destroy his stronghold of Thangorodrim.

And yet, this is a Pyrrhic victory, and hence, the sorrow. In the final battle, the Elven city of Beleriand is drowned under the sea, two of the three Silmarils are lost forever and many of the Noldor become exiled in Middle-earth where they either perish in later wars with Sauron during the Second Age or remain in diminished form until the end of Third Age.

And it is this, more than any other aspect of the legend, that was derived most obviously from Tolkien's experiences of war. The sense that there is never a complete victory and that all triumph is always tarnished with loss is a powerful element in Tolkien's universe. Throughout the entire epic cycle, victory is always gained at a grievous price, success is always at least partly tempered with failure. A tinge of sadness, of fragility and impermanence underlies everything about Middle-earth.

This pessimism even extends to the most romantic episode in 'The Book of Lost Tales'. In the 'The Lay of Beren and Lúthien,' a story containing hints of *Romeo and Juliet* and *Tristan and Isolde*, a man, Beren, son of Barahir, the chief of the First House of the Edain, stumbles upon the Elven princess Lúthien, daughter of Thingol Greycloak, King of the Elves of Doriath as she dances in the woods. They fall in love and together play a pivotal role in the fight against Morgoth. They claim back one of the Silmarils from Morgoth's stronghold but at the moment of triumph, Beren is attacked by a wolf unleashed by the enemy and he dies in the arms of his lover. Lúthien Tinúviel, the immortal Elven princess, chooses to die as a mortal woman and so to follow her beloved Beren.

Tolkien probably wrote this story during the spring of 1918, several months after his first son, John, was born and he was inspired to begin the story after Edith danced for him in the woods near one of their temporary wartime homes, in Roos, Yorkshire. Consequently, Tolkien always associated 'The Lay of Beren and Lúthien' with himself and Edith. In his mind, the struggles of the couple he describes in the story mirrored the real life battles he and Edith had fought and won. Of all the things he wrote, 'The Lay of Beren and Lúthien' was his favourite, and when Edith died, fifty-three years after the story was written, Tolkien insisted her gravestone should carry the inscription:

EDITH MARY TOLKIEN
1889–1971
Lúthien

The stories that now filled his notebook meant a great deal to Tolkien, but he then had no clear idea what he was going to do with them. As we shall see, later in his career, when *The Hobbit* had become a success, Tolkien tried extremely hard to have *The Silmarillion* published, and it is easy to see why that work was special to him. Into it he had poured so much of himself, things he loved, things he feared and things he hated. Clearly, it was a very personal document, and it became a work which dominated his life. He never really could bring himself to finish it. Even as an old man, only months before his death in 1973, Tolkien was still making amendments and alterations to the text, still filling in the details of the epic. And even during those early years when the first notebook had been filled to over-brimming and his tales of Middle-earth had begun to spread to many new volumes, he knew this was his great act of sub-creation. By the early 1970s, he could not bring himself to admit the tale was complete because it had long-since taken on a life of its own and absorbed him into it. He had grown to identify himself with the story almost too much.

In 1918, as he left the army behind and began to forge a career, life as an academic, a husband and a devoted father lay ahead of him. He could only hope the work that had occupied him for almost two years would one day receive the attention he knew it deserved. Although he had no way of knowing it, the writing of the first draft of *The Silmarillion* was simply the beginning of the struggle and his attempts to become a published writer were to take many strange and wonderful turns during the decades to follow.

CHAPTER 6

Climbing the Ladder

Victory Day brought with it both incredible joy and relief. At one o'clock in the afternoon, Big Ben struck for the first time in four years. Hundreds of thousands of Britons poured out onto the streets and in Central London the roads were jammed with celebrating crowds throughout the day and into the chill night. One observer declared it was like 'a giant school let out'.

By the end of the conflict, ten million men, women and children had died and the war had bled dry the resources of the great nations of Europe. But it had also changed the face of Western civilisation. The Prussian Empire, one that had taken a thousand years to form through war and marriage, had dissolved in little over fifty months. And from the ashes of this Empire, four 'new' countries were created by the victorious nations – Austria, Czechoslovakia, Hungary and Yugoslavia. With one voice, the people of Europe vowed they would never slide into such slaughter again.

Tolkien was in Hull when the news came through, but he had no intention of staying on in the army a moment longer than he needed to. He had already asked for permission to return to academic life and in the meantime he had been offered a job in Oxford. Within weeks his request had been granted. He was free to pick up Edith, baby John and the ever-present Jennie Grove from Penkridge where they had been living since the spring and together they travelled on to Oxford, the place Tolkien had long considered home.

The job, Tolkien's first, was as a philologist for *The New English Dictionary* then being compiled in Oxford in a set of tiny, musty rooms in the heart of the Old Ashmolean building on Broad Street close to the centre of the city.

It was a rather poorly paid appointment but it served the purpose of getting Tolkien back to Oxford in gainful employment, and even in early 1919 when he began work, he probably knew this was just a temporary position.

The New English Dictionary was a massive project that had begun life in 1878 in the hands of a devoted editor named James Murray who had died in 1915 after dedicating forty years of his life to the project.[1] The first twenty-two years of the project had taken the compilers through the letters A to H and they were now in the second phase covering the remaining letters of the alphabet. Tolkien was assigned to work on a few of the words under 'w'.

It was the sort of work that required meticulous attention to detail and a deep understanding of language, but it was extremely dull. Tolkien had the linguistic skills to excel at the job, but he knew that he should be working within the broader canvas of an academic career. Tolkien was assigned just a few words at a time and needed to thoroughly research their roots and meaning. He had to find intricate links between these English words and their equivalents in a dozen different languages, including ancient languages (such as Anglo-Saxon) and to trace the way they evolved. Only a tiny fraction of this material would appear in the finished copy, but the compilers believed that everything that could be known about a word should be known so that the two or three lines that would appear in the dictionary would be accurate and definitive. Often, research for a single word would take Tolkien a week to study and report in full.

During their first few months in Oxford, the Tolkiens rented a small flat in St John's Street close to the Ashmolean Building. It was cramped and uncomfortable, but soon Tolkien was able to take on private tuition at the flat and this supplemented his rather meagre salary, so that by the summer of 1919, he decided they could afford to rent a small house not far away in Alfred Street.

This marked a vast improvement in the family's quality of life. There was plenty of room, they could employ a maid, and most importantly for Edith, they could get her piano out of storage, dust it down and give it pride of place in the drawing-room. It was also much more practical as a venue for teaching university students, and Tolkien had the great advantage of being able to take on female students from the women's colleges because the presence of his wife and Jennie Grove meant the young ladies needed no chaperone.

Indeed, Tolkien discovered that he was actually a very good teacher. He was popular with his students, their work greatly improved and he enjoyed this new role. By the following spring, with a clutch of students booked ahead for the rest of the academic year, Tolkien calculated that he could give up the job at *The New English Dictionary* altogether.

He must have felt uncharacteristically confident because Edith had just announced she was pregnant with their second child, but it also coincided with Tolkien realising that what he really wanted was to build a career as an academic. He had discovered he had a gift for communicating his own enthusiasm for his subject and he knew that working as a philologist outside a university, such as the job offered by the *The New English Dictionary*, was definitely not for him.

In the summer of 1920, Tolkien learned that the position of Reader in English Language at the University of Leeds had fallen vacant after the Professor of English there, F.W. Moorman, had died in a drowning accident. Without mentioning anything to Edith, he applied for the position and was astonished when a letter arrived in Alfred Street inviting him to an interview.

He had had few expectations of getting this far and when he was invited for an interview he thought he would be up against a collection of much more experienced candidates and so have little hope of success. But after spending a day at the university and getting on extremely well with the man who had invited him there, the new Professor of English, George Gordon, he began to think that he might after all be in with a chance. A few days later, the official offer arrived in the post and Tolkien had to break the news to Edith that they would have to move.

She was understandably upset, for she had allowed herself to believe their peripatetic life was now over and that they would settle in Oxford, a city she had grown to like. But it was clear they had no choice. For Tolkien, this was a great step up the ladder, and it simply could not be rejected.

The city of Leeds is not a pretty place and never has been. The centre of the city was dominated by grim, terraced houses (referred to as two-up-two-downs because they comprised of just four rooms). Each house had a tiny, concrete yard and they were packed into narrow, treeless streets. The university was equally unappealing – today it would be called a red-brick university – far from the splendour of Oxford.

For Tolkien, the first few months in this new job were particularly depressing. With Edith remaining in Oxford to have the baby, he was obliged to live in a tiny bed-sit close to the university. Each weekend he would travel to Oxford by train late on a Friday and return on the Sunday. Indeed, things were so miserable for him he applied for two other academic positions. The first was the Baines Chair at the University of Liverpool, the other was a newly created position, the De Beers Professorship at the University of Cape Town which was supported by the famous diamond mining family.

Tolkien was passed over by the English Department in Liverpool, but he was staggered to hear that the position in Cape Town would be his if he wanted it. He must have thought long and hard about this while sitting in his poky little room during that freezing cold winter. He could remember nothing of his early years in South Africa, it had become for him almost a legendary past, but although exciting, a move to Cape Town would bring with it its own problems.

Just as he was trying to decide the best course, Edith gave birth to their second child, Michael, and shortly afterwards she decided she was ready to make the journey north. Tolkien had found 11 St Mark's Terrace, a small house close to the university, and early in 1921, the family moved in. It seemed obvious he could not expect Edith to agree to a move abroad and so he let pass the offer from Cape Town.

In later years, Tolkien often wondered whether he had made the right decision over this. Before he had gained a footing in his career and had become a successful writer he mused upon the fact that this could have been their big chance to make something exciting of their lives. But, to the surprise of both Ronald and Edith, with the arrival of spring and the family united in Leeds, they found they were starting to enjoy life there.

From the perspective of Alfred Street, Oxford, the prospect of the move had filled them with dread, but for quite different reasons each of them found much to like about Leeds. Edith preferred the less formal atmosphere of the city over the rarefied environment of the Oxford colleges and she quickly made friends with the wives of Ronald's colleagues.

The English department run by George Gordon was small but growing. The university had none of the riches of the Oxbridge colleges and Tolkien had to share an office with Gordon and the Professor of French, the three of them squeezed into a space a quarter the size of the sumptuous rooms provided for an Oxford don. The windows were dirty, the paintwork flaking and the views no match for the lush quads and ancient sandstone of Exeter. But surroundings and creature comforts are not everything. Tolkien liked and respected Gordon and quickly grew fond of his English students. Most of them came from local cities, many from lower-middle-class families and they were mostly hard working. Plentiful experience of elitism at Oxford had shown him that wit and urbanity had their place but when married to laziness and arrogance, they produced little of value. In some ways, the northern lads who studied English at Leeds reflected an aspect of Tolkien's own personality, his stoicism and dedication. These men had had to overcome birthright just as he had.

And things got better still. In early 1922, a young academic whom Tolkien had taught two years earlier in the little house in Alfred Street arrived at Leeds University to take up an appointment as a junior lecturer in the English Department. Eric Gordon (no relation to George Gordon) was an exceptionally bright, scholarly fellow who shared Tolkien's obsession with ancient languages. He had been a Rhodes Scholar, and back in Oxford, he and Tolkien had enjoyed many an enjoyable conversation outside of official tutorial time.

Soon they were collaborating on publications. Their first was a glossary for a vast collection of Middle English extracts that was published late in 1922, but then they began to work on what was to become Tolkien's first significant published effort, a new edition of the Middle English poem *Sir Gawain and the Green Knight*. Written by an anonymous West Midlands poet around 1380, the poem is an alliterative romance, in which the protagonist, one of King Arthur's knights, Sir Gawain, survives two tests. The first is to behead the evil Green Knight; the second, to resist the temptation to commit adultery with the wife of a certain Lord Bertilak.

It was a personal favourite of both Tolkien and Gordon, and was one of the mainstays of undergraduate Middle English courses. When it was finally published by the Clarendon Press of Oxford in 1925, it was immediately instated as the standard college text and remained so for many years.

But Tolkien and Gordon were also friends and they did much to enliven the English faculty at Leeds. They created a Viking Club for tutors and students. This bore no relation to many of the other clubs and societies with which Tolkien had been involved. There was the common intellectual thread offered by the study of Norse and other ancient languages and traditions, but it was meant really to be fun, a relief from academia. The participants spent most of their time writing bawdy verse which was read aloud over large quantities of beer in the college bar and it served to make Tolkien and Gordon just about the most popular teachers at the university.

Meanwhile, Tolkien's domestic life continued to become more complicated, his responsibilities greater. Early in 1924, Edith had fallen pregnant again, a fact that had not pleased her. The prospect of raising three small children in the tiny house in St Mark's Terrace was not a happy one and they soon moved again to a larger home not far away at 2 Darnley Road, West Park. There is little doubt Tolkien could have remained in Leeds his entire career, and for many reasons, he and the family could have been happy there. He was certainly not earning much but was making a little extra income marking School Certificate exam papers during the summer vacation. They could just about afford short holidays at nearby seaside towns each summer and there was a chance they might soon be able to buy a small house of their own. Tolkien was further encouraged when, in 1924, a new professorship was created in the Leeds English Department. He was appointed and took the Chair in October, just a month before the couple's third child, Christopher Reuel, was born.

This new appointment may have been enough to keep Tolkien in Leeds for some time. It came with more money and it was an important advancement, yet, there was something missing in his career. He could not help feeling he could do better for himself and his growing family. It was certainly a noteworthy achievement to have become a full professor by the relatively tender age of thirty-two, but there was no escaping the fact that it was in a small, provincial university. Although he said nothing,

Tolkien had his sights set upon higher things, a position in London perhaps or one of the Oxbridge colleges.

He did nothing about it, but then, early in 1925, an ideal opportunity presented itself. The Professor of Anglo-Saxon at Oxford, William Craigie, had accepted a seat in the United States and the most coveted position in Tolkien's field was suddenly up for grabs. Naturally, he could not resist.

Three other candidates were approached, all more experienced and better placed for the job than Tolkien, so in spite of his ambitions, it looked as though he would be staying in Leeds for some time. But then one of the candidates decided not to apply, another was offered it and turned it down, which left Tolkien and one other candidate, Kenneth Sisam, who had been one of his tutors at Exeter ten years earlier.

The selection panel deliberated long over the placement. Sisam was by far the more experienced man and he was popular at the university. Tolkien was something of an unknown quantity. There was also an element of snobbery and elitism that influenced some of the panel into viewing Tolkien's present professorship at Leeds University as somehow less worthy than it was. But Tolkien had friends too, and indeed, the man who had given him his first academic job, George Gordon, had himself moved to Oxford two years earlier and was now Professor of English Literature there.

After protracted debate, the votes of the selection panel were split evenly between Sisam and Tolkien, but, influenced by Gordon, the Vice Chancellor, who had the casting vote, came down on the side of the young professor from Leeds.

There is no doubt Tolkien was genuinely staggered. In his resignation letter to the Vice Chancellor of Leeds University he made it clear that, with so little experience, he had had no idea he would have been offered such an illustrious job and that he had instead expected to remain in his happy position at the university for many years to come.

For Edith, it meant yet more upheaval, but it was a remarkable leap forward for Ronald and she was thrilled for him. She had begun to settle in Leeds but in the back of her mind she had suspected they would not be living there for ever, that her brilliant husband would not accept second best for long.

CHAPTER 7

A Don's Life

As Tolkien stepped off the Leeds train at Oxford station, he must surely have paused for a moment to contemplate just how far he had come in such a very short time. He had stood on this spot just sixteen years earlier when he had arrived in Oxford, a schoolboy attempting to pass the university entrance exam. He had been love-sick and forlorn, and he had failed. But a year later, he had returned to try again and in the autumn of 1911, he had entered Exeter College. Now, here he was in October 1925, the newly appointed Professor of Anglo-Saxon. He was alone again at the station (Edith and the boys were staying in Leeds while he established himself in the new job and found an appropriate home for the family), but in all other ways, his life was transformed. As far as his academic life was concerned, he had made it; he had reached the pinnacle of his profession.

For the first few months in Oxford, Tolkien was incredibly busy, but also extremely happy; it felt like a home-coming. He was thrown straight into teaching and administrative duties, and there were other new roles for him, for, as a professor in the Oxford English faculty, he was now part of a very active social scene within the university. He was required to attend dinners and to represent his faculty, to meet visiting dignitaries and to be seen to participate enthusiastically in college politics. To do otherwise would have been considered bad form and might have started tongues wagging. On top of this, he also had to find a suitable home for the family, but of all his new tasks this was a job he was quite used to.

Late in 1925, Tolkien found a large, comfortable house in leafy Northmoor Road in the academic heartland of Oxford just north of the city centre and its grand university buildings. Number 22 Northmoor Road was an attractive new house with a beautiful, large garden. Rose bushes climbed around the front door and a stone path wound its way to a tree-lined road almost totally devoid of traffic. It was a perfect place in which to raise a family and, soon after Christmas, Edith and the boys – John now aged eight, Michael, five and Christopher, just turned one – moved in. Finally, they had found some stability and the Tolkiens stayed in Northmoor Road until 1947. Their only move during that time was to the next-door house, Number 20 when they bought it from the publisher, Basil Blackwell, in 1929.

Thanks to the fact that Oxford was almost untouched by German bombers during the Second World War, Northmoor Road, about a mile from the city centre, is little different today to the way it was during the 1930s. The two houses each occupied by the Tolkiens look much as they did when the Professor of Anglo-Saxon and his growing brood lived there. It remains a street in which academics raise their families, although nowadays few of them stay for anything like the two decades the Tolkiens did. Number 20 Northmoor Road is a larger house, but remains far less aesthetically pleasing than Number 22. It is covered with grey pebble-dash, just as it was when the Tolkiens bought it, and its asymmetric design is not gentle on the eye, although the sprawling gardens make up for much.

The move to Oxford marked a significant change in the lifestyle of the Tolkien family. Gone now were the claustrophobic houses, the begrimed streets of a northern industrial city. For once, Edith felt they had found the perfect house and her husband had the perfect job. As for Tolkien, there was no longer the grim visage of brickwork through his office window, no need for shared offices. He cycled to work along quiet, tree-lined streets until he emerged onto St Giles, the broad sweeping avenue that links North Oxford to the city centre. Merton College, the place the English Faculty considered its headquarters, backs onto Christ Church Meadow which sweeps down to the Cherwell. In summer, the college gardens are ablaze with multi-coloured flowers. Meetings in college were sedate affairs at which tea was served in china cups and servants offered biscuits.

Tolkien settled into his new role immediately. He was expected to deliver a series of lectures each year and these required little preparation because in essence the course was little different to the one in Leeds thanks to the fact that George Gordon had modelled his faculty on Oxford's. Some lectures were held at Pembroke College (to which he was officially affiliated), but more often than not they took place in the Examination Schools on The High.

The lecture halls of the Examination Schools are vast, high-ceilinged affairs, richly decorated with stucco columns and with walls painted in pastels. The wooden floorboards echo to every footfall and the lecturer's voice resonates. Some lectures, such as those on Mediaeval Literature, were always packed because every student in the English school was required to attend. At other times, Tolkien taught small groups on specialised subjects. He was never very strict and was prone to drift off the subject, so that for some students it became something of a game to see how long they could take their lecturer away from the curriculum. One former student recalled how he thought at the time that Tolkien was 'as mad as a hatter' because he would suddenly leave the subject of the lecture and start talking about goblins and elves, half mumbling to himself and half talking to the class.

Tolkien loved an audience and relished lectures in which he could really express himself. He had a deep, abiding love for his subject and he was superb at conveying this to his students, so that few could forget his impassioned and forceful delivery.

Of all Tolkien's lectures, those on *Beowulf* were, for many, the most memorable. At the start of the lecture series he would walk silently into the room, step up to the podium and suddenly burst into the opening lines of *Beowulf*, almost shouting the words, filling the lecture hall with the booming stanzas. His face was contorted as he delivered the powerful words in the original Anglo-Saxon: 'Hwæt wē Gār Dena in geārdagum, þēeodcyninga þrym gefrunon, hu ða æþelingas ellen fremedon.' ('So, the Spear-Danes in days gone by and the kings who ruled them had courage and greatness. We have heard of those princes' heroic deeds.')

It made a startling impression. The poet, W.H. Auden, who was a great admirer of Tolkien and corresponded with him from the mid-1950s, attended one of the *Beowulf* lectures as a student and said once in a letter to his former tutor that he had never forgotten the way he had stunned the audience with the dramatic impact of the piece and how it had remained with him ever since.

What made Tolkien such a good teacher was his exuberant personality. He could be introverted, even insular at times, but he was a natural communicator whether it was on a one-to-one basis such as in his tutorials with students at home or with an audience like those he held spellbound during lectures on such an arcane and complex subject as Anglo-Saxon. This was summed up well by the writer, Desmond Albrow, who, many years after the event, recalled how as a young man he had met Tolkien in his study in Northmoor Road. 'He was a professor,' Albrow wrote, ' who looked like a professor . . . Tolkien wore cords and a sports jacket, smoked a reassuring pipe, laughed a lot, sometimes mumbled when his thoughts outstripped words, looked in those days to my idealistic eyes like the young Leslie Howard, the film actor. There was a sense of civilisation, winsome sanity and sophistication about him.'[1]

Tolkien was something of an actor. At King Edward's he had enjoyed school plays and as an undergraduate he had dabbled with drama. In the clubs and societies of which he was a prominent member he would proudly deliver a speech, enter a debate or read a sample of his own fiction without any sense of inhibition, and as an old man he even enjoyed recording himself reading in Elfish using an early home tape recording system.

He loved dressing up and more than once he took delight in terrifying his neighbours in Northmoor Road by charging down the street dressed as an axe-wielding Viking before cycling off to a fancy dress party in college. Although from middle-age he claimed he did not like or approve of drama and found the modern theatre vulgar, he had a wonderful sense of dramatic delivery. When the mood took him, he could easily cast-off the outward appearance of the stuffy, rather clichéd model don and unleash a suppressed mischievousness. Once, in an Oxford shop, the assistant was taking a long time to pay attention to him and was carrying on with whatever it was she was doing. So, to get his revenge, when it came time to pay, Tolkien handed the woman his false teeth along with the loose change.

During a brief period in the 1930s when the family owned a car, Tolkien proved to be at best an erratic driver. Their first car, nicknamed 'Jo' after the first two letters of its registration number, was a Morris Cowley built just a few miles from Northmoor Road at the Cowley car plant. Tolkien had a series of minor accidents in the car, but they were enough to convince Edith she would be safer using public transport and most of the time, she refused to get into the car when Tolkien was driving. Most frightening was his habit of ignoring traffic signals and when crossing a main road simply heading for a side street without looking and yelling, 'Charge 'em and they scatter!'

Tolkien's easy manner with other people was useful to him in his new position, for to succeed as an academic in a faculty position, one needed the talent and temperament for playing politics as well as mastery of one's own discipline. The professorship also came with administrative duties, which Tolkien found dull in the extreme. He hated petty-mindedness and he loathed bureaucracy and red-tape, but when an issue meant a great deal to him, he could fight his administrative corner as well as anyone.

One such battle occupied Tolkien almost from the moment he arrived. The School of English Language and Literature was, in many respects, an unhappy company of men and women.

Unlike many subjects with a core syllabus of equal interest to all, many students (the philologists) were more interested in language than literature. These students resented having to read set texts from Chaucer, Shakespeare and other icons of the literary tradition, while at the same time, the English Literature group could see little reason to study ancient poems such as *Beowulf*.

Tolkien believed that during the final year of the English Language and Literature course, students should be allowed to specialise in their own field of interest. The English Literature devotees could say goodbye to Middle and Old English and concentrate upon more modern texts, while those fascinated with the pre-Chaucerian literary canon could likewise dispense with the need to pore over anything that had been written after the fourteenth century.

It is surprising perhaps that such a simple and clearly logical improvement should have met with any opposition, but it certainly did. In fact, in 1925 when Tolkien first suggested the curriculum change, almost nobody in the School supported him. But gradually, he succeeded in persuading many of the die-hard traditionalists that his scheme would be an improvement. Admittedly, it took six years before the reforms were implemented, but within the academic world of the time, this was a lightning-strike revision. Tolkien operated well in the Senior Common Room and he was a persuasive talker. He was neither flatterer nor aggressive proselytiser, but simply knew how to network.

In parallel with these diverse duties, Tolkien also played the role of the family man. In 1929, some four years after settling in Oxford, he and Edith had a fourth child, the daughter Edith had longed for, Priscilla. But as much as this baby brought the family great happiness, she was also another small burden to add to Tolkien's growing stock of responsibilities. He was thirty-seven and at the pinnacle of his academic career. Being a professor at Oxford carried kudos and social status, but it was not terribly well paid, and he was obliged to continue marking School Certificate exam papers (which he did every summer for some twenty years).

In fact, the impression one gets from Tolkien's diaries and letters between 1925 and the late 1960s suggests he was always working in some capacity, and that his schedule was gruelling. He awoke early and often saw at least one student in Northmoor Road before heading off to Oxford to deliver a lecture. There were frequent faculty meetings to attend and endless university administration to deal with. After lunch he would sometimes deliver another lecture or return home to mark term papers or student essays. There were always courses to prepare, advice to be given to colleagues, letters to write, committees to attend. On top of this, in common with most academics, Tolkien was expected to contribute to the literature of his field by publishing papers.

However, Tolkien had no great love for writing for fellow academics. He had a pleasant enough time during the early 1920s compiling the new edition of *Sir Gawain and the Green Knight* with Eric Gordon in Leeds, but he never much liked writing to order or to fulfil the imperatives of his academic position. Even so, he produced a respectable body of work and even succeeded in making readable and interesting what, in most other hands, could have been extremely dry studies. He wrote frequently for *The Review of English Studies* and *The Oxford Magazine* and many other literary journals. He completed a key study on a mediaeval English text called *Ancrene Wisse and Hali Meiohad*, an account of which appeared in *Essays and Studies by Members of the*

English Association, published by the Clarendon Press in Oxford in 1929, and he was a regular contributor to the *Transactions of the Philological Society*.

These things filled his working life as an Oxford professor, but of course, there was always another side to his intellect that needed an outlet. As much as he enjoyed his academic work, it did little to channel his volatile and many-faceted imagination. So, late at night when the family was asleep, he donned his writer's cap and submerged into a fantasy world.

Of course, it takes a special strength to pick up a pen after a full day of mentally demanding work, but Tolkien had the self-discipline and the drive to sit at the desk in his study from around 10 p.m. until one or two o'clock in the morning wrestling with convoluted plots and beautifully chiselled characterisations. Then, after a few hours' sleep, each new day, the cycle began again.

There was also the family, to whom Tolkien was devoted. Somehow, he always managed to find time for his children, no matter how great the demands upon his energies. He was an extremely affectionate father, and, unusually for the time, he was not at all embarrassed to show it. He often kissed his sons in public, and in the many hundreds of letters he wrote them at different stages of their lives, he always addressed them in the most loving of terms, such as 'My Dearest', and he invariably signed off 'Your own father' or 'With all the love of your own father'.

One of the ways in which he expressed his affection was by each year writing them a letter 'from Father Christmas'. Each told the children of the latest adventures of Father Christmas and his seasonal preparations and were accompanied by lavish illustrations. These letters have been lovingly preserved by the

Tolkien family and in 1976, they were gathered together for publication as *Letters From Father Christmas*.

Tolkien composed the first letter in 1920 when John was three and he may have been inspired to write it because he had rediscovered in his papers a letter his own mother had written to Father Christmas on his behalf when he was two. The envelope for Tolkien's first letter to John was addressed: Mrs Tolkien and Master John Francis Reuel Tolkien, 1 Alfred Street, Oxford, England, and inside was a letter describing Father Christmas's house along with a carefully produced illustration. From then on, each year, the envelope carried a newly designed and painted stamp, and inside could be found news from the North Pole recounting the latest trials and tribulations of Father Christmas. Gradually, the tales became more elaborate and a cast of characters, including the Great Polar Bear, the Great Seal and the Snow-elves were featured.

As a collection, the letters from Father Christmas are a beautiful heirloom and chart the course of the family as it changed with the passing years. By 1924, the letters to John had become letters for both John and Michael. After this, and for the next few years, the addressees are 'John, Michael and Christopher Tolkien' and by 1929, the envelope reads 'J&M&C&P Tolkien, 22 Northmoor Road, Oxford, England', with the letter addressed to 'Dear Boys and Girl'. But then, as time passes and the boys grow up, we have envelopes marked for fewer and fewer Tolkiens, until 1938 when Christopher, now aged fourteen is deemed too old for such things and Priscilla, nine, becomes the sole recipient. This is how it remains until 1943 when Priscilla's last letter is signed off 'Very much love from your old friend, Father Christmas.'[2]

Tolkien clearly loved composing these letters and he relished making up other tales for his children. Some of these were devised on holiday and began when one of the children noticed a roadside notice or street sign, or they met someone unusual. One series involved the tireless Major Road Ahead who was constantly trying to catch the shady and inscrutable Bill Stickers (from a sign that read 'Bill Stickers Will Be Prosecuted').

In 1925, Tolkien composed a story for John and Michael (Christopher was still a small baby) which began when Michael lost a toy dog on a beach, and this grew steadily into a complex collection of adventures called *Roverandom*. The main character was a dog called Rover who was turned into a toy by a wizard and then lost on the beach before being rescued by Psamathos Psamathides, the sand-wizard. Tolkien wrote down this set of stories and illustrated them with watercolours. One of the best of these paintings (preserved today in a collection held by the Bodleian Library in Oxford) was called 'The Gardens of the Merking's Palace' which accompanied an adventure in which Rover travels under the sea.

Other favourites included a series of stories about two mysterious characters called Maddo and Owlamoo who had featured in Michael Tolkien's childhood nightmares. Maddo was an armless gloved hand that could part the bedroom curtains and climb up and down them in the dark, and Owlamoo was an ugly owl that perched on top of the wardrobe. Another tale involved a Dutch doll owned by Michael, and there were still more involving a tiny fellow called Timothy Titus.

This period was a highly creative time for Tolkien and his fertile imagination was stimulated by the positive reactions he always got from his own children. He produced quite a large collection of drawings and illustrations, pictures of dragons, goblins and other strange creatures. Another popular creation was Mr Bliss, a tall, thin man who owned a yellow car and got into all matter of scrapes. Tolkien was particular pleased with this tale and made a fair copy which he had bound.

The character of Tom Bombadil also first appeared during this time, and a series of tales in which he is a central character was later published as *The Adventures of Tom Bombadil*. These also involved Goldberry, a family of badgers, Old Man Willow, and the Barrow-wight, who in this story was the ghost of a long-dead monarch buried under the Berkshire Downs.[3] Although Tolkien had no idea that one day these characters would appear in the story of the Ring, Bombadil (and indeed Goldberry and the others) hardly changed between this first appearance and the form they took in *The Lord of the Rings*.

Tolkien also spent a lot of his spare time producing water-colours of dragons, some of which provided the basis for his later paintings used to illustrate *The Hobbit*. Tolkien's vision of the dragon was heavily influenced by his childhood love of the *Red Fairy Book* by Andrew Lang which contained a particularly dramatic dragon tale called 'Sigurd and Fafnir'. One of Tolkien's best illustrations from the 1920s was a watercolour of a coiled dragon to which he added a caption based upon a quotation from *Beowulf*, 'hringboga heorte gefysed', ('the heart of the coiling beast was stirred').[4] Over a decade later, a few months after the publication of *The Hobbit* in 1937, Tolkien delivered a Christmas lecture for children, 'On Dragons', at the University Museum in Oxford and he used this painting as a slide to illustrate the talk.

When we survey Tolkien's work and consider in particular the erudition and depth of a masterpiece such as *The Silmarillion*, it is easy to forget how much he enjoyed writing for children and this must have been in no small measure due to the fact that he had four of his own. *The Silmarillion* and *The Lord of the Rings* are ostensibly adult books (although the latter has always been enjoyed by all age groups), but Tolkien thoroughly enjoyed developing stories that had started life as spontaneous oral tales told at bedtime or used to help alleviate the tedium of a long journey. And he always greatly valued children's reactions to his stories. As a famous author, he took particular delight in giving public talks for children and took pains to reply to any young person who wrote to him concerning his books. According to a lady who, as a child, was a neighbour of Ronald and Edith's, Tolkien would often try out his stories on her and the other children who played in the street.

And so, this was the Tolkien in his middle years; a professional scholar and teacher, a family man and a conjurer of dreams and fairy tales. Viewed from afar, his life was orthodox and rather plain, but his inner world, the world of sub-creation was a ferment, the very opposite of his conventional façade. This was the private man who moulded legends and shaped an entire mythology. But, before we consider this and the results of his labours, we should first turn to yet another aspect of his personality; J.R.R. Tolkien, the man's man who relished the company of like-minded imaginative souls in an exclusive man's world.

CHAPTER 8

A Man's World

Tolkien and C.S. Lewis first met on 11 May 1926 at a meeting of the faculty of English at Merton College. Tolkien had been Professor of Anglo-Saxon at the University for little more than two terms and Lewis had only recently been appointed Fellow and Tutor in English Language and Literature at Magdalen College.

At first they seemed rather wary of one another and Lewis confided to his diary: 'Tolkien managed to get the discussion round to the proposed English Prelim. I had a talk with him afterwards. He is a smooth, pale, fluent little chap . . . thinks all literature is written for the amusement of *men* between thirty and forty . . . No harm in him: only needs a good smack or two.'[1]

This is a rather odd recollection of their first meeting and sadly we have nothing from Tolkien with which to compare it. If we ignore the rather silly, arrogant style, it says much about

Tolkien at the time. This was the period when he was first campaigning to alter the structure of the English course at Oxford and the way Lewis describes Tolkien successfully managing to get the conversation round to the subject he wanted confirms what we know of him already – that he was a good talker and a proselytiser. Already it seems that some in the faculty were becoming weary of Tolkien's convictions, and for some time after they first met, Lewis was far from supportive of his plans.

The other strange comment comes from Lewis's reporting of Tolkien's feelings about the uses of literature. Tolkien was of course a rather old-fashioned man and had strong views about the correct roles of men and women in society, but the comment that literature was 'written for the amusement of *men* between thirty and forty' seems quite out of character. Perhaps Lewis put words in his mouth, or maybe it was mere bravado, for Tolkien had some experience of intellectual women. Within his own family, his Aunt Jane, with whom he had lived for a short while in 1904, was one of the first women to obtain a science degree and he considered her a quite remarkable woman.

By the time they met, Lewis and Tolkien had much in common. Lewis was the younger by almost seven years, but both men had fought in the trenches, and although he was not familiar with Icelandic in the way Tolkien was, Lewis was fascinated with the arcane intricacies of Norse mythology and with Old English literature.

But they had come from very different backgrounds and been brought together by their intellectual brilliance. Lewis was the son of a successful Belfast lawyer. His parents had christened him Clive Staples, but from childhood he had called himself Jack and this is the way his friends addressed him throughout his life.

He had been educated at the exclusive Malvern College and then won a scholarship to University College in 1916. He was an exceptional scholar and took a First in Classics in 1920 and followed it up two years later with another First (in Greats); a truly remarkable achievement especially when we consider the fact Lewis fought in the war and was wounded in action in 1918.

Perhaps because of his relatively privileged background, Lewis came across as more urbane than Tolkien, his interests were more wide-ranging, and in many ways, he was a far more unconventional character. While Tolkien was a husband and a father to four children, Lewis was leading an entirely different sort of life, one that was considered bohemian, almost bizarre by the standards of the time. He was unmarried but shared a home with a much older divorcee, Janie Moore, a poorly educated Irishwoman whom Lewis had met during the war when she was forty-five and he was just nineteen. They lived in a large, rambling house called The Kilns close to Shotover Hill about five miles from the centre of Oxford. Lewis lived there for thirty-three years from 1930 until his death in 1963 and it was mostly a merry place, filled with books and papers. There was a large pond in the garden where Lewis and Tolkien often swam in summer.

But, whenever Lewis referred to his mistress at all, he called her 'Mrs Moore' and she was both mother and lover to him. She was also something of a mystery to Lewis's friends. Jack never took Mrs Moore to social functions and many of those who knew Lewis well met her only rarely when she happened to be in when they visited The Kilns. Tolkien, who by the late 1920s, was one of Lewis's closest friends and confidants, knew almost nothing about the woman except that she seemed to have some strange emotional hold over Jack. Many in Oxford considered her to be something of a simpleton because, from the odd mention Jack made of her, she seemed to talk largely gibberish and was known to be almost insanely possessive of Lewis.

The close friendship that grew between Tolkien and Lewis was inevitable. Many of the other dons were rather dull characters who had little in their lives other than their work. (In one of his earliest books, *The Pilgrim's Regress,* Lewis lampooned the type as 'Mr Sensible', defining them as witty and intelligent but narrow minded and shallow.) Lewis was keen to write fiction and poetry and had grand plans. In this respect, he found a kindred spirit in Tolkien. Also, each was attracted to a form of camaraderie into which they had been immersed since schooldays, a man's world which had gained greater significance to them during the war. But their friendship also developed because of a shared intellectual background and through measured criticism of each other's literary efforts.

Within a few months of their first introduction, the two men took to meeting regularly in Lewis's rooms in Magdalen, a drably furnished, shabby suite. Heavy velvet drapes adorned the windows, the desk was piled high with papers and books lay scattered about the floor or in piles propped up against the door. Often, they would sit by the fire late into the night discussing literature or history, each reviewing the other's manuscripts.

Soon after they first met, Tolkien loaned Lewis a draft of *The Gest of Beren and Lúthien* (what later became *The Lay of Beren and Lúthien*) and Lewis filled the margins with constructive comments. He seems to have realised quickly that Tolkien could be sensitive to criticism, and so instead of blunt commentary, Lewis mocked his own criticisms about *The Gest of Beren and Lúthien* by writing them under the guise of fictitious critics 'Schick',

'Peabody' and 'Pumpernickel', each of whom had a few words to say.

But perhaps Lewis need not have been so concerned. He was right to judge his friend as sensitive to criticism, but equally Tolkien could certainly accommodate the views of those whom he respected. Many years earlier, his friends in the T.C., B.S. had subtly nudged him away from what they perceived as misguided directions, and by the late 1920s, with two of his oldest friends gone and Lewis now large in his life, there were few men he respected more. Tellingly, when the manuscript of *The Gest of Beren and Lúthien* came back, Tolkien noted every single comment and almost totally rewrote the piece.

But, if literature had been the spur to their relationship, it soon developed in other directions for they also liked good conversation with other men, strong beer and reading aloud to each other from ancient texts and their own writings.

Only a few weeks before their first meeting during Tolkien's second term as Professor of Anglo-Saxon he had formed an Icelandic reading-group called the 'Coalbiters'. The name derived from the Icelandic word *Kolbíter* which means 'those who in winter get so close to the fire they bite the coal' and its purpose was solely to bring together those interested in the traditional Icelandic sagas which were then read aloud by the members.

By the autumn of 1926, Tolkien had invited Lewis to join the Coalbiters and although he knew almost no Icelandic, he was keen to learn and gradually took on more and more ambitious passages to read aloud. Amongst the Coalbiters, Lewis was not the only novice scholar of Icelandic. Some members were linguistic experts, including G.E.K. Braunholtz, the Oxford Professor of Comparative Philology and R.M. Dawkins, the

Professor of Byzantine and Modern Greek, but some others
were even less expert in ancient languages than Lewis. An
English don from Exeter College, the aristocratic Nevill Coghill,
knew no Icelandic at all and Tolkien's old boss at Leeds
University, the Professor of English Literature at Oxford,
George Gordon, was also only a keen beginner.

As with all such clubs, it was as much an excuse for meeting
with friends, sharing evenings drinking beer and having some
light relief from the pressures of the working day as it was serious study. But the original objective of the group was to read
through all the major Icelandic sagas, which, by the early 1930s,
they had succeeded in doing. Consequently the Coalbiters began
to wind down and Tolkien and Lewis become members of
another literary club called the Inklings. Founded by an undergraduate, Edward Tangye Lean, the club met each week in
University College.

Lean was also editor of the university magazine *Isis*, and an
ambitious young author who had started the club so that members could read to each other their unpublished work. In 1933,
Lean left Oxford to begin a career in journalism and broadcast-
ing and his club stopped meeting, but within a term, some of
the original members, including Tolkien and Lewis, decided to
start meeting again and adopted the old name for their informal
gatherings in Lewis's rooms in Magdalen. No one really knows
why they used the name Inklings, but both Tolkien and Lewis
liked it because of its ambiguity, the fact that it implied members were grappling with 'big ideas' and that it also suited
academics and writers whose lives had been built upon large
quantities of ink.

The earliest meetings of the Inklings took place each
Thursday evening in Lewis's spacious rooms in Magdalen, but

by 1939 they had also begun to hold regular Tuesday morning meetings at a pub on St Giles called the Eagle and Child (affectionately known by all as the Bird and Baby).[2]

The pub has been extended since those times and the room in which the Inklings met was once part of the back of the pub. Today, it has become something of a shrine to the Inklings with photographs of Tolkien, Lewis and Charles Williams adorning the walls. Those partaking of 'the inklings Tour' conducted each Wednesday morning during the summer months stop off here to soak up the atmosphere. On the wall by the bar is a large plaque that reads:

C.S. Lewis

His brother W.H.L. Lewis, J.R.R. Tolkien, Charles
Williams and other friends met every Tuesday morning
between the years 1939–62 in the back room of this
their favourite pub. These men, popularly known as 'The
Inklings', met here to drink beer and to discuss, among
other things, the books they were writing.

This was not the only pub the Inklings frequented, they enjoyed the King's Arms near the Bodleian Library, the White Horse, and the Mitre in the centre of Oxford, but as the plaque says, the Bird and Baby was their favourite. Here, Tolkien first read to his friends extracts from what he called 'The New Hobbit', *The Lord of the Rings*, while Lewis told them of Narnia, of his cosmic mythology and one of his most acclaimed creations Screwtape and the apprentice devil, Wormwood.

All these men have gone now, but if you stand in the Bird and Baby before any other patrons arrive, if you ignore the traffic outside and the hum of the coolant system for the Australian lager and the publican gearing up the sound system for the students, you might just be able to imagine Tolkien ('Tollers' as they called him) leaning back in a chair and cupping the bowl of his pipe, his head wreathed in smoke as Lewis reads from some crumpled pages in front of him. Around the table sit three or four other Inklings, Hugo Dyson, Nevill Coghill and Christopher Williams perhaps. Each listens intently, sipping occasionally at their pints of beer.

The core of the Inklings consisted of some seven or eight contemporaries. Lewis and Tolkien were the founders, Nevill Coghill, Lewis's older brother Warren (Warnie) and Hugo Dyson, Professor of English Literature at Reading University, also attended early meetings along with a doctor friend, Robert Havard (known, for some mysterious reason, as Humphrey). Charles Williams joined later, in 1939. Not all of them were literary men. Warnie was an army officer and a graduate of Sandhurst, but he began to write history books during the 1940s; Humphrey was a Catholic and an Oxford man, which endeared him to Tolkien, but he had no literary leanings other than being thoroughly admiring of the efforts of his friends; Nevill Coghill was a Fellow at Exeter and a scholar of Middle English who gained academic acclaim for his translation of Chaucer's *Canterbury Tales* and became Professor of English Literature at Oxford in 1957. He was also greatly interested in the theatre and managed many lavish productions in Oxford. Most famous was a spectacular outdoor *Tempest* during the summer of 1949 performed on a stage constructed next to a lake behind Worcester College. Coghill was tutor to W.H. Auden and, during the period in which he attended meetings of the Inklings at the Bird and Baby, he also taught Richard Burton who acted in several Coghill productions.

Of course it was a terribly exclusive club. The membership changed little except when Lewis encountered someone new and invited them along when they were next visiting Oxford. Any member had to fit several criteria; they had to be a good conversationalist, interested or involved in writing, they had to enjoy drinking, be a friend of C.S. Lewis, but most crucially, they had to be male.

No women ever gained admittance to this most select of men's clubs. According to legend, in 1943, the writer of detective novels and plays on religious themes, Dorothy Sayers, turned up at the Bird and Baby expecting to be invited to join the men around the table, but she was politely asked to leave.[3] It was very important to these men that the Inklings remained an exclusively male preserve.

Lewis captured well the atmosphere of Inklings meetings in letters to friends and in his essays. They usually met in the evening, but he, Tolkien and Williams often read to one another over a morning smoke in Lewis's rooms. 'Picture to yourself,' Lewis wrote, 'an upstairs sitting-room with windows looking north in the "grove" of Magdalen College on a sunshiny Monday morning at about ten o'clock. The Prof and I, both on the Chesterfield, lit our pipes and stretched out our legs. Williams in the arm-chair opposite to us threw his cigarette into the grate, took up the pile of extremely small, loose sheets on which he habitually wrote – they came I think, from a two-penny pad for memoranda – and began.'[4] Elsewhere, Lewis described typical meetings involving at least half a dozen Inklings as 'raucous affairs' and imagined that any passerby would have thought they were talking about 'bawdy affairs rather than theology'.[5]

Today, it is perhaps easy to underestimate the influence of the

Inklings. Professor Kilby, Curator of the Wade collection in which many of Lewis's papers are kept, knew Tolkien briefly during the 1960s and has written: 'The Inklings as an organisation is more our conception after the fact than it ever was in reality.'[6] By this he was asserting that the group of individuals that met in Oxford pubs and discussed literature, religion or whatever took their fancy did not think of themselves as a literary group in the way, say, the Bloomsbury Group did. But this does nothing to detract from the fact that they *were* immensely influential. In 1997 (soon after the first polls naming Tolkien as the most popular author of the century and placing *The Lion, the Witch and the Wardrobe* high in the ratings), journalist Nigel Reynolds commented: '[the poll] suggests that the Inklings, a 1930s Oxford drinking club, has been a more powerful force than the Bloomsbury Group, the Algonquin set in New York, Hemingway's Paris set or the W.H. Auden/Christopher Isherwood group of writers of the 1930s.'[7]

For Tolkien, the halcyon days of the Inklings probably lasted until the end of the Second World War, by which time he was struggling through the final third of 'The New Hobbit'. But within a few years, his relationship with some of the other members had begun to sour. Evidence of this waning interest comes from the fact that the final parts of what was to become *The Lord of the Rings* were not read at meetings of the Inklings and his fellow members were left with Frodo and Sam at the borders of Mordor.

Between 1946 and 1947, when Tolkien was attending fewer meetings, the Inklings began to gather less frequently in Lewis's rooms and instead made for another pub in Oxford called The Roebuck (now Oz Bar) in Market Street. This venue was unofficially divided into two. Upstairs was a large room with heavy velvet drapes at the windows, a bar, a piano and a small kitchen where food was served and it was almost exclusively a university domain. Downstairs was the public bar.

The Inklings met there almost every week, but Tolkien at least was not very interested in this sort of place for it had none of the gentility of the Bird and Baby. In fact it would appear that at the Roebuck more drinking than reading was done, because the abiding memory of the townsfolk who kept to the public bar was the sound of First World War soldiers' songs sung so loudly they could be heard through the ceiling. Lewis always did enjoy a sing-along, but it was not really Tollers' thing.

Tolkien and Lewis were close for perhaps twenty years from 1926 to about 1946, but then their relationship began to cool until, by the early 1950s, almost none of the old warmth remained. Meetings of the Inklings continued until perhaps a year before Lewis's death in 1963, but by then Tolkien had long since stopped attending and the erstwhile friends met only very rarely. The reasons why the relationship fell apart are as complex as the friendship itself, and in order to try to understand it we should consider some of the less attractive aspects of Tolkien's character.

For many years, Tolkien had been fond of Hugo Dyson and Warnie Lewis. He had remained close to Christopher Wiseman and had as a youth formed an unusually intimate bond with the other members of the T.C., B.S. He also enjoyed many cordial relationships with other academics at Oxford, but for Tolkien, Jack Lewis was a very special friend, to whom he could open up his heart, from whom he could accept detailed criticism, and of all the Inklings, he viewed himself and Lewis as being the most like-minded and intellectually equivalent. But Tolkien was a very jealous man who was unusually possessive of his friends. At the same time, he became easily resentful of them if they gained recognition and success.

Lewis was aware of Tolkien's insecurities and inclination towards jealousy. As early as 1939, he was able to write to his brother, Warnie, describing how Tolkien's 'trials, besides being frequent and severe are usually of such a complicated nature as to be impenetrable'.[8]

Jack's feelings for Tolkien were never as intense. He had unbounded respect for him, enjoyed his company enormously and gained much from their relationship, but at the same time, he was an altogether more colourful, unorthodox individual than Tolkien. Living with the distinctly odd Mrs Moore, Jack did not have the conventional family lifestyle of his friend. He had many more close friends than Tolkien, and in some respects he possessed a more liberated mindset and was able to enjoy a freer personal life. These differences added dynamism to the friendship, but starting from the late-1930s, three things slowly came between the pair: Lewis's religious conversion, Lewis's commercial success, and finally but perhaps most importantly, Lewis's friends.

Lewis had been raised an Ulster Protestant, but by the time he had reached adulthood he had largely discarded any form of religious faith. Tolkien only became aware of this gradually, but when he did, he quickly began to see it as in some way his duty to enlighten his friend to the mysteries of religious doctrine. As a consequence, they had many long conversations on the subject of religion.

Although Lewis would have called himself an agnostic during the mid-1920s, he had thought deeply about religion. Soon after the war, he had reached what he called a 'New Look' concerning religious orthodoxy. In this philosophy he considered the Christian doctrine as a myth just like any other. But gradually, this view began to change. By the time he met Tolkien in 1926, he was growing confused over some of the deepest questions of faith, and initially at least, Tolkien's orthodoxy added to this confusion.

Lewis found it difficult to square the fact that his new friend was one of the most interesting, intellectual and intelligent men he had ever met and yet he was a devout Christian – and a Catholic to boot. He could have dismissed as wishful thinking Tolkien's deeply held convictions, but he did not. He tried to separate intellect from faith, to propose that a person may have a highly tuned intellect but that their faith derived from something quite separate and more powerful, although this did not support closer scrutiny.

Instead, Lewis went completely the other way. Although Tolkien could not really be said to have converted Lewis, his portrayal of his own religious beliefs and his capable explanations of subtle nuance and meaning did much to make Lewis reconsider. During the first five years of their friendship from 1926 to 1931, Lewis's stance on religion moved a considerable way. By the end of this period, he had concluded that there was a God, but his vision of the divine was not an orthodox Christian one. It was more akin perhaps to the God of many eastern religions, almost a Pantheist God, a God that was the source of inspiration, a well-spring of Nature, far from any Biblical portrayal.

Of the many fruitful and intense conversations Tolkien and Lewis had, there was one that stands out as a turning point in their debates and marks the point where Lewis turned from agnostic to believer.

It was a Saturday evening, 19 September 1931. Lewis and Tolkien's friend Hugo Dyson (who was also a Christian) was making one of his frequent visits to Oxford and had dined with Jack and Tolkien at Magdalen. He was quite aware of the many conversations his two friends had had on the subject and was keen to join them. After dinner, the three of them went for a stroll and the conversation naturally turned to Christianity. Lewis had become entrenched in his Pantheist vision of God and because of this he could not begin to embrace orthodox Christianity, which at its heart requires a belief in Christ and an unflinching conviction that Jesus was sent to die upon the cross in order to save our souls. Lewis could accept none of this as being anything other than myth. He, like Tolkien, was a scholar of ancient mythologies, of tales of heroes and of pagan moral salvation. To him, the story of Christ was simply just another legend, another myth no more accurate or meaningful to him and the modern world than any other. And at their root, he believed, myths are of course, lies.

Tolkien listened carefully to what his friend said and when Lewis reached this conclusion, he threw up his arms as if to say 'So, how then can you believe the Christ story to be anything but an ancient legend?' Then Tolkien came back with an argument that changed the course of Lewis's life.

Myths, he declared, are most certainly not lies. Myths derive from a kernel of truth and portray very specific cultural meaning. Christianity is based upon what Lewis considered the 'myth of Christ'. Very well then, Tolkien argued, call it a myth if you want to, but it was constructed upon real events and it was inspired by a deep truth. Ultimately, no myth was a lie, Tolkien believed, and the 'myth' that lay at the core of Christianity provided a route to follow for the non-materialistic aspect of every human being, an in-road to a deeper, spiritual truth.

Revelation did not come instantly, but it is clear that this conversation set Lewis thinking about the problem of faith in a quite different way to the one he was used to. Lewis never accepted some aspects of Christian orthodoxy; it seemed his intellect always stood in the way of his faith. He once wrote to a friend: 'How could I – I of all people – ever have come to believe this cock and bull story?'[9] Nevertheless, within two weeks of his debate with Tolkien and Dyson, Lewis was writing to a friend, Arthur Greeves, telling him that he had moved from his long-held convictions to a new position in which he could finally embrace Christ; in other words, he now considered him-self 'a Christian'.

As much as it shows how Tolkien influenced Lewis's reli-gious thinking, the conversation that September evening also offers a fascinating insight into the way the two men intellectu-alised and how this process fed their writing. The idea that Christianity is a true myth lies at the heart of what Lewis went on to spend the rest of his literary career describing. It is the principle behind his famous Narnia books (which Tolkien detested) and his science fiction trilogy, *Out of the Silent Planet* (1938), *Perelandra* (1943), and *That Hideous Strength* (1945). By linking Christ with an intellectual thread with which Lewis was very familiar (the meaning of myth) it was almost as though he could first intellectualise religion and from there let it become instinctive, a passion.

Ironically, this important conversation in September 1931 marked a new intensity in the relationship between Tolkien and Lewis, but it also planted the seeds of their later falling out. Tolkien had hoped sincerely that Lewis would adopt Catholicism, and even two years later, he was able to write in his diary that his friendship with Lewis 'besides giving constant pleasure and comfort, has done me much good from the contact with a man at once honest, brave, intellectual – a scholar, a poet and a philosopher – and a lover, at least after a long pilgrimage, of Our Lord'.[10]

But Tolkien had seriously misjudged his friend. Instead of approaching Catholicism, Jack returned to his roots, to a form of Irish Protestantism which of course, Tolkien loathed. When the man he had helped find God then became 'one of the enemy' and not only that, but a famous convert, their friendship began to crumble.

For his part, Lewis had no liking for Catholics or Catholicism. He and his brother, Warnie Lewis, often referred to Irish Catholics as 'bog-trotters' and when Tolkien made mention of his religious devotions or slipped into talking about what Lewis saw as arcane and frankly ludicrous religious practices, he could barely reign in his disgust.

But, because they were both writers, Lewis's conversion became especially painful for Tolkien. From finding God, finding Christ and becoming a believer, Lewis immediately leapt into the role of Christian apologist, a role that also made him famous far beyond Oxford. With what Tolkien considered indecent haste, Lewis had published *The Pilgrim's Regress: An Allegorical Apology for Christianity* and *Reason and Romanticism* (1933). Later, *The Screwtape Letters*, largely written during 1940–1 while on air-raid duties, was serialised in a Christian magazine and then found international success in book form when it was published in 1942. Tolkien disliked these books and believed, probably with some justification, that Lewis had not given himself time to come to a clear understanding of his religious outlook, that he had rushed his thoughts into print without allowing them to mature.

During the rest of the 1940s and on into the 1950s, Lewis produced a long succession of commercially successful books each quite different in character covering a range of genres, but each carrying forward the underlying theme of using allegory to portray his religious viewpoint. *Out of the Silent Planet* and, later, the Narnia books beginning with *The Lion, the Witch and the Wardrobe*, all ploughed the same furrow of religious allegory.

Lewis dedicated *The Screwtape Letters* to Tolkien, and in the personal copy for his friend he added 'In token payment of a great debt'. But ironically, Tolkien did not care for the story, seeing it as rather trite and too hastily put together. Yet, his true objection to it was actually more personal. In many ways, Tolkien was almost a fundamentalist Catholic. He believed the devil and his demons really did exist and that it was therefore rather foolhardy to make light of such serious matters.

But, Tolkien's greatest scorn was reserved for Lewis's most famous and successful work, the Narnia Chronicles. Lewis began to read these at Inklings' meetings during the spring of 1949. The Inklings had all been entranced by Tolkien's reading of *The Lord of the Rings* during the decade that he had taken them from Hobbiton to the borders of Mordor, but now Lewis was working through his own mythology at a staggering pace and presenting lengthy passages which had often been written in a matter of days. Such haste was one cause of annoyance for Tolkien, but he also hated the story and found it filled with contradiction and inconsistency. He applied exacting standards to himself and he expected the same quality and integrity from his friends.

Tolkien did nothing to hide his disgust and forthrightly declared at meetings that he really did not like *The Lion the Witch and the Wardrobe*. One of Lewis's pupils, Roger Lancelyn Green, had begun to meet occasionally with the Inklings and heard some of Lewis's reading from an early draft of the book during meetings which Tolkien refused to attend. Later, when Tolkien bumped into Green in the street and the student began to talk about Lewis, Tolkien declared, 'I hear you've been reading Jack's children's story. It really won't do, you know!'[11]

But there was more to this than Tolkien being offended by Lewis's writing speed. By the mid-1940s, Lewis had become a famous writer. His Screwtape books had sold almost a quarter of a million copies and his science fiction novels were rolling off the press at the rate of one a year garnering more acclaim and global recognition. *The Hobbit* had done very well, but now its author was struggling with some sort of sequel and he could find no publisher interested in the project that really mattered to him, *The Silmarillion*. Salt was rubbed in the wounds when, a few months after finishing *The Lion, the Witch and the Wardrobe*, Lewis had publishers beating a path to his door trying to get the rights to the book. There is no coincidence in the fact that by October that year, the Thursday meetings of the Inklings in Lewis's rooms in Magdalen ended and the group met less frequently and with less formality and then only in Oxford pubs.

To add another turn to the screw, Tolkien also began to suspect that Lewis had 'borrowed' from him. He believed there were echoes of his ideas in Lewis's books and that Lewis had reworked and reused some of his names. An example was Lewis's 'Tinidril' which was, Tolkien suspected, a combination of his own 'Idril' and 'Tinúviel'. Tolkien's personal copy of Lewis's *Perelandra* (*Voyage to Venus*) contains a rather caustic note in his own hand that reads 'A bottle of sound vintage (?) I hope!'[12]

Lewis had a wide circle of contacts and acquaintances and once in a while he would encounter a new person about whom he quickly grew very excited, almost to hero-worship. Then he would try to thrust this person upon his long-established friends. He did this many times during his relationship with Tolkien, but the most irritating occasion for Tolkien was when Lewis first met the writer Charles Williams. Within days of knowing Williams, Lewis was telling his Oxford friends what an amazing man he was. He described Williams as 'an ugly man with a rather cockney voice. But no one ever thinks of this for five minutes after he has begun speaking. His face becomes almost angelic. Both in public and in private he is of nearly all the men I have met, the one whose address most overflows with *love*. It is simply irresistible.'[13] These were typically over-the-top comments from Lewis, but Charles Williams was to become more than a passing interest and soon rivalled Tolkien in Jack's affections.

Williams was the oldest of the three and already fifty by the time he first met C.S. Lewis in 1936. He had had a rather che- quered education which had begun well enough with a scholarship to St Albans Grammar School and then an award to University College, Oxford, beginning in 1901 some fifteen years before Lewis. By all accounts he was a promising student, but then, after spending two years at Oxford, Williams's father hit financial difficulties and the family could no longer contribute to his fees so he was forced to leave without obtaining his degree. He then worked for the Oxford University Press and published a succession of novels, non-fiction books and collections of poems and plays.

By 1940, Charles Williams had written twenty-seven books and had come to Lewis's attention when he discovered a copy of Williams's recently published *The Place of the Lion*. By 1939, Williams had moved to Oxford where he and his wife and son spent the duration of the Second World War. From this time on, he began to see a great deal of Lewis, whose friendship and advice he valued greatly. Writing to his wife in 1939, Williams said of his new friend: 'I have fled to C.S. Lewis's rooms . . . he is a great tea-drinker at any hour of night or day, and left a tray for me with milk and tea, and an electric kettle at hand.'[14] Much to Tolkien's chagrin, he was soon inviting himself to regular Monday talks at the Eastgate Hotel which Lewis and Tolkien had been enjoying alone each week for more than ten years.

Lewis quickly became almost inseparable from Williams and began campaigning to have him accepted as an official lecturer at the university in spite of the fact that he had never been awarded a degree. In the face of opposition from almost all quarters, Lewis succeeded in this (largely thanks to the severe shortage of qualified teaching staff during the War) and was later instrumental in acquiring for Williams an honorary MA at Oxford.

In spite of, or perhaps because of Lewis's adulation, Tolkien was never entirely comfortable with Jack's new friend. Charles Williams was viewed by some as a rather arrogant, self-possessed man who in the company of the Inklings seemed to need to over-compensate for his fractured education and Tolkien certainly did not much care for the man's character. Tolkien also disliked William's writing, especially *The Figure of Arthur*, an account of the Arthurian legend.

Tolkien also seems to have been constantly suspicious of Williams's religious and philosophical stance, much of which was diametrically opposed to Tolkien's own. Charles Williams was a mass of contradictions. He was at once a devout member of the Church of England, but almost obsessively fascinated with mysticism and the occult. He had joined the famous mystical group known as the Order of the Golden Dawn which counted the notorious Aleister Crowley as a member, but on Sundays he attended church and said his prayers. These two aspects of his philosophical and spiritual interests made for an interesting blend when expressed poetically, but Tolkien, who had harboured little sympathy for Protestants since childhood, could find little in common with a Protestant who was also interested in the Hermetic tradition, devil worship and black magic.

Worse still, Williams appears to have had quite serious sadistic tendencies. Although, as far as anyone knows, these were never expressed physically and he was said to have been a devoted and loving husband to his wife, Michal and their son, Michael, he expressed himself vividly in his poetry and in his novels. In a poem entitled 'Antichrist', he wrote:

> My mind possessed me with delight
> To wrack her lovely head
> With slow device of subtle pain.[15]

When combined with his attraction to the occult, such sadistic impulses added an exciting intensity to his writing, but according to some of his friends, they often felt Williams was only just in control of his emotions, able to rein in his darker side only with a great effort of will.

All of this would have made it difficult for Tolkien and Williams to become friends without the complication of their respective relationships with Lewis, but clearly, Tolkien simply felt jealous and usurped by Williams. The best that could be said about the relationship between Tolkien and Williams is that they tolerated each other, and familiarity changed this little. They spent perhaps two evenings a week together for something like six years, but were never able to trust each other, and Tolkien often felt extremely uncomfortable in Williams's presence.

None of this seems to have made any sort of impact upon Lewis. He was thrilled by Williams's rather edgy character and adored his mind. Indeed, Lewis seems to have lived under the misunderstanding that his friends all felt the same way. 'By 1939, Williams had already become as dear to all my Oxford friends as he had to me,' he wrote.[16] This appeared in an essay of Lewis's that was part of a memorial collection written by some members of the Inklings and their friends called *Essays Presented to Charles Williams* published in 1947 (two years after Williams's death in 1945). However, some measure of Tolkien's intolerance of Williams is revealed in a comment he added to his own copy of the book (to which, ironically, he had also contributed). In the margin, he wrote, 'Alas no! In any case I had hardly ever seen him till he came to live in Oxford.'

Tolkien often ignored or contradicted Lewis's enthusiasms and he considered his friend a very impressionable man as well as a rather poor judge of character, but he was also a stickler for accuracy, especially on the printed page, and this comment was made when he and Lewis were approaching the nadir of their relationship, but it also seems to have derived from strong personal sentiment. To a journalist many years later, Tolkien remarked of Williams, 'I have read a good many of his books but I don't like them . . . I didn't know Charles Williams very well.'[17]

By the end of the 1940s, the Tolkien–Lewis friendship was almost over. Jack and Tollers had become alienated by their very different religious viewpoints and Tolkien had grown irritated by Lewis's commercial success. The introduction of Charles Williams into the inner circle had caused great resentment and loosened bonds still further, but then, in 1952, a year after the death of Janie Moore, Lewis finished things off when he met and fell in love with Joy Gresham.

This new person who had suddenly sprung into Lewis's life destroyed the last vestiges of the old friendship. Joy Gresham was a writer who had enjoyed moderate success and was married to another writer, a reformed alcoholic named Bill Gresham. Like Lewis, she had experienced a religious conversion and, in 1952, she visited England and met Lewis for the first time. They became close very quickly, fell in love, and after Joy had returned to America to obtain a divorce, she came back to England with her two young sons and was soon installed at The Kilns as Lewis's lover.

Four years after they met they were married at the Oxford register office. None of Lewis's friends was in attendance, and many of them (including Tolkien) only heard about it in a report in *The Times*. Tolkien was by all accounts devastated he had not been told by Lewis himself.

But by then, Lewis knew he could never rekindle the relationship he had once enjoyed with Tolkien. There was now a sea of resentment between them and Lewis knew what Tolkien's reaction would have been to his decision to marry. Tolkien hardly knew Joy Gresham, but for many reasons, he strongly disapproved of her. First, she was an outspoken, strong-willed and independent American woman, not at all the type Tolkien was fond of. She was a divorcee with two young children and she was a Jewess who had only recently converted to the Presbyterian church, an orthodox doctrine just about as far removed from Tolkien's Catholicism as it was possible to be. Worse still, she was a writer who had begun to craft the sort of books Lewis had been writing, adding her energies to what Tolkien would have considered Protestant propaganda. Ironically, Edith Tolkien did become friends with Joy Gresham.

By the time Jack and Joy were married, Tolkien was seeing his erstwhile friend only very rarely. In 1954, Lewis accepted the Professorship of Mediaeval and Renaissance English at Cambridge and so he was in Oxford less frequently. He remained on cordial terms with Tolkien and wrote a glowing review for *The Lord of the Rings*, which he had first read in manuscript form when, at the very end of 1949, in one of the concluding acts of their shared intimacy, Tolkien had loaned it to him and asked for his opinion. And yet, when Joy died in 1960, leaving Lewis bereft, the two old friends could not rekindle their feelings and did not seek each other out.

When Lewis died in November 1963, Tolkien declined all invitations to write an obituary and he refused to contribute to a memorial collection of essays. Indeed, he rarely spoke of Lewis and his only documented comment about the ending of their long friendship came as a rather acerbic reference in a letter written shortly after Lewis died. 'We were separated first by the sudden apparition of Charles Williams,' he declared, 'and then by his [Lewis's] marriage.'[18]

It was a sad footnote to what had been a relationship as productive as it was intense, a friendship that had made each of them better men.

CHAPTER 9

To *The Hobbit*

For Tolkien, the 1930s and 1940s were the most creative decades of his life. It was the time during which his inspirational ideas and his literary work blossomed. It was a time during which the loose, fragmentary ideas for children's stories took on a form that would reach a wide audience and it marked the period in which he found a sound footing as a writer.

No one is quite sure when he began to write *The Hobbit*, not even Tolkien himself. Like *Mr Bliss*, *Roverandom* or the Father Christmas letters, it became a bedtime story for his younger children and we may only assume that after the initial inspiration that came while marking exam papers, Tolkien ruminated on the idea and let it flower as an oral tale that was then written down. In 1937, a few months after *The Hobbit* was first published, Christopher Tolkien mentioned in his letter to Father Christmas that his father had read *The Hobbit* to the children years before and only the ending was not then typed out. This

is confirmed by the fact that Tolkien loaned Lewis the manuscript minus the final chapters *before* the Inklings and while the
Coalbiters were still reading their Icelandic sagas, placing the
earliest conception of the book at sometime around 1931.

After Tolkien's own family, Lewis was probably the first to
read the story and he was immediately entranced. Writing to his
friend Arthur Greeves, he declared:

> Since term began I have had a delightful time reading a
> children's story which Tolkien has written. I have told you
> of him before: the one man absolutely fitted, if fate had
> allowed, to be a third in our friendship in the old days,
> for he also grew up on W. Morris and George
> Macdonald. Reading his fairy tale has been uncanny – it
> is so exactly what we would both have longed to write (or
> read) in 1916: so that one feels he is not making it up
> but merely describing the same world into which all three
> of us have the entry . . . Whether it is really *good* is of
> course another question: still more whether it will
> succeed with modern children.[1]

Indeed, much of the inspiration for *The Hobbit* came from
Tolkien's early life, the books he read as a child, the fantasy
games he played. On a superficial level, there are hints and
markers from his younger days: his Aunt Jane lived in a cottage
in Worcestershire that was called 'Bag End' by the locals and
dragons featured prominently in Andrew Lang's stories. Tolkien
had written of dragons in his earliest children's stories composed when he was teaching in Leeds. Most significant was a
series of poems he called 'Tales and Songs of Bimble Bay', one
of which, 'The Dragon's Visit', described a dragon attack on

the sleepy Bimble Bay and involved a 'Miss Biggins'. It is also clear that much of the spirit of the Father Christmas letters went into the writing of *The Hobbit*. This was noticed by the family's literary friends who had been shown the Father Christmas letters. One of them, fellow philologist Simonne d'Ardenne has commented: 'Those lovely letters were the origin of *The Hobbit*, which soon made Tolkien famous, and the starting point of the later fairy tale for grown-ups, the great trilogy of *The Lord of the Rings*.'[2]

But when Lewis wrote, 'one feels he is not making it up but merely describing the same world into which all three of us have the entry', he meant that Tolkien (like Lewis and, presumably, Greeves) had retained strong images of a fantasy world cultivated in childhood. Tolkien was the perfect *type* to have created a character like Bilbo and a place like the Shire.

After his books had become famous, Tolkien was quite happy to declare that he was a hobbit. It was meant half as a joke, but there is a degree of cross-over between Tolkien's character and that of a typical hobbit. Indeed, in many respects, Tolkien was not so very different to Bilbo Baggins. Tolkien distrusted and, at times, despised the twentieth century. He was something of a Luddite who believed that science and technology had done nothing worthwhile to change the lot of humankind. He resisted owning a car until it became a practical necessity and Edith got her way (and even then they got rid of it after a few years). He never owned a TV and he listened to the radio only rarely. He disliked modern literature, music and theatre and had no time for contemporary politics. It might be said that he did not really wish to live in the modern world at all and that this disapproval was in part a spur for his creativity; he much preferred Middle-earth.

But on a more prosaic level, the hobbit is a type, a type not unlike many of the people Tolkien knew and grew up with. Hobbits are modelled upon a set of types of English men and women now almost extinct, denizens of the pre-Second World War Middle England, like actors in pre-war British movies, Richard Hannay, the hero of *The Thirty-nine Steps*, perhaps.

Bilbo Baggins is a middle-class Englishman who, like Tolkien, frowns upon progress and innovation. Bilbo likes his pipe and his comfy chair and is only slowly persuaded to take part in any form of adventure. But, when he does become involved, he turns into a hero, the blood of the Somme courses through his veins. A hobbit like Sam Gamgee represents the working-class Englishman, the Tommy of the trenches, the barrow boy or the butcher's assistant, whistling as he cycles to work.

The Hobbit began with a flash of inspiration, a revelatory moment, perhaps, as legend has it, when Tolkien was day-dreaming and saw a hole in his study carpet. But from that initial creative impulse, he began to think backwards. 'In a hole in the ground there lived a hobbit.' Fine, but what was a hobbit? And why did he live in a hole in the ground?

To answer these questions, Tolkien had to take the story back several stages, to find out who these creatures were and to build a set of characteristics for them and so images of the people he knew — his relatives in Birmingham, the stoic students in Leeds, the privates in the trenches with whom he would have liked to have made friends, the dons at High Table, the grocer in the covered market in the centre of Oxford — they all went into the melting pot.

For some time, the manuscript of *The Hobbit* remained incomplete and half-forgotten, placed in a desk drawer and ignored.

And so it may never have seen publication except for the fortunate fact that Tolkien did occasionally open the drawer and lend the incomplete manuscript to trusted family friends and close associates such as Lewis.

In an early version, Bilbo was going to sneak into the dragon Smaug's lair to stab him and some other important details were different: the dragon was called 'Pryftan' and the name 'Gandalf' was given to the chief dwarf, while the wizard was called 'Bladorthin'. It is possible the creation of the Inklings encouraged Tolkien to open that drawer and dust off the pages, but even then, the final chapters were still to be written down and the end of the story had been left trailing with the dragon about to die but with no description of the final scenes on paper. Gandalf probably obtained his name and Bladorthin was dropped after readings in Lewis's rooms when Tolkien decided to take names for all the dwarves from a collection of ancient Icelandic poems, the *Elder Edda*.

One of the people who was shown the manuscript was a former student named Elaine Griffiths who in 1936 was working in Oxford on a revision of a translation of *Beowulf* for the London publishing house of George Allen and Unwin. One of Elaine Griffiths' old college friends, Susan Dagnall, who had read English at the same time as her and was now an editor at George Allen and Unwin, came to Oxford to discuss the edition of *Beowulf*. Over lunch, the two women fell into discussing old times and Elaine mentioned that Professor Tolkien had written a wonderful children's story which he had lent her. She suggested Susan Dagnall should visit Tolkien that day and see if he would let her have the manuscript.

To Susan Dagnall's surprise, Tolkien was only too pleased to lend her his book and she headed off to Oxford station with a promise she would return it as soon as possible. Her curiosity piqued, she read the manuscript on the train journey back to London and a few days later she returned it to Tolkien with a letter explaining that she thought it had great potential but it needed to be finished before she could pass it on to her superiors in the publishing company.

Enthused by this news, Tolkien set to work right away. It was early August 1936 and perfect timing for him. It was the 'Long Vac', he had almost finished marking his annual pile of School Certificate papers and college would not resume for almost two months. Michael Tolkien, then nearly sixteen, had cut his hand badly on a broken window at school, but he was able to help his father with typing the new version using one hand, and by 3 October, just in time for the beginning of the academic year and more mundane business, the revised and completed version of *The Hobbit* was ready to send to Susan Dagnall. On the front of the manuscript Tolkien had typed 'The Hobbit, or There and Back Again'.

Susan Dagnall was thrilled with the new manuscript and showed it to the company chairman Stanley Unwin. He liked it immediately but wanted to gauge the reaction of someone of the age it was written for and so he passed it on to his ten-year-old son, Rayner, who for a fee of one shilling was persuaded to write a short report on the book. The boy concluded that it would be of great interest to children between five and nine.[3]

Within a week, George Allen and Unwin wrote to Tolkien to inform him they would like to publish his book.

Tolkien had supplied Susan Dagnall with a set of maps to accompany the manuscript and the publishers thought some of these would be appropriate for inclusion, but Tolkien had some grand and adventurous ideas for the book that could not be met. His maps had to be redrawn because the originals contained too many colours. He also wanted a general map of the part of Middle-earth in which the story is set to go at the end of the book and for Thror's map to be inset into the text of Chapter One. Tolkien rather naively proposed that this be printed using invisible ink so that it would appear when held open to the light.

Tolkien also offered George Allen and Unwin a set of illustrations for the book, adding a note to say, 'The pictures seem to me mostly only to prove that the author cannot draw.'[4] But, in spite of his self criticism, the editors and Stanley Unwin thought highly of Tolkien's drawings and wrote back to say they wanted to use eight of them printed in black and white.

By February, the proofs of *The Hobbit* were ready and in Tolkien's study in Northmoor Road. But he had an eye for detail and needed to constantly rework so that reading these was no simple matter. Instead of merely refining the text, Tolkien decided to make major revisions. Learning of this, the publishers tried to dissuade him by mentioning that it would prove very expensive and that it would be his responsibility to pay for any changes. Undeterred, Tolkien went to great lengths to ensure that the new sentences always fitted precisely into the space left by the old.

His particular gripe with the uncorrected proofs was actually a reasonable one. He did not like the way he had made so many asides to the reader and spent some time cutting these and changing the text.[5] But other problems came from inconsistencies in the geography and chronology of the story all of which took some considerable alteration and correction to put right.

In the end it took him over two months of effort during the

spring of 1937 to get the proofs into shape. He had made the book considerably better, but by the time the manuscript arrived back at the offices of George Allen and Unwin in London, the publishers had grown rather exasperated with Tolkien and realised that for all his talent as a storyteller, the professor's need to deliberate over every word and to pick apart and rework everything he had written was a source of considerable frustration.

The next problem arose over the publication date for the book. For many good reasons, George Allen and Unwin wanted to publish in late September. This would be a perfect time to capture the Christmas market for children's fiction and it would give them time to set and print the book after so many delays at the proof stage.

Tolkien preferred a June publication. The reason for this came from the fact that during the year in which he had been revising and perfecting *The Hobbit* he had been holding a grant to pursue his literary studies (a Leverhulme Research Fellowship). He had been working on his academic papers while completing his novel in his spare time, but Tolkien was worried that his fellow dons would suspect him of using university funds to finance his career as a writer of children's stories. If the book came out in June, Tolkien argued, it would be difficult for anyone to claim that he had been working on it during the period of the grant (which ran one year from October 1936).

Stanley Unwin realised Tolkien was worrying unnecessarily and would not allow his commercial instincts to be compromised. The book finally reached the bookshops in late September 1937 and was sold out by Christmas. Tolkien's colleagues were hardly aware of it until it was reviewed in *The Times*, and according to Tolkien's own reports to Stanley Unwin, they reacted with 'surprise and a little pity'.[6]

This might seem like an odd reaction unless one is familiar with the personality of many dons. Oxbridge is renowned for its 'bitchiness' – a characteristic of many academic institutions – but most pronounced within the hallowed halls of Oxford and Cambridge. The tone of many dons has always been one of mockery towards almost everything they encounter and for many it is a form of self-defence, a way to bolster an innate but misplaced sense of superiority. Tolkien knew this, he was right to expect ridicule, but there is no denying the pleasure it gave him when his book could not simply be ignored by his colleagues. 'I am constantly asked how my hobbit is,' he told Unwin. 'The professor of Byzantine Greek bought a copy, "because first editions of Alice [*Alice in Wonderland* written by another Oxford academic, Charles Dodgson] are now very valuable".'[7]

The Times' review that so impressed Tolkien's contemporaries was composed by C.S. Lewis, who wrote:

> All who love that kind of children's book which can be
> read and re-read by adults should take note that a new
> star has appeared in this constellation. To the trained eye
> some characters will seem almost mythopoeic . . . Tolkien
> has the air of inventing nothing. He has studied trolls
> and dragons at first hand and describes them with that
> fidelity which is worth oceans of glib 'originality'.[8]

A few days before this review Lewis had already announced his verdict, in the *Times Literary Supplement*. In this, he declared, 'No common recipe for children's stories will give you creatures so rooted in their own soil and history as those of Professor

Tolkien – who obviously knows much more about them than he needs for this tale.'[9]

Fearing perhaps that the reviewer's identity would be revealed and be viewed as suspect, Tolkien told those who knew it was written by his friend that Jack was the most scrupulously honest man he had ever known, that his sentiments were always genuine and that he would not have written these things if he had not believed them, simply to help sales. This was doubtless true, and indeed, Lewis never stopped promoting Tolkien's work, even after their friendship cooled. In his book, *Of This and Other Worlds*, written in the late 1930s, he said of *The Hobbit*:

> It must be understood that this is a children's book only in the sense that the first of many readings can be undertaken in the nursery. *Alice* is read gravely by children and with laughter by adults; *The Hobbit* on the other hand, will be funniest to its youngest readers, and only years later, at a tenth or a twentieth reading, will they begin to realise what deft scholarship and profound reflection have gone to make everything in it so ripe, so friendly, and in its own way so true. Prediction is dangerous, but *The Hobbit* may well prove a classic.[10]

A decade later, Lewis remarked:

> *The Hobbit* escapes the danger of degenerating into mere plot and excitement by a very curious shift of tone. As the humour and homeliness of the early chapters, the sheer 'Hobbitry' dies away we pass insensibly into the world of epic.[11]

Even before *The Hobbit* had been published in Britain, it had gained the attention of a major American publishing house. The editor assigned to the book at George Allen and Unwin, in London, Charles Furth, wrote to Tolkien in May 1937 to tell him that Houghton Mifflin of Boston wanted to take on US publication. Furthermore, they wanted a set of colour illustrations to accompany the text and wondered if Tolkien could supply them.

Tolkien was delighted and said that he would like to attempt to deliver the pictures but was nervous that the publishers might not feel they were good enough. By this time, Furth and the other staff at Allen and Unwin had grown accustomed to Tolkien's manner and that in some ways he was not the easiest author to work with. Back in February, they had been astonished by the detail of Tolkien's critical appraisal of the proofs of his black and white illustrations for *The Hobbit*. In a letter to them he pointed out that the prints were good except for two problems with 'the Troll' illustration. One of the outlines of a background tree was slightly broken and some of the dots around the fire in the centre of the picture had not reproduced well.

Because of many other demands, Tolkien was pushed for time, but he also did not like the idea of anyone else illustrating his book and told Furth that if he couldn't produce satisfactory artwork he must at least be guaranteed a veto on anything the Americans did, because he had a 'heartfelt loathing' for everything the Disney Studios produced.[12]

For some reason, this letter was then forwarded onto Houghton Mifflin, unedited. When Tolkien learned of this he was extremely embarrassed. However, the editors in Boston seemed quite unaffected by Tolkien's unsolicited comments and no less keen to acquire the rights and to publish as quickly as possible. By August 1937, he had overcome any insecurities he had about his artistic ability and managed, in spite of a heavy workload of exam papers and administrative duties, to produce five colour illustrations for the book. These were 'Rivendell', 'The Hill: Hobbiton-across-the-water', 'Bilbo awoke with the Sun in his eyes', 'Conversation with Smaug' and 'Bilbo comes to the Huts of the Raft-elves'. Houghton Mifflin used all except the last of these in their first edition and Allen and Unwin included them in their second edition in early 1938.

Tolkien was very pleased with these pictures and was thrilled by the second impression of *The Hobbit*, but once again his publishers came in for more criticism over their efforts. On the jacket flap for the first edition, Stanley Unwin had written a blurb that ran:

> J.R.R. Tolkien has four children and *The Hobbit* was read aloud to them in nursery days. The manuscript was lent to friends in Oxford and read to their children. The birth of *The Hobbit* recalls very strongly that of *Alice in Wonderland*. Here again a professor of an abstruse subject is at play.

Innocent enough one might think, but Tolkien tore into it, writing three pages of criticism of this simple paragraph. The book had not been read in nursery days because his eldest, John, was thirteen when he heard the story and he hadn't 'lent' the book to anyone, and those who had read it had certainly not read it to their children. Tolkien bridled at the suggestion Anglo-Saxon was abstruse, although actually Unwin was being more inaccurate about the author of *Alice In Wonderland*, Charles Dodgson, a mathematics lecturer. Tolkien went on further to argue that Dodgson had not actually been a professor, but a college lecturer (a distinction that means the world to an Oxford don). He also did not like the idea of being a professor at play.

This letter demonstrates one of the major difficulties Tolkien and his publishers now faced. *The Hobbit* and Tolkien's other fiction sprang from a very particular character. Tolkien was picky, obsessive and must, at times, have been quite insufferable to work with. But he was also other-worldly, completely unable to sympathise with anyone working within the publishing business, or any other; indeed, the entire business world was utterly alien to him. Tolkien was used to taking his time to perfect his writing. He loved re-writing and re-arranging his ideas on the page. He lived inside his work and few things existed beyond it save his academic life, his family and his close friends. He saw no need for Unwin's blurb, he had no concept of the need to capture the public's imagination, he could not understand why anyone would compare *The Hobbit* to *Alice In Wonderland*, and so he picked over the minutiae and missed completely the idea that the public require hooks, reference points, markers. From his ivory tower in Oxford, he did not look down upon the masses, he just believed everyone thought the same way as he did.

This led to problems beyond the relationship he had with his editors. When *The Hobbit* turned out to be a great success during the winter of 1937, Stanley Unwin naturally hoped for a sequel. Tolkien too was especially keen to follow it up and was beginning to fantasise that this breakthrough in his writing career might change the Tolkien family's fortunes enormously for the better. As early as October 1937, only weeks after *The Hobbit* was published, Tolkien was already feeling optimistic. In a letter to Stanley Unwin he expressed a hope that he might soon be able to forget the marking of exam papers, a poorly-paid chore that had already robbed him of seventeen summers, and that he could do the work he loved most and to gain sufficient financial rewards from it. And indeed, *The Hobbit* sold well over the Christmas season, and as 1937 turned into 1938, it gained some attention in the national press, so there seemed to be plenty of reasons for Tolkien's optimism. More good news came early in 1938 when the American edition was published and was received as warmly as it had been in Britain. That spring Tolkien won the *New York Herald Tribune* award for the best juvenile book, and, determined not to lose impetus, he tried to get to work on a follow-up.

But, in part because Tolkien could not think commercially or turn his mind to what the market required of him, his road to international success was to prove a slow and frustrating one. But at the same time, this painful journey was to produce something far more important than a mere sequel to *The Hobbit*.

CHAPTER 10

The War and the Ring

The Hobbit arrived in a troubled world. Of course, the world is always troubled, but during the autumn of 1937, less than twenty years after the slaughter of the Great War, civilisation stood once more poised before the abyss. That spring, Guernica in Spain had been obliterated by the Fascists, and in September, the Japanese levelled Shanghai killing many thousands. Perhaps this is one of the reasons for the success of Tolkien's book, it offered an alternative reality, a world that was 'real' in that it offered violence and intrigue, good and evil, but set in a universe without bombs and mortars, fire-bombing and goose-stepping Nazis.

But if 1937 had brought a succession of horrors, 1938 was no better, and while some tried to pretend there would be no global conflagration, no repeat of the last generation's terrible mistakes, most knew that war was inevitable. In September 1938, a weak and unrealistic Prime Minister, Neville

Chamberlain met Hitler and returned home to declare there would be 'peace in our time'. Five days later, Hitler invaded Czechoslovakia. In response, Britain and France began to rearm and the level of anxiety and dread grew steadily palpable. Within twelve months, Britain was at war with Germany, and this time the whole of Europe was a battlefield.

Oxford fared better than almost any other British city during the Second World War. Hitler considered Oxford such a beautiful place he wanted to preserve it at any cost and had in fact earmarked it as his future seat of government. So, thanks to a rare pact between the warring nations, it was agreed at the start of the war that in exchange for the RAF never dropping bombs on Heidelberg and Göttingen, the Luftwaffe would leave Oxford and Cambridge untouched.

But the citizens of Oxford suffered many of the privations of the rest of the country. There were food shortages and fuel rationing and one could never be quite sure if Hitler would stick to his word. Even so, Oxford was considered something of a safe haven. It was a long way from the coast and therefore more difficult for German bombers to reach, and in the event of an invasion it would probably have been one of the last places to fall. National treasures were stored there taken by truck and train from London and elsewhere, and before the Blitz, some twenty-thousand women and children were evacuated to Oxford and the surrounding villages.

The Tolkiens took in evacuees to fill the bedrooms now left empty in their large house in Northmoor Road. Only Priscilla and Christopher were at home; Tolkien's eldest son, John was training for the priesthood in Rome and then evacuated back to England; Michael enlisted in 1939, but spent a year at Trinity College, Oxford before becoming an anti-aircraft gunner. Later in the war, Christopher was stationed in South Africa with the RAF.

To a large extent, Tolkien's life changed little. There were far fewer students at the university, but lectures went on. He still had to mark examination papers and fulfil his administrative duties and meetings of the Inklings continued as though nothing was happening in the rest of the world. Tolkien and Lewis were joined most times by Williams, Lewis's brother Warnie and Humphrey (Dr Havard). Hugo Dyson often made it from nearby Reading University and Coghill was still a keen member. In fact, the war years probably mark the apogee of the Inklings. Admittedly, the presence of Charles Williams rather spoiled things for Tolkien, but for these men the Inklings offered an escape from the harsh reminder that, for the second time in their lives, their country was entangled in military conflict, that beer and tobacco were becoming hard to come by and that many of the students they liked might never return to the lecture theatre just as many of their own friends had failed to do twenty years earlier.

For Edith, this was a particularly unsettling and depressing time. Her sons were away facing danger and her husband was as involved with his male friends as he had always been. Edith had been forced to accept the fact that a large part of Ronald's life did not involve her. Indeed, in many ways, it excluded her. She did not like many of her husband's male friends and she avoided them. Whenever Jack visited the house in Northmoor Road, there was a frostiness between him and Edith, as though they could simply not communicate with one another, and just about the only point of contact between the world of the Inklings and Edith Tolkien's existence came from the fact that their family doctor and fellow Inkling, Dr Robert Havard, was also a family friend who played with the children and actually conversed with Edith.

Furthermore, Edith disliked and distrusted almost all the wives of the other dons Tolkien associated with. Many of them were from wealthy families and they lived in grand houses that made 20 Northmoor Road look very modest. Edith was acutely aware of her roots and the fact that she had not come from an upper-middle-class family, that she was poorly educated compared with many of the other dons' wives. For the sake of her husband she tried hard to be sociable, she gave teas and luncheons and tried to make conversation and to break through the social iciness, but after a while she gave up and decided that that aspect of Oxford was not for her. Gradually Edith gained a reputation for being insular and uninterested and was consequently left to her own devices.

And, in many ways, this suited her. She had her family and her home and she was satisfied if not thrilled by the course her life had taken. She was still resentful of the fact that her husband had forced her into Catholicism and she attended church only rarely. Tolkien grew more pious as he grew older, but he did not try further to impose his beliefs on Edith. Her lack of commitment certainly frustrated him and their very different religious views remained an issue between them until the start of the Second World War when the couple had a major row and all the resentments and frustrations came out into the open.

The argument was probably precipitated by the stress caused by the war and the breaking up of the family unit. Edith was anxious and could perhaps already visualise what she thought would be a very lonely future. Priscilla, who was ten at the outbreak of war, was at school, the boys were either away or about to leave home and Tolkien was usually spending three evenings a week with his friends; and when he was not out drinking and chatting with his cronies he was working. He was also expected to play his part in the war-effort and he, along with many of the other academics (including Lewis and Williams), was required to spend evenings and nights as members of the Air Raid Protection service (the ARP) watching the skies for Hitler's bombers. There seemed to be little room for Edith.

As well as these personal difficulties, Tolkien could barely maintain the family's comfortable lifestyle. The four children had been a constant drain on his financial resources – private education and then university fees and medical bills during the days before the National Health Service were crippling. Tolkien was acutely aware of the financial shortcomings of a career in academia. He had not gone into university life for the money, but as the family grew and the demands grew, the loathing for the annual ritual of marking exam papers mounted and Tolkien saw some of his contemporaries earning money from journalism and publishing books, he began to hope that his own literary efforts might alter the course of his fortunes.

The Hobbit had been a success for Tolkien, but it did not make him huge sums of money at this time. He learned in 1938 that the American publishers had sold three thousand copies of the book and in England it had sold around the same number during its first year in the shops. The money this provided was useful but it did not change things greatly. A little more money came from a steadily growing collection of publishers around the world, but The Hobbit only became a huge money-spinner after the success of The Lord of the Rings in the mid-1960s.

The Hobbit had received critical acclaim and it had drawn attention to Tolkien. People in the media and in the publishing world began to know his name and Tolkien quite understandably started to think that he could capitalise on his success. Proof of his new status came from the fact that when, in the autumn of 1937, he mentioned to Stanley Unwin that his friend C.S. Lewis had written a novel, the publisher was immediately interested in seeing it. The novel (*Out of the Silent Planet*) had already been turned down by one publisher, and indeed, after receiving an unfavourable report from their reader, Unwin also passed on it, but it illustrated to Tolkien that he was being taken seriously.[1]

Within weeks of the publication of *The Hobbit*, Stanley Unwin was aware that the book was doing well and that Tolkien could become a new literary force. People, he believed, would soon be wanting to know a great deal more about hobbits and their world, and he wrote to Tolkien to tell him so. However, Unwin, a man of great experience and an expert businessman, also knew that authors very rarely broke through with their first published book and that they needed to sustain an initial impetus and produce a string of successful titles, so he was naturally keen for Tolkien to follow up his success with a sequel, a 'New Hobbit'.

And indeed, Tolkien's study was a veritable treasure-trove of literature. There on his desk lay copies of some of his children's stories and alongside these there were piles of papers, notes, typescripts, maps, drawings, poems and prose that told of the First and Second Ages of Middle-earth, of heroes such as Beren, Gil-galad and Elrond, stories of elves and the Valar, stories about the evil of Morgoth and Sauron. Could he find here the 'New Hobbit'?

On 15 November 1937, Tolkien met Stanley Unwin for a private lunch to celebrate the publication of *The Hobbit* and to discuss future plans. Tolkien took along with him a mixed bag of work including the Father Christmas letters, a collection of children's stories, a copy of the prose version of *The Silmarillion* (the 'Quenta Silmarillion') and an unfinished version of the poem 'The Gest of Beren and Lúthien'. He had already offered George Allen and Unwin his children's story *Mr Bliss* and although Tolkien's editor did not feel it was the right thing to follow *The Hobbit*, he was sufficiently interested to encourage him to have another look at it and to see if it could be adapted into something more appropriate for publication.

It is likely Stanley Unwin didn't really know what to make of the selection of writings Tolkien gave him. The Father Christmas letters were clearly attractive but they could not be published as a sequel to *The Hobbit*. Such a collection would have to be printed with the colour illustrations and that would make it a prohibitively expensive venture. 'The Gest of Beren and Lúthien' must have been totally baffling to Unwin, and *The Silmarillion*, which was then a bundle of stories, some incomplete and seemingly unconnected with each other (or indeed anything else), must have presented an even more confusing offering. What Unwin wanted was another novel-length adventure involving Bilbo and dwarves and elves, wizards and trolls that was set in Middle-earth; another mission for Bilbo the burglar perhaps.

Unwin dutifully took the manuscripts and promised to have them read. He was a genuine and honest man who had built an impressive publishing business by taking chances and doing his best never to let opportunities slip through his fingers. Professor Tolkien had already proved himself with *The Hobbit*; who could tell what other treasures sat in the drawers of his office back in Oxford?

George Allen and Unwin's reader, Edward Crankshaw, was predictably confused by the material passed onto him, but he did see some sense of magic amidst the flow of words. However, it was clear this material was not what Unwin was after and Tolkien was worldly-wise enough to realise it too. 'The Silmarils are in my heart,' he wrote Unwin, and his manuscript would remain private and close to him for many years to come.[2] And indeed, Tolkien would have been shocked if Unwin had been interested in publishing *The Silmarillion*. He was not at the right point in his career to have this book published even if it was in a more cohesive state. It was a piece of work that might have come from a totally different author to the creator of *The Hobbit*. It would have made no sense to publish this in the wake of a successful children's book and it would have confused his public. But beyond this was the personal factor that in 1938 Tolkien was not mentally prepared for his masterpiece to be edited by an outsider. In his heart he knew the book was not even close to completion, that it needed many more years of preparation and growth before it could offer the reader a satisfying image of Middle-earth and the Lands of the West. *The Silmarillion* was still too personal a document, it was imbedded too deeply in his soul.

In the meantime, he would have to turn his mind and his proven talent for children's literature to fashioning a more conventional story that would again engage his readers. In mid-December, Tolkien received the news that the material he had given Unwin was not appropriate for a sequel (but was not actually rejected entirely), and by 16 December he replied that he would give his attention to the matter of thinking up a new hobbit story but that he had no clear idea what he should write or where he could take the characters and ideas laid out in the original.

The next day, Tolkien's editor, Charles Furth wrote to him to say that demand for *The Hobbit* was so great they had to rush through a second printing and that in order to get the books to the shops they had to use a private car to pick up the copies from the printers in Woking. Whether it was this or something else that prompted him is unclear, but that day, Tolkien had a flash of inspiration and began to make notes on a new hobbit story. By 19 December, he was able to tell Furth that he had already written the first chapter of a new book and that he was calling the chapter 'A Long-expected Party'.

It was a great start, but then it had come to him during the Christmas vacation with no exam papers to mark and little administration to attend to. Tolkien knew he was good at beginning stories, but that it was quite another thing to keep up the momentum. Tolkien had always found it impossible to write to a deadline or to do anything creative unless the muse took him.

An example of this comes from one of his academic projects. During the early 1930s, he had been working on a translation of three poems *Pearl*, *Sir Gawain and the Green Knight* and *Sir Orfeo* to be collected into a single volume. By the early 1960s, this task was finally completed and his publisher was only waiting for a Preface to the book which Tolkien had already been promising them for several years. Successive editors tried everything to propel Tolkien into writing this simple short piece to open the book, including asking his friends to nudge him into writing, but nothing worked. Eventually they gave up and the book was only published posthumously with a Preface written by Christopher Tolkien.

But in 1937, something kept pushing Tolkien along with his thoughts for a 'New Hobbit'. That 'something' was probably a collection of different motivations. A large aspect of his drive certainly came from the excitement of starting something new and fresh, but it is undoubtedly true that he just could not allow himself to let things go after such a fine introduction to a wide readership. We must also accept that there was a certain rivalry between Tolkien and Lewis. At this time they were still great friends. Charles Williams had appeared on the scene but was not yet living in Oxford and intruding (as Tolkien perceived it) into the Tolkien–Lewis axis. The Inklings were at their most productive and Lewis was churning out manuscript after manuscript, writing both fiction and non-fiction. He was also contributing to magazines and newspapers, and within the social circle of which Tolkien and Lewis were the leading lights, Lewis was considered to be the one most likely to set alight the world of letters.

Most crucially, Lewis was a quick worker and seemed to have a boundless energy and a whirlpool of ideas to draw upon. Before *The Hobbit* was published, Lewis had already seen two of his non-fiction books in print, *The Pilgrim's Regress* and *The Allegory of Love* and he had written *Out of the Silent Planet* in a matter of a few months during 1937.[3] Tolkien was irritated by Lewis's speed and he worked in a very different way; he was meticulous, a perfectionist who found it difficult to let anyone see his work until it had been re-worked and revised many times.

Surprisingly perhaps, Tolkien and Lewis had, around this time, discussed writing a book together. Lewis had first suggested the idea because he believed there were too few books published that they each liked and so they should compose their own. Lewis decided he would write a book about space and Tolkien would cover the subject of time. From this came Lewis's *Out of the Silent Planet*, but after completing four chapters, Tolkien gave up on his project, a book called *The Lost Road* in which a father and son travel through time and become involved with the downfall of Númenor.

Lewis's admiration for his friend was certainly another force that pushed Tolkien into working on his fiction. He nagged and encouraged him with his well-judged criticisms, he spurred him on and pulled him out of his frequent dry spells. Many years later, Tolkien told Lewis's biographer, Walter Hooper, that he had written *The Lord of the Rings*, 'to make Lewis a story out of *The Silmarillion*'.[4] To another writer, he declared, 'But for the encouragement of C.S. Lewis I do not think that I should ever have completed or offered for publication *The Lord of the Rings*.'[5]

So, several forces were pulling Tolkien in different directions simultaneously. He wanted to get on with a sequel to *The Hobbit*, for the health of his ego he *needed* to get on with it, he could perceive the potential of making money from his efforts and would have loved to have been able to give up some aspects of his academic career (in particular the dreaded marking of exam papers) to concentrate solely on writing. But at the same time, he could not change the way he thought and the way he worked. Fortunately, Tolkien was the sort of intellectual who could retain a detailed mythology in his head and he could make sense of disparate notes and cross references so that a story could grow without him losing the thread or indeed the energy and the impetus to finish what he had begun. During the twelve years in which *The Lord of the Rings* developed from a vague sequel into a full-blown and independent creation, the effort would be pockmarked with delays and retrogressive decisions, entire months, even years would pass with nothing done interspersed with spells of furious creativity. Many times, the entire idea was shelved temporarily and a completely new project envisaged. But Tolkien's great ability to focus and to visualise on an epic scale held the project together.

Fired up by this new beginning, Tolkien spent the rest of the

Christmas vacation of 1937 polishing 'A Long-expected Party' and had a typed copy with his publishers by early February 1938. In an accompanying letter he suggested to Stanley Unwin that he should pass it on to his son Rayner, a boy who had, after all, been such a good judge of *The Hobbit*.

This opening to *The Lord of the Rings* is almost like an extra chapter of *The Hobbit* (indeed, this could be said for much of the first 150 pages of *The Lord of the Rings*), and in essence, little was changed between this version and the final one in the finished book. The only real differences are that the character who later became Frodo appears as Bilbo's son and his name is not Frodo but 'Bingo' (after a toy owned by one of Tolkien's children), and as he was writing this chapter Tolkien was only dimly aware that he could incorporate into this new story the ring that Bilbo had found in *The Hobbit*.

Rayner did read this opening chapter and was enchanted by it. Within a few days of receiving the short manuscript, Stanley Unwin had written to tell his author of its positive reception and encouraging him to press on with the idea. Buoyed up by this and his own enthusiasm for what he had written, Tolkien continued immediately so that after three weeks' work he had reached the end of Chapter Three and had begun to shape the central themes of the book.

This first draft was still very much a 'New Hobbit', although in Tolkien's mind, the mood and feel of the book was becoming something altogether different. The key early chapter, 'The Shadow of the Past' (Chapter 2 in the finished version), packed with exposition and background detail, was not written until sometime later, but by February or March 1938, the ring had become central to the story and Tolkien had concluded that some form of quest linking the hobbits, the ring and the Dark

Lord, Sauron (who had been mentioned briefly in *The Hobbit*), should provide the backbone of the story.

But then, in June 1938, came the first break in Tolkien's work pattern. He was beset with problems. His friend, the fellow linguist Eric Gordon, died suddenly at the age of fifty-two and the usual batch of summer exam papers had arrived again, but Tolkien was also struggling with the direction in which his creation was moving. He was racing ahead with the story but had no clear idea where it was taking him. However, something must have fallen into place in his thinking because a month later he was back on course again and had worked out the main plot structure for the story.

He had come to realise that the central theme was based upon the idea that Bilbo's ring was the one ruling ring, once owned by Sauron, 'the necromancer' of *The Hobbit* who now wanted it back. The story would revolve around the forces of good in Middle-earth who would, by destroying the ring, prevent Sauron from achieving his goal, and, during July and August 1938, Tolkien put these explanatory ideas into the crucial early chapter, 'The Shadow of the Past', in which Gandalf explains the history of the ring to Bilbo.

In August, the family went on holiday to the seaside town of Sidmouth. Here Tolkien had a rush of creativity and took the story to the Prancing Pony where the hobbits first meet Aragorn. The writing block had been freed and Tolkien wrote furiously but still the story and the way it was progressing remained thematically confused. Tolkien had established the central thread of the tale and could visualise a middle and an end to accompany his beginning but the problem lay with the fact that this tale was now neither a children's story nor a serious adult novel. An indication of this confusion comes from the very names Tolkien was then employing. 'Strider' was a hobbit called 'Trotter' and Frodo was still 'Bingo'. The tale seemed inexorably to fall between stools because although it included many of the characters featured in *The Hobbit*, the spirit of the book was entirely different. This story dealt with grand themes that kept suggesting a larger panorama, the first hints of something epic in stature.

At this juncture, Tolkien could have gone off in a number of different directions. Perhaps it would have been easiest for him to have moulded the story into a 'New Hobbit'. After all, he had Stanley Unwin pushing him down this road and Tolkien too wanted another book in the shops. He was desperately hard-pressed financially and told Unwin of his difficulties in a letter written during the summer of 1938 in which he declared that he was only managing to keep his head above water by working all hours on examination marking. He knew that his time was precious and that a quick book might help him and the family through their immediate problems. But, greatly to his credit, he chose not to take this path. Instead, he had glimpsed a grander vision and he wanted to see what treasures could be unearthed there.

That autumn, Tolkien threw off the last vestiges of a plot that would suit a 'New Hobbit' and he began calling his new fiction, *The Lord of the Rings*. By this time he had worked out that Frodo would be responsible for the fate of the ring and that in order to destroy Sauron's power and prevent him dominating Middle-earth for ever, the ring must be voluntarily destroyed in the Crack of Doom in the heart of Mordor.

Late 1938 was a productive time and the story moved on rapidly. Early in 1939, Tolkien began to prepare a lecture he had agreed to deliver on 8 March 1939, the Andrew Lang Lecture at the University of St Andrew's in Scotland. Andrew Lang was the collector and author of fairy stories that had had a great influence upon Tolkien, and so it seemed appropriate that he should choose as his subject, 'On Fairy Stories'.

As well as this lecture being a masterpiece of analysis of a literary form so close to Tolkien's heart, it served to focus his own thoughts about his new work. Within any culture, fairy stories derive from a rich resource of tradition and myth; they are droplets of narrative taken from a great ocean of history and legend. *The Hobbit* is a classic example of this, a tiny story about a few individuals but with overarching themes, and, at its periphery, the vaguest hint of something far grander still. Tolkien had begun to write *The Lord of the Rings* with the idea that he would compose another tiny story; perhaps it would tell the tale of another adventure with Bilbo and the dwarves, or maybe he could tell another little story about others who lived in Middle-earth. But he soon realised that Middle-earth was a much bigger place than had been revealed to him and his readers in *The Hobbit*. Middle-earth had a history and a geography, there were many strange and wonderful lands that lay beyond Mirkwood and the Misty Mountains. But more importantly, Tolkien had already created the grand mythology, the history and the geography, much of the legendary past and the supportive framework for a little tale; he had already written *The Silmarillion*. And of course, when Tolkien realised that he had this grand panorama to draw upon, he concluded that this new tale, *The Lord of the Rings*, need not be such a small story involving the same characters as those in *The Hobbit*. He had an entire world as his playground, why hold back?

By September 1939, the Hobbits had reached Rivendell and the plans for the fellowship were being laid out. Meanwhile, in

Oxford, the declaration of war on the 3 September had quickly begun to reshape the lives of everyone. Hundreds of thousands of sandbags were piled up against buildings, gas masks were issued to all citizens, railings, baths and saucepans were offered as metal for reshaping into guns and tanks, and everyone had to be especially vigilant about the black-out. In the centre of the city, cellars and mediaeval tunnels running under the colleges were converted into air-raid shelters, including one in the lowest basement of the new Bodleian Library which could, in the event of an air-raid, house 1,100 people. The Examination Schools were requisitioned for use as a military hospital and the cricket pavilion at Jesus College was converted into a temporary day-nursery. Around the city, as elsewhere in the country, signs went up with slogans such as 'Waste not Want Not', 'Dig for Victory' and the outrageous 'Keep Mum – She's not so Dumb'. On the edge of the city at the Cowley car plants, tanks and aircraft rolled off the production line.

In the study of 20 Northmoor Road, Tolkien could, with an effort of will, blot out this grim world and submerge himself in the fantasy of Middle-earth. Here there were troubles aplenty but they were of the type Tolkien felt more comfortable dealing with. Paper was short, so much of the first draft of the middle sections of *The Lord of the Rings* was written on the back of examination papers and odd scraps of paper lying around the office, Tolkien's neat compact writing filling every available space.

However, it was inevitable that the war would slow Tolkien's progress. There were fewer students to teach, but the demands of his job changed little and he now had the added responsibility of helping with the war effort in every way he could. Tolkien's overwhelming feeling about the war, and an opinion shared by almost all of his friends, was that it was an utterly ridiculous waste of life, time and energy. Hadn't the world learned anything from the last war?

There is no question Tolkien was a patriot, he loved his country, but he never really considered himself 'British'. Instead, he saw himself as most definitely 'English'. His ancestors had left central Europe some two hundred years before he was born, but he did not approve of the concept of the British Empire and still less the British Commonwealth and he identified himself with an older tradition linked to the ancient heart of England. Naturally, he loathed Hitler whom he considered a 'ruddy little ignoramus' and was furious that the great German people, as he viewed them, could be corrupted by so worthless an individual.[6]

This sorry state of affairs was brought home to Tolkien even before the war began. In the summer of 1938, George Allen and Unwin forwarded a letter to him from the German publishing house of Rütten and Loening requesting the rights to publish *The Hobbit.* In the letter, they asked Tolkien if he could tell them whether or not he was of Aryan extraction.

Tolkien was outraged by this because he realised that what the publishers really wanted to know was whether or not he was Jewish. Yet, he also realised the editors at the publishing house were only doing what they were forced to do by government regulations and so, taking the advice of Stanley Unwin, Tolkien wrote two letters to the German publishers and sent both onto George Allen and Unwin, leaving them the choice of which to pass on to Rütten and Loening. One letter was obviously more forthright than the other, but each responded to the question with righteous indignation. Stanley Unwin authorised the forwarding on of the more toned-down of the two letters. Surprisingly perhaps, the Germans did not seem to take offence and still wanted to buy the rights to translate *The Hobbit.*[7]

Because of the war, work slowed so that by the end of 1940, now some three years into the project, Tolkien had reached only part way through what would eventually become Book II of *The Lord of the Rings*, and here, with the fellowship of elves, hobbits, dwarves and men having just discovered Balin's tomb, writing stopped for an entire year.

The reasons for this hiatus are not known. Tolkien's son Michael was seriously injured in January 1941 and hospitalised; Tolkien's war duties intensified and he was more than usually distracted by academic responsibilities, but he nevertheless succeeded in maintaining his interest in the story and was able to pick up the thread again late in 1941.

Clearly though, there were many times during the writing of the first half of *The Lord of the Rings* when Tolkien had no definite idea where the story was taking him. At this stage, Lothlórien and Rohan did not exist and Treebeard was a hostile figure and was responsible for imprisoning Gandalf rather than Saruman who also had not been thought of.

A further year of writing brought Tolkien to the chapter called 'Flotsam and Jetsam' (originally Chapter 31 or Book 3, Chapter 9 in the published version) and at this stage, around December 1942, he believed the entire story was only six chapters away from its conclusion. But then, during the spring of 1943, as he tried to bring the story to an ending in which all the loose ends were tied up and the inter-linking themes satisfactorily dealt with, he began to realise he had miscalculated and that the story could not be reined in this way; and so, once again, the work stopped abruptly.

To get the tale to this stage, Tolkien had been using *The Silmarillion* as a guide. Throughout the first half of *The Lord of the Rings* there are detailed references to past Ages, songs are sung and poems read in which whole sections of *The Silmarillion* are alluded to and this adds tremendous substance and depth to the book. Two examples come from a early section of *The Lord of the Rings*. In Chapter 11, 'A Knife in the Dark', Aragorn brings a wealth of historical detail into the story all built upon an existing section of *The Silmarillion* and later, in Rivendell, Bilbo sings a song of Eärendil based on the poem Tolkien had written more than twenty years earlier (in which Eärendil was originally named Earendel). But the more Tolkien dipped into *The Silmarillion* to fish out treasures, the more he found and the more he found the closer the connections became between the two works.

As time moved on and Tolkien slowly unravelled the story of the ring, new sub-plots, new threads and entire themes presented themselves. Tolkien found himself quite unable to ignore them and so, even without pushing the story forward with new pages of the tale itself, he was finding himself absorbed with tributaries that turned into brooks and streams while the river had been halted in its course. Of course, this was to bear fruit, just as it had done during 1938 when the story of the ring first began to unravel. It was a rare and complex alchemy and the brew could only ferment in its own time.

And yet the strain was growing. To Tolkien it must have seemed the effort was interminable. On the one hand he felt a deep attraction to this story; it was a partner to his cherished *Silmarillion* and had become almost as important to him. But on the other, the years were passing. Unwin had lost sight now of a sequel to *The Hobbit*. Tolkien had been trying to sustain their hope with letters declaring that the end of the 'New Hobbit' was not far off. But knowing how much of a perfectionist Tolkien was and how he could not let go of things easily, his editors had come to believe the new book would never be in their hands. Things were made even worse in 1942 when, for a while, *The Hobbit* went out of print because the warehouse holding the stock of copies was destroyed in an air-raid.[8] Tolkien was as frustrated as his publishers, and he felt it more personally; but he could only work within his limitations.

For Tolkien, the autumn and winter of 1943 was the worst period in the gestation of his great tale. He had stopped working on the book altogether and seemed unable to pick it up again. Part of the problem stemmed from the fact that he had become so entangled in minutiae that he had lost sight of the plot. It was not lost, just confused. Where was he to take the story? How could he guide his characters to a satisfactory dénouement?

Tolkien was not consciously aware of the reason for his difficulties. If he had stopped to analyse what he was doing, he would have concluded that his obsession with detail was simply the way he worked. He would have been right to conclude this and, as we have seen before, this great talent was in part responsible for the magical quality of *The Lord of the Rings* and *The Silmarillion*. The determination to investigate every aspect of a story and to colour the background with rich shades makes Tolkien's work that much more profound and more satisfying than any other in the genre. But it also meant he was tortured by what he was doing. He did not fully realise it but he was becoming buried by the complexity of the tale and the barrage of detail so that he could no longer see things clearly. And, as often happens with such things, a small incident in the everyday world of the conscious mind triggered something deeper within his subconscious and freed the shackles.

One of Tolkien's neighbours in Northmoor Road, the elderly

Lady Agnew met Tolkien on the pavement outside Number 20 and happened to mention she was worried about a poplar tree outside her house. She had had it cut back and many of its branches lopped off and now she believed that it was a safety hazard, that it could fall onto her house in a storm. Tolkien, who had always loved trees, thought Lady Agnew was being ridiculous and gently persuaded her that the tree should stay, that the house would be swept away long before the tree could damage her property. That night, Tolkien dreamt about the incident and when he awoke he had a complete story in his mind and wrote it out very quickly, almost as a stream of sub-conscious thought.

The story was *Leaf By Niggle* and it was a perfect allegory of Tolkien's own predicament.[9] In the story, the central character, Niggle, is a painter obsessed with refining the most minute details of a painting he has been working on for many years. He knows that time is running out for him and that he will soon die but he is constantly being distracted and never gets to complete his picture during his lifetime. The story then shifts to Niggle's time in purgatory and the discovery that his painting has been re-created there so that he may finish it before travelling on to heaven.

It is a very neat and touching little story, a favourite in the Tolkien household, and, according to Priscilla Tolkien, the most clearly autobiographical of all her father's writing. And in its way it was also a tonic for him, cathartic, and in a sense liberating. For perhaps a year after writing *Leaf By Niggle* Tolkien pressed on, painfully slowly. He had found a new burst of energy but he was working now with three separate plots following the progress of the broken fellowship. He confided in his son Christopher, who was then serving with the RAF at Standerton in the Transvaal, that each page was an agony and that getting back into the swing of things had become a real trial for him.

During the summer of 1944, Tolkien worked on steadily and by July he had brought the story to the end of Book IV (what would later be the end of the second volume, *The Two Towers*). At this point, Frodo has been captured by orcs, Merry and Pippin are set to play their part in the great battles that lay ahead and Aragorn and Gandalf have adopted their mantels of power and stand ready to fulfil their destiny. But although Tolkien was not fully aware of it even then, he was still only three-quarters of the way through the story. But suddenly, during the autumn of 1944, all work on the book once again ground to a halt. This time it seems Tolkien was simply exhausted with the task.

This break lasted more than a year, the longest hiatus since the book was begun almost eight years earlier. The war in Europe ended on 7 May 1945 and Christopher Tolkien returned from South Africa to resume his undergraduate studies. For a time, Lewis was his tutor, and by the autumn, Lewis had proposed that Christopher Tolkien become a full member of the Inklings, 'quite independent of my presence or otherwise' as his father put it.[10] Of all Tolkien's children, Christopher was the one most closely associated with his father's writing (and he is today literary executor and editor of his father's work), but he is also a very good reader: indeed, C.S. Lewis claimed he could read *The Hobbit* and *The Lord of the Rings* better than their creator.

That summer, Tolkien was appointed Merton Professor of English Language and Literature and he preferred the less formal atmosphere of Merton over his old college, Pembroke. It meant a small pay rise, but did little to alleviate the family's rather depressed financial situation. Soon after his appointment, he applied to rent a college house, but it took until March 1947 before one became available.

The Tolkien boys were all now away from home: John was working as a priest and living in the Midlands, Michael was married with a son and Christopher was an academic, so the family no longer needed a house the size of 20 Northmoor Road and the sale of the property would do much to supplement Tolkien's future income. However, the house that was to become their home for the next three years was by no means ideal. Number 3, Manor Road was a small, ugly, modern building, and most distressing for Tolkien, he lost his spacious and comfortable study only to have it replaced by a tiny attic room with a low ceiling.

During the two years that had passed since the end of the war, Tolkien had nudged his story on little by little so that by the summer of 1947 he felt ready to show a portion of it to his favourite critic, Rayner Unwin, the son of his publisher, who was by then an undergraduate at Oxford. On 28 July, Tolkien met Stanley Unwin for lunch in London and handed him Book I of *The Lord of the Rings*. Rayner read it in a matter of days and was captivated. He declared in his report that it was a rather strange book, very different to *The Hobbit* and not really for children. However, he suspected that if adults could overcome their inhibitions to this sort of story they would gain a great deal from it and that it was certainly something George Allen and Unwin should publish.

Tolkien was greatly encouraged, but he still procrastinated over finishing the book. The plot had been worked out and the threads were there to be tied up, but Tolkien simply could not bring himself to draw a line under this epic tale that had occupied his mind on and off for a decade. Just as he had earlier become obsessed with every detail of *The Silmarillion* and was unable ever to say it was truly complete, he had now become so absorbed with the world of Middle-earth, so enmeshed in this alternative reality, he could not take the characters to the last page, nor even to the final chapter.

He had the entire story written by the end of 1947, but for the next two years he reworked it and rewrote entire sections. He went back and inserted explanatory passages and he tied up all the loose ends. Finally, during the autumn of 1949, he made himself stop. He had retyped the entire saga and at last it was fit to be read. And the first person he thought of for this task was his friend, C.S. Lewis.

Chapter 11

Entangled

Lewis had of course already heard most of *The Lord of the Rings*, as it was read aloud at meetings of the Inklings. But, in its entirety, it presented a grand vision, a panorama he had never experienced before and he told Tolkien this in a letter full of praise and admiration. He could have pointed out flaws but these had been commented upon already over beer at the Bird and Baby or around the fire in his Magdalen rooms, and besides, compared with the majesty of the finished work, they were, he believed, trivial.

Immediately after finishing the book Lewis passed it onto his brother Warnie. He took three weeks to finish it, but when it was done, he declared in his diary, 'Golly, what a book! The inexhaustible fertility of the man's imagination amazes me. A great book of its kind.'[1]

So, it was finished. What now? Amazingly, although *The Lord of the Rings* was ready to be edited by the end of 1949, another five years were to pass before the book was finally published, a delay caused by misunderstandings, hard-nosed stubbornness and Tolkien's naivety and unworldliness.

As he finished *The Lord of the Rings*, Tolkien came to the conclusion that he now wanted both this and *The Silmarillion* published as associated volumes. He rightly perceived the two as intimately linked and believed that they should be produced by the same company and, if not published at the same time, then certainly close together. He could not tolerate the idea of *The Lord of the Rings* being split into sections and was now so bound up with the entire mythology, he could not have easily tolerated a single word being changed. As he told Stanley Unwin, 'It is written in my life-blood . . .'[2]

But to complicate things further, Tolkien had lost faith in his publisher. The primary reason for this lay with his belief that Sir Stanley Unwin (he had been knighted in 1946) had no real interest in *The Silmarillion*. Tolkien had presented him with the book on several occasions, and although he had not received a flat 'no', he thought that his great work was not being taken seriously.

But actually, Unwin had hardly been given a chance. Back in 1937, Tolkien had presented him with the 'Quenta Silmarillion' and this had been scrutinised, but largely misunderstood, by the company's regular reader. During the intervening decade, Tolkien had brought up the subject of his masterpiece but gave no hint to Unwin that it might need substantial redrafting and reworking. However, most importantly, Tolkien had confused Unwin with what he was actually doing. Having long-since given up ever seeing a sequel to *The Hobbit* by the end of the war, Unwin could only hope Tolkien would one day surprise him with a wonderful new book. Stanley Unwin's son Rayner had read some of Tolkien's work-in-progress during 1947 and he had been suitably enthusiastic, so why, Unwin must have wondered, was Tolkien now persisting with talk of this other, rather peculiar book, *The Silmarillion*? To a businessman like Sir Stanley Unwin it was obvious that if *The Lord of the Rings* was as good as his own son suggested, then Tolkien and his publishers should concentrate upon that and maybe talk about this other project later.

This of course was not at all the way Tolkien perceived things. To him, *The Silmarillion* and *The Lord of the Rings* were one book, a singular entity, and any editor or publisher he was to work with had to understand that. And, to complicate things still further, in early 1950 Tolkien decided that, for two major reasons, George Allen and Unwin were not doing their job as well as he would have liked.

First, Tolkien was very disappointed with the first post-war edition of *The Hobbit* which appeared without the colour plates that had so enhanced the second edition of 1938. The plates had proven too expensive and too difficult to produce because of war restrictions, but Tolkien seemed to ignore this, or else he failed to understand the simple economics involved.

But Tolkien's second criticism of his publishers was more serious. When, in 1938, they had persisted in attempting to find something that could act as a form of follow-up to *The Hobbit*, he had shown them a short tale called *Farmer Giles of Ham*. It was very different to *The Hobbit*, but was an enchanting story set in what Tolkien described as 'The Little Kingdom' (in fact Oxfordshire and Buckinghamshire in the heart of England and close to his home). George Allen and Unwin wanted to publish the story right away but there followed delay after delay and the scarcity of paper during the war meant that it did not see publication until 1949. When it did, it was something of a disappointment. Flushed with confidence thanks to the continuing success of *The Hobbit*, the publishers had printed five thousand copies of the story, but by the spring of 1950, they had sold only two thousand copies and Stanley Unwin had to confess to Tolkien that it was not yet the great success they had all hoped it would be.

Tolkien blamed his publishers squarely for the initial failure of *Farmer Giles of Ham* and believed they had not promoted it sufficiently. This assessment was probably true in part, but there is also the undeniable fact that although the story is charming, it was only ever going to have a modest impact (and then only thanks to the attention its author was later given by fans of *The Lord of the Rings*).[3]

However, none of this would have made much difference if Tolkien had not met and been impressed by an editor who seemed to show the sort of interest in his entire collection of work that he believed was lacking at George Allen and Unwin. This editor was a young man named Milton Waldman who worked at Collins publishing house in London and had been introduced to Tolkien through the writer's friend and fellow Inkling, Gervase Mathew, who had enthused over Tolkien's epic narrative. When Waldman heard that this was nothing less than a sequel to *The Hobbit*, he immediately contacted Tolkien and asked to see some of his material.

But Tolkien didn't send him the manuscript of *The Lord of the Rings*. Instead, as a test, he offered him *The Silmarillion*. If Waldman was interested in this, he reasoned, then he would show him *The Lord of the Rings*. Waldman was as stunned by *The Silmarillion* as all its few readers had been. Captivated by its beauty, he told Tolkien he was interested in trying to get his company to publish it. And so, impressed, Tolkien then sent him *The Lord of the Rings*.

After reading Tolkien's latest epic Waldman realised he had hit a very rich seam indeed, but he was also working to a hidden agenda. Although he was genuinely interested in all of Tolkien's work, what Waldman and his boss, the publisher William Collins, really wanted was the rights to Tolkien's already successful book, *The Hobbit*. To encourage Tolkien to leave Unwin Milton Waldman told him that Collins, who were also stationers and printers, would have no problem getting supplies of paper and were therefore far better placed than George Allen and Unwin to publish such a hefty pair of books as *The Lord of the Rings* and *The Silmarillion*.

Tolkien was convinced. His contract for *The Hobbit* had stipulated that he must give his publishers two months to accept or reject a sequel and he felt satisfied that their refusal to take *The Silmarillion* and their acceptance of *Farmer Giles of Ham* had freed him from any contractual obligations. He did however feel a moral obligation, especially to Sir Stanley, whom he considered a close acquaintance if not exactly a friend, and to Rayner Unwin who had only ever been supportive of his work. Because of this, he decided he could not make a clean break with George Allen and Unwin and tried instead to simply put them off, to dissuade them from taking *The Lord of the Rings*.

Tolkien wrote to Unwin explaining that his new book had run out of control. Combined with *The Silmarillion*, he told him, his mythology now ran to over one million words, and he had begun to wonder whether anyone would actually be interested in such a monstrous thing. Unwin asked if it could not be split into several volumes, and in reply Tolkien made it clear he could never allow such a thing.

But Tolkien had miscalculated. By playing so hard to get, he had merely succeeded in making Unwin more interested in what he had written. Meanwhile, he remained in touch with Waldman and told him how he was handling Stanley Unwin, reporting that he hoped he would soon be free from his publishers without them even seeing anything he had written.

But of course, Rayner Unwin had already seen some of *The Lord of the Rings* a few years earlier and understood the potential of the book. In a letter to his father he suggested that *The Lord of the Rings* was complete enough on its own and did not need *The Silmarillion* as a companion volume and that there may be material in the latter that could enhance the former. He went on to point out that a competent editor could work with Tolkien to extract such appropriate material, that they could publish *The Lord of the Rings*, and then, after a reasonable period of time, drop *The Silmarillion* altogether.

Rayner had not meant for this letter to be seen by Tolkien, but Sir Stanley included his son's comments in a letter he sent to the author a few days later. Naturally, Tolkien was furious and had to draft and redraft his reply several times before he could frame his anger sufficiently well. Barely keeping his cool, he gave Unwin an ultimatum; either take both books or neither.

Faced with such a choice Unwin could do nothing but let Tolkien go. He wrote expressing his genuine regret that they could not come to an understanding and that the author had forced him into turning down his work and that if he had waited a while they may have been able to reach a suitable compromise. However, it was now clear to all concerned that the relationship had fallen apart. Tolkien wanted to be free of George Allen and Unwin so he could follow through with the interest shown by Waldman; Unwin did not want *The Silmarillion* and could not be forced into accepting it.

Tolkien was now free both contractually and, he believed, morally, and so he gave a commitment to Milton Waldman and William Collins that they could publish his work. But then he immediately confused the matter by informing Waldman that he expected the completed version of *The Silmarillion* and *The Lord of the Rings* together to come in at around one million words. A puzzled Milton Waldman pointed out that the manuscript for *The Lord of the Rings* was about half a million words in length and *The Silmarillion* was only about one hundred and twenty-five thousand words long. It was then Tolkien dropped his bombshell — that he considered *The Silmarillion* only partially finished and that it would require a huge effort to prepare it for publication, an effort requiring the addition of *more* material. This was not quite what Waldman had had in mind; he was about to tell Tolkien that *The Lord of the Rings* needed substantial cutting.

When Tolkien was told this, he was genuinely shocked. He had believed that he had found a sympathetic publisher who understood how he worked and appreciated that his mythology could only be adequately explained if there were no restrictions on the length of the books and the level of detail he demanded. But, rather than trying to reach a compromise with his new editor, Tolkien decided it was the right time to send Waldman several new sections of *The Silmarillion*, which he posted to the London offices of Collins without explaining either where they were to be placed in the main manuscript or how they linked with the rest of the book.

It's possible that even at this stage something could have been salvaged from this disastrous new beginning, but it was not to be. In the summer of 1950, Waldman left for Italy where he spent most of each year. He left Tolkien in the hands of others in the London office of Collins, but they had no understanding of what had transpired and could make neither head nor tale of the strange bundle of papers pertaining to Professor Tolkien. Waldman was due to return to England for a few months in the autumn of 1950, but the trip was postponed when he fell ill in Italy.

And so, Tolkien's relationship with Collins fell apart. Waldman made efforts to correspond with him and was rewarded with a long and detailed synopsis of the entire mythology which Tolkien hoped would help clarify any ambiguities in the incomplete epic and illustrate how the books were unified and indivisible except as two volumes – *The Lord of the Rings* and *The Silmarillion*.

But it did little good, and by early 1952 Tolkien was losing hope. Throughout the year he had been preoccupied with academic work and the family's move from Manor Road to a house in the centre of Oxford, 99 Holywell Street, but once settled there, Tolkien's thoughts had turned back to his book. Sadly, the interest of Waldman and Collins had by then evaporated, and to exacerbate the situation further, the price of paper had increased dramatically in 1951, making the publication of a Middle-earth mythology an even greater gamble for a publisher than it had been two years earlier. In frustration, Tolkien wrote to Collins offering them a similar ultimatum to the one he had imposed upon Stanley Unwin – they must either accept his work as it was and completely unexpurgated or return it forthwith.

A few days later, Tolkien's manuscripts were on his desk once more and for the first time since the late-1930s, he was without any form of relationship with a publishing house. The time had come, he now realised, to shift his perspective and to re-evaluate the situation. A few months earlier he had celebrated his sixtieth birthday and his work was no nearer publication than it had been when he had finished writing *The Lord of the Rings* almost three years earlier. He thought of his own creation, the character, Niggle, and how he had only seen his work completed in heaven; if he was to see published the mythology to which he had devoted so much time and energy, he must act now. He must eat humble pie, and for once, he must compromise.

In June, Tolkien wrote to Rayner Unwin explaining the way his book had become entangled and wondering if he and his father Sir Stanley would still be interested after so long. Rayner Unwin replied immediately to arrange a meeting in Oxford, and in September he picked up the manuscript from Tolkien's house in Holywell Street.

Now there was no question of publishing the entire mythology and Tolkien agreed that *The Lord of the Rings* would have to be split into three separate volumes and published over a period of at least twelve months. But even then Rayner was concerned. His feeling was that George Allen and Unwin must definitely publish the book, he considered it a work of genius, but he also had almost no confidence in its commercial potential. Although *The Hobbit* was still selling, Tolkien had lost any cachet he once had from the initial burst of enthusiasm for hobbits and Rayner Unwin thought that a book as dark, as detailed and as long as *The Lord of the Rings*, a book he could not visualise fitting into any existing genre, would only appeal to a very small section of the market.

Rayner was now deeply involved with the family business and he was left alone to make the decision over *The Lord of the Rings* because his father was in Japan. Nevertheless, after doing some calculations, he still felt anxious enough to seek his father's advice and via telephone and telegram, he explained that he believed the book would lose the company up to £1,000, but that they should still publish it as a prestige title that would gain them great literary kudos. Stanley Unwin agreed and between them they decided to offer Tolkien a deal in which they would pay no advance for the book and no royalty, but they would enter into a profit-sharing scheme. This meant that George Allen and Unwin would cover the costs of production, distribution and advertising and if there was any profit to be made it would be split fifty-fifty with Tolkien.

Tolkien accepted the offer immediately. By this time, he had come to the conclusion that he was never likely to make very much money from his writing and he simply wanted to see his book in print and given due attention.

The year 1953 was a very busy one for Tolkien. He and Edith had never been very happy in Holywell Street. The house at Number 99 was a beautiful old building and it was extremely well placed – a short stroll from college in Merton Street and five minutes from the shops and the covered market near Carfax – but the volume of traffic ruined things, especially for Ronald. He hated the car with a vengeance, but at least in Northmoor Road he had suffered few of its intrusions so close to home. Now, cars and lorries sped past their front door in Holywell Street night and day.

To escape the traffic, they moved to a new house in Headington. Today, Headington is an eastern suburb of Oxford, but then it was almost a separate town and the house at 76 Sandfield Road lay in a quiet side-street. But if by moving there the Tolkiens had hoped to escape the car they had miscalculated because Headington was one of the main centres of development around Oxford during the 1950s, so that within a few years, their quiet cul-de-sac was opened up to become a through road and the neighbourhood was rapidly covered in concrete and tarmac.

During the move, their third in six years, Tolkien was busily attending to final revisions of the text of *The Lord of the Rings* and checking proofs. Although he had always claimed that the only natural break for separate volumes of his mythology was between *The Lord of the Rings* and *The Silmarillion*, with Rayner Unwin's guidance he did find a way to split the book neatly into three volumes. But when this was done the question of subtitles became a major issue debated at considerable length. Eventually, they settled upon *I: The Fellowship of the Ring*, *II: The Two Towers* and *III: The Return of the King*, although this last was wrangled over interminably because Tolkien preferred the subtitle, *The War of the Ring*.[4]

Tolkien was still working full-time at the university, and the work-load was almost crippling. Rayner had not asked for cuts, but in typical fashion, Tolkien agonised over every single word of the massive manuscript. He also had to compose a set of detailed Appendices culling appropriate material from *The Silmarillion*, and he needed to produce family trees, timelines and a set of maps.

The publication date for *The Fellowship of the Ring* was set for the summer of 1954, and after much pleading on Unwin's part, Tolkien finally managed to submit his perfected draft in April 1953, ready for the slow process of production. By October, the publishers wanted maps to be made ready for the printers as quickly as possible, but by this point Tolkien was overwhelmed, the new academic year had begun and he was trying to revise and rework the manuscript for *The Two Towers*. Fortunately,

Christopher Tolkien was around to help and he prepared the maps from the confused set of images his father had drawn hastily many years earlier. Towards the end of the year, Tolkien found time to produce a set of jacket designs which the publishers used as a basis for the final cover. On olive grey paper the design shows the One Ring surrounded by the fire-letters of its inscription and surmounted by the Red Ring, Narya, a design which is still used today for some editions.

Finally, all was ready and George Allen and Unwin, still bereft of confidence, ordered a print run of just three and half thousand copies pegged at a price of twenty-one shillings per volume. To boost the publicity campaign, they employed three well-known authors to write blurbs for the jacket of the book. One was C.S. Lewis, the other two were famous fans of *The Hobbit*, Naomi Mitchison and Richard Hughes.

Lewis's blurb read: 'It would be almost safe to say that no book like this has ever been written. If Ariosto rivalled it in invention (in fact he does not) he would still lack its heroic seriousness.'[5]

In August 1954, *The Fellowship of The Ring* finally reached the bookshops.

CHAPTER 12

The World of
Middle-earth

This book is like lightning from a clear sky. To say that
in it heroic romance, gorgeous, eloquent and unashamed,
has suddenly returned at a period almost pathological in
its anti-romanticism, is inadequate . . . Probably no book
yet written in the world is quite such a radical instance of
what its author has elsewhere called 'sub-creation'.[1]

This was one of the first reviews of *The Lord of the Rings* to appear
and was written by none other than Tolkien's friend C.S. Lewis
who, in private, was even more unrestrained with his praise,
telling friends that *The Lord of the Rings* was as long as the Bible
and not a word too long.

Soon there appeared review after review, a continuing stream
of comment and opinion about Tolkien's great work which has,
over the ensuing years, swelled to a flood.

Lewis was by no means the only one to consider Tolkien's

book a masterpiece. The reviewer in the *Manchester Guardian* declared that Tolkien was: 'one of those born story-tellers who makes his readers as wide-eyed as children for more'.[2] And in *Country Life*, reviewer Howard Spring enthused, 'This is a work of art . . . It has invention, fancy and imagination . . . It is a profound parable of man's everlasting struggle against evil.'[3] More support came from *Truth* which carried a review by A.E. Cherryman in which he wrote, 'It is an amazing piece of work. He has added something, not only to the world's literature, but to its history.'[4] And closer to home, the *Oxford Times* reviewer made the prescient point that, 'The severely practical will have no time for it. Those who have imagination to kindle will find themselves completely carried along, becoming part of the eventful quest and regretting that there are only two more books to come.'[5]

Another early convert was Bernard Levin who considered *The Lord of the Rings* 'One of the most remarkable works of literature in our, or any time. It is comforting in this troubled day, to be once more assured that the meek shall inherit the earth.'[6]

But others were less impressed. In the *Daily Telegraph*, Peter Green called it 'a shapeless work' and that it: 'veers from pre-Raphaelite to Boy's Own Paper'.[7] While in the *Sunday Times*, the reviewer questioned whether the book was written merely 'for bright children'. But the most disgruntled of Tolkien's reviewers was Edwin Muir who claimed in the *Observer* that he considered the book 'remarkable', but criticised Tolkien for the fact that 'his good people are consistently good, his evil figures immutably evil: and he has no room in his world for a Satan both evil and tragic'.[8]

When *The Fellowship of the Ring* was published in the United States that October, it received another set of patchy reviews, but found an avid and vocal supporter in the shape of the literary giant, W.H. Auden, who wrote in *The New York Times* that 'no fiction I have read in the last five years has given me more joy'.[9] And a month later he added more weighty support when in a radio interview, he declared: 'If someone dislikes it I shall never trust their literary judgement about anything again.'[10]

In November 1954, the second volume, *The Two Towers*, was published in Britain. This garnered another wide-ranging selection of reviews and Tolkien was surprised to learn that because he had left the story with Frodo held prisoner in the Tower of Cirith Ungol many readers and reviewers could hardly wait for the last instalment. The reviewer in the *Illustrated London News* pronounced that 'the suspense is cruel'. And Lewis waded in with another glowing review for *Time and Tide* in which he wrote: 'When I reviewed the first volume of this work, I hardly dared to hope it would have the success which I was sure it deserved. Happily I am proved wrong . . . The book is too original and too opulent for any final judgement on a first reading. But we know at once that it has done things to us. We are not quite the same men. And though we must ration ourselves in our re-readings, I have little doubt that the book will soon take its place among the indispensables.'[11]

It was only after the third volume was published on 20 October 1955 that the critics could properly assess the work in its entirety and make their overarching pronouncements. For many, their opinion had been settled with the reading of the first volume. Those who loved *The Fellowship of the Ring*, adored the entire work and those who found serious fault in the first volume retained their prejudices and dislikes through to the bitter end. And the criticisms were varied and fulsome. Edwin Muir, who succeeded in greatly irritating Tolkien with his barbs, wrote an article for the *Observer* entitled 'A Boy's World' in which he pronounced:

> The astonishing thing is that all the characters are boys masquerading as adult heroes. The hobbits, or halflings, are ordinary boys; the fully human heroes have reached the fifth form; but hardly one of them knows anything about women, except by hearsay.[12]

The then well-known American author, Edmund Wilson, was far more blunt when he wrote that *The Lord of the Rings* was 'balderdash' and 'juvenile trash' and went on to make the ill-judged observation that he thought the book would only appeal to British literary taste.[13]

Clearly, from its very first appearance, *The Lord of the Rings* stimulated strong emotions. It was immediately a book both beloved and loathed, a book that split the literary fraternity with seeming randomness. Opinion could not be divided between those with 'highbrow' or 'lowbrow' tastes, and in spite of Wilson's jaundiced opinion, there was no apparent demarcation along national lines. Furthermore, the criticisms were (and remain) incredibly wide-ranging.

The first type of criticism seems to have come from those who simply set their faces against the book. Reviewers often have a personal axe to grind, which may usually be put down to simple jealousy, a need to show-off to one's peers, or just a dislike of someone or something connected with an author or a particular book. It seems this last was the reason Edwin Muir turned against Tolkien before he had even read a word of *The Lord of the Rings*. In his first review (Muir reviewed each of the volumes as they appeared) in the *Observer* of 22 August 1954, he had commented: 'This remarkable book makes its appearance at a disadvantage. Nothing but a great masterpiece could survive the bombardment of praise directed at it from the blurb.'

This was written during a more naive age than the one we live in today, an age when journalists were not so used to the barrage of information and hyperbole associated with a typical, modern book launch. Indeed, the very word 'hype' was one used rarely in those days. Yet, Muir was being deliberately oblique, for what really irritated him was the praise offered by C.S. Lewis, whose own work he disliked intensely.

By the 1950s, Lewis had many enemies and although he also had many hundreds of thousands of fans around the world, some journalists and literary figures despised his books. Lewis knew this and when he was asked by Tolkien's publishers for a contribution to the blurb for *The Lord of the Rings*, he warned Tolkien that this might not actually be good for him, that in some quarters he was a hated man and that Tolkien should think carefully before approving his offering.

Curiously, it was only after opprobrium was heaped upon Tolkien and its source clearly identified as those who hated Lewis that Tolkien realised that his friend had not been exaggerating. He seems to have been quite unaware just how unpopular Lewis was in some circles, but perhaps he also could not resist fine words in print from Lewis, who was by then a famous writer.

But aside from the personal attacks derived from silly feuding and animosity, Muir did go to great lengths to explain his criticisms and in fairness we should address them. His primary objection was in a sense to do with what he perceived as an immaturity in the authorial voice. He couches this in eye-catching phrases, insisting upon relating the lead male characters to boys, but it cannot be denied that perhaps the weakest aspect of *The Lord of the Rings* is the way Tolkien deals with romantic emotions. Tolkien is faultless in his portrayal of heroism and what he may have considered 'high emotion', but it is certainly true that he deals with any relationship between the sexes with extreme clumsiness.

This stems from the fact that Tolkien really did not feel comfortable writing about women and he displayed none of his usual fluidity of language when he needed to write a scene in which men and women interact in any way. We must remember that he was an old-fashioned man with many Victorian views. As we saw earlier, his own vision of romance was influenced by the books he had read and he was quite aware that he did not know how to write convincingly about anything sexual. Of all his writings, his personal favourite was 'The Lay of Beren and Lúthien'. It is a wonderful tale, but it contains no sexual energy which is what Muir complained was missing in *The Lord of the Rings*.

However, there is a caveat to this. If Muir had good reason to criticise this aspect of Tolkien's work, he was also wrong to make such a great deal of it. Admitting that *The Lord of the Rings* was 'a remarkable book', the reviewer had allowed his dislike of Lewis and Tolkien's failure to write convincingly about romance and sex to overshadow the other great achievements of the book.

The lack of subtlety in the remarks of men like Edmund Wilson are more puzzling. They may have been provoked by jealousy, but it is also likely that Wilson and others simply 'didn't get it'. *The Lord of the Rings* was almost completely unique, readers (including professional critics) had almost nothing with which to compare it, nothing to measure it against. Furthermore, when Tolkien's books appeared in the mid-1950s they were utterly unfashionable. Modernism was at its most popular and Tolkien's writing was considered by some to be irredeemably, almost perversely, old-fashioned.

And of course, it was. That was Tolkien's style; his writing had its roots in an ancient form. Even during the 1950s, plot was becoming *infra dig*, style was taking centre stage, but it was a modernist style, not the archaic or the fairy story form that was Tolkien's.

We will return to the critics in Chapter 14, but as well as surveying the opinions and the early critical appraisal of Tolkien's creation, we must take a closer look at some of the themes and conceptual threads that weave the fabric of Middle-earth. We need to address a plethora of questions that spring from any reading of *The Lord of the Rings* and *The Silmarillion*. There are many puzzles. Where is Middle-earth? Do the Ages of Middle-earth relate in any way to the history of our world? Why is it that amongst Tolkien's million words or more on the subject of Middle-earth, the word 'God' does not appear even once? Did Tolkien have a message in his writing and his descriptions of his mythical world? And if he did, what was this message? And, ultimately, we have to address a question that probably irritated Tolkien more than any other linked to his work: is Tolkien's mythological world allegorical?

Middle-earth is, without doubt, a distorted version of Earth. More specifically, the countries in which *The Lord of the Rings* is set and in which the action takes place are a distorted version of Europe. Tolkien himself made this very clear. When asked about the geography of Middle-earth, he declared, 'Rhûn is the

Elvish word for east. Asia, China, Japan, and all the things which people in the west regard as far away. And south of Harad is Africa, the hot countries.' When asked, 'That makes Middle-earth Europe doesn't it?' Tolkien replied, 'Yes, of course – north-western Europe . . . where my imagination comes from.'[14] When questioned by a journalist as to the location of Mordor, he replied, 'roughly in the Balkans', and in a letter written while on holiday in Venice in 1955, Tolkien described the city he was visiting as 'Gondor'.[15]

Hobbits are English, and the Shire is an aspect of England. A journalist who spent some time with Tolkien during the 1960s, Clyde Kilby, learned this directly from Tolkien. 'When I asked him if there were hobbits in the earlier ages,' Kilby reported, '. . . he plainly answered that there were none because hobbits were English, a remark which both confirms geographical delin-eations and has wide temporal implications. As to the geography, we were once driving a few miles east of Oxford on the London Road and Tolkien pointed out little hills to the north of us that, he said, were just right for hobbit territory.'[16]

Looking at the broader canvas, it would seem likely that Númenor is based upon the legendary Atlantis, or perhaps the older legend of Mu. The Atlanteans were thought to possess an advanced civilisation, to be superior to common men and to have mystical powers. When asked where Númenor was, Tolkien didn't hesitate. 'In the middle of the Atlantic,' he said.[17] Interestingly, modern research points to the fact that Atlantis, Mu or some other ancient civilisation may have once existed in an island state in the mid-Atlantic.[18]

The Silmarillion and The Lord of the Rings together represent an alternative history of the world, but one that stops just before recorded history begins. It seems likely that Tolkien had some form of Atlantean legend in mind along with the Norse paradigm. According to legend, the Atlanteans enjoyed a longer life-span than humans who succeeded them, they were greatly skilled and gifted seafarers. Some believe that Europe was colonised by the Atlanteans and that they also planted the seed of the Egyptian civilisation. In *The Silmarillion*, the Númenoreans, banned by the Valar from travelling West to the Undying Lands, head eastward to Middle-earth during the Second Age and begin to colonise; they too have longer life-spans than other men and are highly civilised.

Ancient legend also describes how the Atlanteans began to believe they were capable of anything and were destroyed by the wrath of God, their civilisation buried under the waves. At the end of the Second Age, the Númenoreans, led by their king Ar-Pharazôn, threaten the Valar by attempting to break the Ban and sail west with a great armada. The Valar call upon the One to destroy the Númenoreans and their entire civilisation.[19]

Tolkien considered his mythology to be a profoundly religious work and perceived *The Lord of the Rings* as a Christian, even a Catholic story. And yet on first reading, this is a conclusion very difficult to understand, for Middle-earth appears to be a wholly pagan world. The only form of prayer is when a 'weak' or 'powerless' individual in desperate need (such as Sam Gamgee in Mordor) calls upon a stronger demi-god and demi-goddess such as Galadriel or Lúthien Tinúviel. When warriors fall and are buried there are no prayers said over their graves. There are no churches or chapels anywhere in Middle-earth. The only 'holy books' are records of elder days. And yet, there are hints of religiosity, even Christian orthodoxy.

The Silmarillion describes the One and offers an alternative Creation before telling of the First and Second Ages, the adventures of elves and men and their fight against Morgoth and Sauron. But, if Tolkien was trying to convey a subtle religious backdrop to his mythology, it appears to have been a confused one, for we get mixed and sometimes contradictory messages.

This is most clear when we try to categorise many of the lead characters and even objects at the centre of the story. Frodo shows Christ-like qualities – he is the bearer of the Ring, burdened with the cross – he is tempted at the Crack of Doom, just as Christ was tempted. Sauron and Melkor (or Morgoth) are clearly figures from Hell, Morgoth, the fallen Valar or black angel, Sauron the fallen Maiar, a devil by any other name. Gandalf is clearly a prophet-figure, but what of Galadriel? She appears only fleetingly, but exerts a powerful presence throughout the second half of *The Lord of the Rings*. She is one of the disgraced Noldor who disobeyed the Valar during the First Age, but there is also perhaps something of the Virgin Mary about her.

This idea was put to Tolkien by his friend, Father Murray. In his reply to the letter in which this was suggested, a few months before publication of *The Fellowship of the Ring*, he thanked the priest for his perceptive interpretations and concurred with the idea that he had placed much of the way he perceived Mary into his drawing of Galadriel.[20]

Yet, the most curious religious aspect of *The Lord of the Rings* is not so much the elements that go to create the central characters but a subtle undercurrent implicit in the telling of the tale, and Tolkien's timing. In Appendix B of *The Lord of the Rings* we are told that the fellowship leaves Rivendell to begin its mission on 25 December. The day Frodo and Sam succeed in destroying the ring, the day it is cast into the Crack of Doom and the new era truly begins is, in the Gondorian reckoning, 25 March. Now although this date has little significance for most people, in the old English tradition (a subject about which Tolkien was quite familiar), 25 March was the date of the first Good Friday, the date of Christ's crucifixion.[21] This then means that the main events in the story of how the Ring is destroyed and Sauron is defeated are played out during the mythic period between Christ's birth on 25 December and his death on 25 March.

There is no reason for this to be planted in the story except as a form of subtle 'hidden message'. Tolkien is imposing his faith upon a pagan world, his characters act out their roles in a non-Christian void, but their 'sub-creator' can move them through a time frame that is Christian – after all, he has the final say.

Beyond this, what Tolkien meant when he claimed his work was Christian and even Catholic in nature was the sense of grace that informs the work. His characters live in a world in which magic is real, in which belief alone can make things happen. This is not simply a question of will power or determination, but thought-made-physical. In Middle-earth, true belief can overcome the stream of reality, it can distort the flow of cause and effect. And, although there is no specific Christianity in any of Tolkien's fiction – no Bibles, no crucifixes, no altars – the 'Christian spirit' is everywhere. The essential core of the story is good versus evil and the triumph of good, but it is also about sacrifice, temptation, self-determination and free-will. Tolkien's friend and supporter W.H. Auden knew this and remarked that, 'The unstated presuppositions of *The Lord of the Rings* are Christian.'[22] The writer Edmund Fuller believed that, 'Grace is at work abundantly in the story' and that 'a thread of prophesy is being fulfilled'.[23]

Tolkien's devotion to Catholicism was probably the most important thing in his life; he was almost a fanatical Christian, a fact that became clear to anyone soon after meeting him. He habitually referred to Christ as 'Our Lord' and possessed an unshakeable conviction in the power of prayer, believing that he had been 'given' stories after praying and that prayers had cured members of his family when they were ill. One friend, George Sayers, said, 'Tolkien was a very strict Roman Catholic. He was very orthodox and old fashioned.'[24] His son John, who became a Catholic priest, has declared that Catholicism, 'pervaded all [his father's] thinking, beliefs and everything else'.[25] It is not surprising, then, that Tolkien was compelled to plant subtle references to Christianity and the biblical tradition into an otherwise pagan tale.

Another matter very close to Tolkien's heart was what he perceived as the destructiveness of modern life and the onward surge of technological progress. His ecological convictions were non-political, driven by a deep personal distaste for many of the trappings of modern living and a distrust of the twentieth century. 'He disliked the modern world,' his son Christopher Tolkien has remarked; 'the modern world meant for him, essentially the machine. One of the underlying things in *The Lord of the Rings* is the machine.'[26] Others have described his anti-modernist attitudes more strongly. 'Tolkien has always spoken . . . as though only fools and madmen would contemplate the twentieth century without horror,' the critic Roger Sale has said.[27] Moreover, the writer Paul Kocher declared that, 'Tolkien was ecologist, champion of the extraordinary, hater of "progress", lover of handicrafts, detester of war long before such attitudes became fashionable.'[28]

Tolkien's anger with the twentieth century is writ large in *The Lord of the Rings*. The ents are one of the saddest creations in literature, for they are doomed, a symbol of a passing age, and the chapter 'The Scouring of the Shire' must have been for Tolkien one of the most satisfying passages he ever wrote.

Indeed, it is clear that Tolkien used *The Lord of the Rings* as a vehicle for attacking his most loathed targets – technologists, modernisers, polluters and inveterate consumers. He created an utterly convincing alternative world in which technology did not exist, what John Clute has described as 'a comprehensive counter myth to the story of the twentieth century . . . a description of a universe that feels right – another reality that the soul requires in this waste-land century'.[29] By doing this, Tolkien was not merely submitting to wish-fulfilment, he was proselytising deeply held convictions and heartfelt sentiments. Colin Wilson made this point forcefully when he wrote:

> *The Lord of the Rings* is a criticism of the modern world and of the values of technological civilisation. It asserts its own values, and tries to persuade the reader that they are preferable to current values . . . it is at once an attack on the modern world and a credo, a manifesto.[30]

From an ecologist's perspective, the character of Saruman (whose name may be translated as 'cunning man')[31] is every bit as sinister as Sauron or Morgoth. We may think of these last two as mystical evil, destroyers of spirit, devils, but Saruman is the embodiment of the corrupt twentieth century. He is the fork-tongued politician, the meddler in the ways of nature, the polluter and the evil scientist. Saruman breeds a particularly vicious strain of orc that has no fear of the light and has the strength of two of Sauron's warriors. He plays with machines and technology and while the heroes of the book are fighting the War of the Ring and saving Middle-earth from Sauron, he is behind the 'modernising' of the Shire. But Saruman is defeated by the triumph of the 'old ways', by Gandalf's naturalistic magic and the 'goodness' of those who work with nature rather than against it. But perhaps Tolkien went too far with this. Perhaps he portrayed his convictions too well because for some readers, *The Lord of the Rings* is, on many levels, pure allegory.

The first to suggest this was Rayner Unwin who read a very early version of part of the story during the summer of 1947. In a report to his father he pointed out that the struggle between good and evil smacked of allegory. Tolkien was unhappy about these remarks and we can probably trace from this response his lifelong insistence that his work was not at all allegorical. However, to be fair to Rayner Unwin, this was 1947, the war was only just won and it might seem likely that the central plot in *The Lord of the Rings*, the struggle between 'the good guys from the West' and the 'baddies from the East' might suggest allegory.

So, let us consider the evidence. First there is this question of the War of the Ring being in some way a reflection of the Second World War.

At first glance, this certainly seems like a possibility. Tolkien was writing his saga during the conflict and even if we consider the argument that he composed some of it before the war and had captured the essence of the tale by 1938, we could counter this by saying that although Europe as a whole was not at war that year, Fascism was very much a powerful force and war was definitely in the air. Furthermore, Tolkien constantly rewrote backwards, reworking and revising early passages, and if he had wanted to write allegorically, he could have easily done so by peppering the text with poignant references to real events after they had occurred.

It is quite easy to find markers of allegorical reference if we search for them. Here are three obvious examples: Tolkien's use of white and black to define good and evil; his decision to make the orc language guttural, which some might interpret as an extreme distortion of spoken German; and of course, most telling of all, the positions in Middle-earth of the warring nations.

A more subtle comment on allegory comes in Book II, Chapter 2 of *The Lord of the Rings*, 'The Council of Elrond', which centres around a complex discussion about what should be done with the Ring. Throughout the discourse it is clear that those working for the forces of good are quite unprepared for conflict and even mighty figures such as Gandalf and Elrond admit to coming only recently to understand the full extent of Sauron's threat. This has been likened to the way in which Britain and the other Allies were ill-prepared for war even though the Nazis had been building their military strength since the early 1930s. Tolkien was writing 'The Council of Elrond' during the very early days of the war.

And then there is the object at the very centre of the story, the Ring of Power, which lends itself to all sorts of allegorical references. Rayner Unwin was the first to propose the idea that it bore similarities to the 'Ring of the Nibelungs' from Wagner's opera. Tolkien retorted that the only thing they had in common was that they were both round.

But really, so few claims of allegory stand up to close scrutiny. Black has always been associated with evil, the conflict between black and white agencies is an ancient one, and indeed Hitler chose black as the colour to represent his regime specifically because of these primitive associations. Furthermore, Germany is some considerable distance from the Balkans, which Tolkien declared to be the European equivalent of Mordor. The orc language could be interpreted as sounding like many other languages and one could argue that with their swarthy looks and slit eyes, orcs bear very little resemblance to SS storm-troopers. In fact, although he may not have realised it, Rayner Unwin was in one respect closer to the mark with his reference to Wagner's Ring Cycle because at least the composer had drawn upon ancient Teutonic myth and legend for his inspiration.

Other proposed allegorical links include the idea that Mordor is in fact Russia rather than Germany. It is certainly true that from long before the Second World War until his death, Tolkien held a deep distrust of Russia and Communism. He was not a very political man, but he suspected Stalin throughout the war, even as Russian soldiers fought alongside British and American troops during the liberation of Europe. And when, immediately after the war, the Russians isolated themselves from the rest of the world and created the Soviet bloc, Tolkien was not at all surprised. However, Russia cannot be Mordor any more than Germany could be, unless Tolkien was imagining a future war on earth, which during the 1940s, was not imagined as even a vague possibility.

Tolkien claimed he hated allegory in whatever shape or form and he vigorously denied the existence of *any* form of allegory in his writing.[32] He confided to close friends that religion had been a great inspiration in the moulding of his characters, but he refused to accept that the plot of *The Lord of the Rings* reflected anything other than merely oblique references to his own experience of war. An example of this is his acceptance that Sam Gamgee represented for him the good, solid, working-class soldier, the trustworthy and faithful private. But in this case, Tolkien was thinking more of his experiences during the First World War and we must not forget that much of the foundation for *The Lord of the Rings* stemmed from *The Silmarillion*, largely composed immediately after the First World War.

But Tolkien went further. He denied that he was making *any* allusion to his ecological concerns in *The Lord of the Rings*. He found particularly galling any parallels drawn between his descriptions in 'The Scouring of the Shire' and the state of England immediately after the War. But to anyone reading *The Lord of the Rings* during the early 1950s (or later by those with memories or knowledge of that time), the links are apparent and undeniable. In Britain between 1940 and the early 1950s, rationing and shortages were common features of society. Prefabs (cheap, easy-to-built or prefabricated buildings) were hastily erected to house those made homeless by German bombs. Industry had to work overtime to rebuild the country and pollution became far worse than it had been before the war; corruption was rife for a while and 'spivs' worked the black market. All of these things were fictionalised in distorted form in the account of the hobbits returning from their own war.

So what are we to believe? To what extent is *The Lord of the Rings* an allegorical work? And why was Tolkien so determined to stamp out the suggestion?

The only logical conclusion is that Tolkien did not deliberately go out of his way to write allegorically but that links with the world in which events were unfolding with dramatic intensity found their way into his work without his realising it. Just as he was starting to write, the tanks began to roll and the world erupted into violence. It was only when some of those who read his work made comparisons with modern history that he came to realise the unconscious allegorical element of his work. For his own reasons, he then chose to resist this suggestion.

And, by trying to understand why he should do this, we may

come to learn much about Tolkien's character and motivations. First, to Tolkien, his fiction was a description of a purer world, a world far from the tarnished Earth of his real life. *The Silmarillion* was, we must recall, his 'mythology for England' and *The Lord of the Rings* was intimately related to this earlier work and drew heavily upon it. The last thing he wanted was for readers to devalue his 'high concept', to demean his grand, timeless epic by relating it to the grubby deeds of modern human life.

The second reason for his determination to refute claims of allegory was more personal. Around the time he was finishing *The Lord of the Rings* and as he was about to place it in publishing limbo for several years, C.S. Lewis had written his first Narnia books. These were of course written as deliberate allegory and Tolkien loathed both the books and Lewis's motives. It is therefore safe to assume that Tolkien would not have appreciated readers or literary commentators painting *The Lord of the Rings* with the allegory brush. For Tolkien, any association between Lewis's writing and his own, in particular any connection that was made between *The Lion, the Witch and the Wardrobe* and *The Lord of the Rings* was to be avoided at all costs.

Tolkien took great exception to any suggestions that his work had been influenced by other writers. His replies to well-meaning letters from fans around the world asking him if he had been inspired by such-and-such a book or by this writer or that were often sprinkled with denials and denouncements and as he grew older, this reaction grew far more pronounced.

A particular example of this is his dismissal of the Victorian writer, George Macdonald, whom he once referred to as 'an old grandmother'.[33] It is perhaps significant that Tolkien's fiction was often compared to Macdonald's.[34] And perhaps we should not ignore the fact that Macdonald was also one of C.S. Lewis's favourites and a writer whom he often cited as an influence upon his own work.[35] Lewis even thought Tolkien owed something to Macdonald and mentioned this in his review of *The Hobbit*.

Even more striking is the way, late in life, Tolkien attacked his most likeable character, Sam Gamgee, whom he had once called a 'jewel among the hobbits'.[36] In a letter to a fan Tolkien once described Sam as 'sententious and cocksure ... He was the youngest son of a stupid and conceited old peasant ... Together with his loyal master-servant attitude, and his personal love for Frodo, he retains a touch of the contempt of his kind (moderated to tolerant pity) for motives above their reach.'[37]

More than almost any other writer, Tolkien poured his own personality into his work. The underlying themes in his fiction – the power of heroism, the importance of honesty and loyalty, the superiority of Nature over technology, the conviction that every victory has its price, the struggle between good and evil as an integral dynamic in the universe – all these things are reflections of Tolkien's deep-rooted beliefs and drives. Of course, Aragorn and Frodo, Gandalf and Sauron too, are alter-egos, but beyond the usual attachments and correspondence between an author and the printed page, Middle-earth is infused with Tolkien's personality.

In the case of Tolkien, this infusion is exceptional for several important reasons. First, Tolkien spent almost his entire life absorbed with Middle-earth. In old age he talked of the fact that some aspects of his later fiction were circulating in his mind as a young boy and we know from surviving documents that he was certainly creating the foundations of his mythology by his early twenties. Tolkien drank, ate, slept and breathed Middle-earth, it was always there in his mind even during the fallow period when work on *The Lord of the Rings* ceased for a year or more, it was there when he was lecturing and marking examination papers, playing with his children on a beach at some English seaside resort or when he was sharing a drink at the Bird and Baby.

The second reason is the fact that, as we saw in Chapter 5, Tolkien wrote his fiction because he *needed* to. He needed to create a fantasy world into which he could absorb himself. He therefore had to be honest about it, honest and plain. And it is perhaps for this reason more than any other that he hated the charge of allegory and did everything he could to remove what he saw as a slur.

Finally, Tolkien's personality, his presence, is so strong in his fiction because he believed that the plot of a story was more important than the style in which it was written. This made him deeply unfashionable at a time when modernism (which places more emphasis upon style than storytelling) was becoming an influential literary force. But Tolkien's desire to tell an honest story in an honest and clear fashion is one of the key reasons for the enormous success of his books and one of the factors that ensures his fans return again and again to reread the mythology of Middle-earth.

CHAPTER 13

The Final Years

The huge success of *The Lord of the Rings* did not change Tolkien's life immediately, and when it had the power to do so it all came a little too late.

However, George Allen and Unwin did not have to wait long to realise that their gamble had paid off and that in fact the decision to profit-share with the author was not actually the wisest one. Within six weeks of its publication, *The Lord of the Rings* had been reprinted, and in early 1956, Tolkien received his first share of profit from the book when a cheque for almost £4,000 arrived at Sandfield Road, Headington. This was more than a year's professorial salary for Tolkien.[1] The cheque that came the following year was considerably larger and for each year (until 1965), sales increased steadily bringing Tolkien larger and larger cheques.

Tolkien's bank account was boosted further in 1957 when a Catholic college, Marguette University in Milwaukee, bought the original manuscripts of *The Hobbit* and *The Lord of the Rings* (along with *Farmer Giles of Ham* and the then unpublished *Mr Bliss*) for £1,250. This new wealth came as something of a shock to the Tolkiens who had struggled all their lives, but it also brought Edith and Ronald security for their remaining years and meant they could splash out on the luxuries they had never before been able to afford.

This success came very late in life – Tolkien was in his mid-sixties when *The Lord of the Rings* made him a bestselling author, he was close to retirement and already looking forward to devoting all his time to working on his other projects, especially *The Silmarillion*, the book that had been at the centre of his creative energies for some forty years.

In many ways, Tolkien had been old before his time. As a young man he had cherished rather anachronistic ideas, and these had never left him. Indeed, as old age crept up on him, many of the good and bad aspects of his personality became exaggerated. His speech impediment became worse so that to some he was almost incomprehensible, a characteristic Tolkien made far worse by having a pipe clenched between his teeth during almost every waking moment. One of his obituaries described him as 'the best and worst talker in Oxford – worst for the rapidity and indistinctness of his speech, and the best for the penetration, learning, humour and "race" of what he said'.[2]

One of his strongest character traits was his pedantic nature. This served him enormously well in making him a successful scholar and it was one of the sources of his greatness as a conjuror of fantasy, but it also made him appear overly critical of so many things. In 1955, the BBC produced a radio dramatisation of *The Lord of the Rings* which was generally believed to be very good, but Tolkien thought it extremely poor and believed he could have acted many of the parts better himself. In 1956, a Dutch publisher was about to publish an edition of *The Lord of the Rings*, but Tolkien found they had translated some of the names incorrectly and held up publication. A few years later, a Swedish publisher infuriated Tolkien with a proposed edition which included a foreword by a Swedish author in which the book was described as allegorical.

Tolkien held very strong prejudices, he had powerful likes and dislikes and, as with so many people, as he grew older, he became more entrenched in his views, more extreme in his feelings. He considered an increasing number of things 'vulgar' or 'absurd', he disliked the French language and French cooking, he disapproved of almost all journalists, he thought many photographers were unable to take a good photograph and that he could do better. He invariably disliked the work of illustrators brought in to produce covers and plates for his books and he considered most publishers to be quite inefficient and poor at distribution and promotion.[3]

He seemed to have an obsessive need to rake over every single detail of anything with which he became involved. When a pair of journalists, Charlotte and Denis Plimmer, interviewed him for the *Daily Telegraph* magazine in 1968, they sent Tolkien the draft of the interview and were treated in response to a two-thousand word dissertation on the piece in which Tolkien took apart almost everything they had written, as though they were students. The Plimmers referred to Tolkien's garage (which had been converted into a work area) as a 'study', but this was apparently inaccurate, and just the suggestion that *The Silmarillion* grew out of Tolkien's predilection for creating languages alone warranted half a page of correction and criticism.

He also became increasingly secretive almost to the point of
paranoia and found it difficult to disclose anything about himself or his past to the many journalists and feature writers who
began to beat a path to his door following the success of *The
Lord of the Rings*. He did not like becoming a cult figure and
could not understand why people were interested in him as well
as his work and declared that he felt people considered him 'a
gargoyle to be gaped at'.[4] In the early sixties he stopped W.H.
Auden writing a short biography of him declaring to the proposed publisher that such accounts should only be written by an
intimate and that it would represent a gross intrusion into his
personal life.

His opinion of modern literature never softened and indeed he
disliked most of the work produced by writers from any era.
Once, when a journalist reminded him that C.S. Lewis had compared him to the sixteenth century Italian writer, Ariosto, Tolkien
retorted, 'I don't know Ariosto and I'd loathe him if I did . . .
Cervantes was a weed-killer to romance . . . Dante doesn't interest me. He's full of spite and malice. I don't care for petty
relations with petty people in petty cities.'[5]

And yet, he was most critical of himself. This was the force
that drove him to rework and to revise and rewrite. He was
acutely aware of faults in *The Lord of the Rings* – the fact that
although five Istari are mentioned, we know in detail about
only two (Gandalf and Saruman), that there was confusion
over who the oldest being in Middle-earth might be – Tom
Bombadil or the ents; that the elf, Cirdan, possesses one of the
great Elven rings of power but appears only fleetingly in the
book. These were deep-rooted faults that could not be cleared
up easily, but Tolkien always harboured plans to write more
books that would explain these anomalies. Once, during the

1960s, when he was asked by his publisher to make revisions to *The Hobbit* for a new edition, he stayed up into the early hours rereading his book and was about to start rewriting the entire thing when he came to his senses and stopped himself. He was a firm believer in the idea that any narrative should first be written as a poem, which is exactly what he did with much of *The Silmarillion*.

And yet, Tolkien never undersold himself, and over many issues he carried the conviction that he was right and others were wrong. This stance was a necessary one for him and essential to his success as an author. He knew he had created something very special with *The Lord of the Rings* and he had the self-confidence and self-belief to pursue his goal for some seventeen years. He was also to be proved right about *The Silmarillion*, which was eventually published in spite of constant rejection by his publishers.

By any measure, *The Lord of the Rings* would have been considered a great success, but then a strange chain of events turned this merely 'successful' book into a global phenomenon.

Early in 1965, staff at an American publishing house called Ace Books had begun to notice how *The Lord of the Rings* had become a hit amongst college students, particularly in California. They then learned that Tolkien's publisher, the Boston-based Houghton Mifflin, had apparently contravened copyright law by importing more than the statutory number of unfolded press sheets from the British publishers. Ace then decided to take a gamble and publish what amounted to a pirated version of *The Lord of the Rings*.

Some time before the edition was ready for shipping, Houghton Mifflin heard about it and contacted George Allen and Unwin in London. An outraged Rayner Unwin realised that Houghton Mifflin had to produce a new paperback edition as quickly as possible, but that in order to do this, the edition had to be revised. So, Unwin travelled to Oxford immediately to talk to Tolkien and to explain the situation so that he could make some relatively minor revision of the text as quickly as possible.

But Tolkien did nothing. The months passed, and by June 1965, the Ace edition was in the bookshops of America. Now desperate to get the official paperback edition in print, Rayner Unwin began to chase Tolkien for the revisions only to learn that the author had not even begun them and had instead made some changes to *The Hobbit*.

The Ace edition was carefully produced and faithful to the original. It had a well-designed cover and most importantly, it sold for just seventy-five cents for each volume, a fraction of the original paperback price. Houghton Mifflin were preparing for legal action, but Ace seems to have taken an extremely cavalier approach to the whole matter and at this stage had no thoughts about paying Tolkien any form of royalty.

Finally, by August 1965, Tolkien seems to have grasped the magnitude of what was happening and realised that if things carried on this way he may never see a penny from the sales of the Ace edition which by all reports was doing great business. He managed to revise the manuscript and get the changes back to Unwin who then passed them on to Houghton Mifflin.

Just before Christmas 1965, a Ballantine edition of *The Lord of the Rings* finally reached the shops. But because they were paying Tolkien a royalty, this official edition was marked at ninety-five cents for each volume and readers were naturally still being drawn to the Ace edition.

From appearing rather complacent about the problem, Tolkien now seems to have become angry about the pirate edition. He had no idea what could be done about it and expected his publisher to take the issue to court; but then, something rather remarkable happened. Tolkien had been a conscientious respondent to any letters that had been sent to him from readers. He had often spent hours writing a single reply and always answered any questions about his work as long as they were asked politely and were intelligent requests for information. This effort now began to pay surprising dividends because in every reply to fan letters from America (now arriving at Sandfield Road in a steadily growing stream), he told of the upset he felt over the Ace edition and how fighting them was distracting him from his work.

With surprising speed, news of this reached a growing fan base and those fans told others, who told others. Within a few months, word was out that the Ace edition should be ignored and the official Ballantine edition was the only one paying the author a royalty. This news soon reached the national press and before long, people who would never otherwise have known of the existence of *The Lord of the Rings* discovered it and were intrigued enough to spend 95 cents to find out more. During 1965, Ace had sold one hundred thousand copies of their edition, but within six months the official Ballantine paperback had topped one million sales, making *The Lord of the Rings* a bestseller in the States more than a decade after it was first published there. By 1968, the book had sold three million copies around the world.

The Ace edition of *The Lord of the Rings* transformed Tolkien's masterpiece into an icon of twentieth-century publishing; not only were Ace forced to agree to an out-of-court settlement to pay all royalties on future sales, they had to make a lump sum payment for all the royalties they had withheld. But more than this, the controversy over their pirated edition pushed Tolkien and Middle-earth into the limelight.

The Lord of the Rings arrived on the campuses of the Western world with perfect timing. It had been written by a traditionalist, betweeded Oxford professor during the Second World War but it struck a chord with a new generation of young people who were then just getting into drugs and what was soon to be called the hippie culture. In 1966, 'Swinging London' was at its zenith, Carnaby Street was in full bloom, the greatest album of the decade, The Beatles' *Revolver* was released and LSD and cannabis were the drugs of choice. That summer, badges appeared carrying slogans such as: 'Tolkien is Hobbit-forming', 'Gandalf for President' and 'Frodo Lives'. Tolkien and Middle-earth societies sprang up in such unlikely places as Poland and Borneo, and American GIs stationed in Vietnam encountered tribesmen carrying shields bearing the Eye of Sauron.

It is not difficult to see why *The Lord of the Rings* was so readily adopted by the hippies. It is set in an alternative reality in which orthodox religion plays no part, where magic makes things happen. It is avowedly anti-twentieth century, anti-technology, anti-bread-head man. But the most important thing about the publicity that Tolkien and his book attracted around the world was that it did not appeal only to hippies, nor indeed young people. It was read by people of all ages, from all sorts of backgrounds. It possesses a universality and it may be interpreted on many different levels and in many different ways (some quite unintended by the author).

And so suddenly, Tolkien found himself at the centre of a

whirlwind of media interest, a cult figure, perceived as some sort of guru. Fan mail that had grown steadily over the years now became a flood and far too much for him to handle personally. He received letters of appreciation from world-famous figures including Hollywood stars and an astronaut, and he even received a letter from a distraught husband who claimed that his wife had fallen obsessively in love with Aragorn. Soon after this letter, Tolkien heard of a dramatisation of *The Lord of the Rings* performed by ten-year-old schoolchildren in Cheltenham and how the boy who had played Frodo could not come out of character for a month. On another occasion, a Member of Parliament visited Tolkien's Headington home and told him '*You* did not write *The Lord of the Rings*.' By which he meant that the author had been given the story by God.[6]

Fans would phone him from California at 3 a.m. because they had forgotten to take into account the time difference. In the summer of 1967, a group of American students travelled to England especially to see Tolkien and camped on the lawn outside his house in Headington, chanting, 'We want Tolkien. We want Tolkien.'

Tolkien was delighted by the popularity of his book, but he was bemused and more than a little disturbed by some of the more extreme reactions of his readers. It's easy to see why. Nothing in his experience had prepared him for this. To Tolkien, the work was the thing and he never understood why anyone should be interested in him, his private life or his past. Edith felt the same way. She tried to act as a buffer between her husband and the outside world so that he could simply get on with his work, but by the mid-1960s she was in her seventies and could do little to deter over-zealous fans and intrusive reporters. By 1968, it had become clear that the Tolkiens could not remain in Headington. They would have to move house and keep the new address secret, they would have to go ex-directory and henceforth be far more circumspect about their plans.

In some ways, it was an appropriate moment to leave Oxford. Since his retirement in 1959 Tolkien had tried to continue working on *The Silmarillion* but progress was slow. He felt bored with life and often grew depressed. He did not like growing old and he missed the diversity of his earlier life. The children had all left home now and had families of their own, most of his old friends had died or lived far away, and worst of all, he felt his energy and enthusiasm for writing seeping away.

Two things kept his spirits up. The first was his faith which had, if anything, grown stronger as he grew older, and the other was Edith. The couple were closer now than at any time in their lives together and Tolkien now had more time to spend with her just chatting about their children and grandchildren or taking her to their favourite restaurants in Oxford. They also had money to enjoy life a little. In 1966 they went on a Mediterranean cruise and in March of that year they celebrated their Golden Wedding Anniversary with a lavish party held in the gardens of Merton College at which the composer Donald Swann performed 'The Road Goes Ever On' – a selection of songs from Middle-earth.

The Tolkiens chose as their new home Poole, a small town adjoining Bournemouth on the south coast. It was a place familiar to them from recent holidays and Edith had friends there, but for Tolkien it must have be quite a culture shock.

They bought a small bungalow a short taxi-ride from the Miramar Hotel in Bournemouth, which had been Edith's favourite destination when they visited the town. She felt infinitely more at home here than in any other place in which they had lived, and the sort of people who stayed there (including many elderly residents) were Edith's kind of people, from similar backgrounds, similarly unpretentious and non-intellectual. Edith enjoyed playing cards with her friends, joining them for tea or simply strolling with her husband along the sea-front past the Winter Gardens and the large comfortable houses that looked out across the English Channel.

The bungalow had a large garden which Tolkien enjoyed tending and the house was of a manageable size. For Edith, the few short years she had in Poole were probably the happiest of her life, but for Tolkien they must have often been torturous. He had no one of his intellectual calibre to talk to, he was gregarious and personable but the constant round of small talk over cream teas must have quickly grown irritating for him. Tolkien though appears to have seen this period as a necessary penance. He felt a deep and genuine love for his wife and in old age he may have grown to realise how unhappy she had been about certain aspect of their lives together. She had hated the university scene, she had liked few of his friends, she had not shared his religious devotion and although she had always been immensely proud of what he had done, she had not been included in his intellectual world. The many afternoons listening to Muzak and conversing with the elderly bourgeoisie of Bournemouth constituted Tolkien's repayment for all the nights he had spent in the Bird and Baby with Lewis or arguing theology until 2 a.m. in Magdalen while Edith slept alone.

Such isolation also seems to have made him increasingly remorseful and he grew to believe, quite inaccurately, that he had neglected his children. In fact, he had doted on them and given them every bit of love he could. 'All his letters,' recalled a close family friend, Simonne d'Ardenne, 'extending over forty years, tell of his concern about his children's health, their comfort, their future; how best he could help them succeed in life.'[7]

And yet, in spite of the lack of intellectual inspiration and the absence in his life of good old, male friends, Tolkien seems to have gradually grown to accept and even to feel a modicum of contentment with the environment in which he now found himself. He was often depressed because he could not work as hard as he had once done and he missed the refined atmosphere of the cloisters and the Senior Common Room, but he cared little for the lack of aesthetics in his new life. When it came to domestic matters, he had always placed practicality over beauty. The house in Northmoor Road was one of the least pretty in North Oxford and the house in Headington was once described by W.H. Auden as 'Hideous, with hideous pictures on the walls'[8] – a remark that had deeply upset the Tolkiens.

It may seem strange that a man so enwrapped in the beauty of language and creator of something so aesthetically pleasing as *The Lord of the Rings*, indeed a man inspired by the great stylist William Morris, should have cared so little about the apparent lack of beauty in his own home. And yet, maybe this is not so odd because for much of his life Tolkien was self-absorbed. He was constantly busy and concerned with so many matters and almost all his energies were diverted to his college life and his internal life – his writing. He lived more in Middle-earth than he did in the real world.

In Poole, he tried hard to work and we can perhaps picture him during the late 1960s at a table in the spare room surrounded by his books and piles of papers. His pipe would be clenched between his teeth as he tried perhaps to tease out the essence of an idea he had written in rough maybe a decade earlier and found again in a long-forgotten file. He would then try to work out how it fitted into his grand mythology. Yet, during Tolkien's final ten years he seems to have made little genuine progress and his epic creation, *The Silmarillion*, was no more organised than it had been during the 1950s. It was growing, but ever more tangentially; ideas would gestate others and from those new trains of thought would take off and interconnect with other complex plots and story lines. Tolkien was every bit as devoted to this mythology as he had ever been and he still visualised it as a myth for England. At one point during the 1950s he had even contemplated dedicating it to Queen Elizabeth II.

By the late 1960s, Tolkien was a multi-millionaire, but a lifetime of counting the pennies meant that he and Edith found it difficult to relax about money. However, they arranged trust funds for their children and grandchildren and having money made the remainder of their own lives and that of their successors much more comfortable. They did not spend lavishly but neither did they deny themselves anything. Tolkien often grumbled about the price of meals in restaurants, but they dined out almost every day and enjoyed rich food and expensive wines. Tolkien also acquired a modicum of sartorial elegance in old age which would have surprised his old friend Lewis. As young men they had both frowned upon any form of stylish or fashionable dress, considering it an expression of latent homosexual tendencies. In Lewis's case this attitude had been exaggerated to the point of absurdity and it was said of him that he was able to make a new suit look old on its second wearing. In his late seventies, Tolkien discovered pleasure in smart silk cravats and hand-made brogues; a change in taste clear to see by comparing photographs of him in old age with those taken when he was a middle-aged don.

Tolkien still received plenty of mail, but now it was filtered through his publishers and he did not have the energy to respond to every single question he was asked as he once used to do. He never lost his interest in ecological issues and, like many old people, during his final years he grew increasingly angry about the way the world was changing, for the changes he saw were, in his view, rarely for the better. He would refuse to continue patronising a favoured restaurant if the route suddenly required them to take a new road that had devastated an attractive piece of countryside, and he was particularly angry when he learned that a cross-Channel hydrofoil was named *Shadowfax* without his permission. On another occasion, on the back of a cheque for the Inland Revenue, he wrote 'Not a penny for Concorde'.

But then, late in 1971, his life changed again. Edith, now eighty-two and increasingly frail, was rushed to hospital with an inflamed gall-bladder. She died a few days later on 29 November.

And so, Tolkien entered the final phase of his life. Deep in mourning he tarried a while in Poole — just long enough to arrange his affairs. He then stayed with family and old friends, gradually and slowly coming to terms with his loss. His son Christopher, who was then a Fellow of New College, helped to arrange for Tolkien to be provided with a flat at 21 Merton Street. The flat was owned by his old college, Merton, and there he had his library of books set upon shelves and a study as well as a rather luxurious living area. He was charged only a nominal rent, provided with free meals cooked by the college chefs, given the services of a full-time house-keeper, free use of a telephone and antique furnishings including a vast Wilton carpet in the living room.

Tolkien was glad to be back in Oxford and included within the academic community as an honorary Fellow, but it was a lonely and sometimes rather desolate existence. He tinkered with his great book, responded to the many kindly letters he received from around the world, was visited frequently by his children and their families and met up with surviving friends. During the spring of 1973, Christopher Wiseman, Tolkien's old pal from the T.C., B.S. and the only other member of the group to survive the trenches, visited him in Oxford and they reminisced, surveying the many years they had remained friends and all that had transpired in their lives and the world beyond. And with his son John, Tolkien visited his brother Hilary who, back in the 1930s, had become a fruit farmer and still lived on his farm in the Vale of Evesham.

During the final years of his life Tolkien was honoured by both the academic community and the world of literature. In the spring of 1972, he attended a ceremony at Buckingham Palace where he received a C.B.E., and that evening, Rayner Unwin held a dinner in Tolkien's honour at the Garrick Club in Mayfair. From the academic community, Tolkien received many honorary doctorates, but the one he valued most came from his own university who, in June 1972, made him an Honorary Doctor of Letters in a ceremony held at the Sheldonian in the heart of Oxford. His old friend and fellow Inkling, Colin Hardie, who was Public Orator for Oxford University, made a speech in his honour.

Tolkien's health had been in decline for several years. In Poole he had begun to suffer from arthritis and gall-bladder infections and from late-1972 he had suffered severe indigestion. He consulted a doctor and X-rays were taken but nothing was revealed. On 28 August 1973, he travelled to Bournemouth to visit friends, Denis and Jocelyn Tolhurst. It was Mrs Tolhurst's birthday and Tolkien appeared to be quite well and even drank a little champagne. But that night he awoke in great pain and was taken to hospital early the next morning. He had an acute bleeding gastric ulcer that had gone unnoticed on the X-rays taken a few weeks earlier. Three days after being admitted to hospital, on Sunday morning, 2 September 1973, Professor J.R.R. Tolkien died aged eighty-one.

CHAPTER 14

The Legend Lives On

During the late 1960s, the journalist Nigel Walmsley wrote of *The Lord of the Rings*:

> The popularity of *The Lord of the Rings* has to be understood in the context of that group which most surely guaranteed its reputation, the young, disaffected section of the Western industrial middle-class of the mid-1960s. The book was a seminal influence on the popular sub-culture of that period, an artefact as commercially enticing as a Bob Dylan record.

He then went on to declare that by 1968, Tolkien's star was in the descendent, that there were 'signs, the surface indicators, of a sharp change in cultural attitude which was effectively to end Tolkien's brief period of coruscating contemporary relevance'.[1]

In writing this Walmsley was being almost as accurate as those who said The Beatles would never make it or that the Third Reich would last a thousand years, because what actually happened was the very opposite of his claims — *The Lord of the Rings* became ever more popular, ever more loved.

This journalist's mistake was a common one. He believed that *The Lord of the Rings* was appealing only to a specific type of person. If it had only been of interest to the disaffected youth of the West then it may, with some justification, have been considered a fashion accessory, a passing fad, but *The Lord of the Rings* appeals to a broad cross-section of people from all cultural backgrounds.

However, as misguided as Walmsley certainly was, he was not alone (and certainly not original) in his misjudged criticisms. Nearly a decade earlier, in 1961, another journalist, Philip Toynbee, had written with unalloyed delight that Tolkien's 'childish books had passed into a merciful oblivion'.[2] During the following years, the huge impact made by Tolkien and his work generated an avalanche of criticism. After 'Tolkien, the fashionable', we had 'Tolkien the racist', 'Tolkien, the sexist', 'Tolkien, the fascist'. The critic, Walter Scheps, called Tolkien's world 'paternalistic', others defined it as 'reactionary' and even, oddly, 'anti-intellectual'.[3] We had those who mocked *The Lord of the Rings*, calling it 'Winnie-the-Pooh posing as an epic' and 'Faërieland's answer to *Conan the Barbarian*' and there are those who have tried to find fault in it or have attempted to make it simply an irrelevance.[4]

This sort of criticism of Tolkien came in a steady stream beginning soon after the first publication of *The Fellowship of the Ring* in 1954, but it reached a new frenzied level in 1997 after Waterstone's decided to canvas their readers to discover which book of the twentieth century was their favourite.

For many, the result came as a shock. Across Britain, 25,000 people voted and more than one-fifth of them placed *The Lord of the Rings* as their first choice, with George Orwell's *Nineteen Eighty-four* in second place. In fact, *The Lord of the Rings* came top in 104 of the 105 branches of the bookshop. The singular exception was in Wales where Joyce's *Ulysses* beat Tolkien into second place. The reaction to this from the literary establishment was immediate and vitriolic.

Susan Jeffreys writing in the *Sunday Times* was mortally offended by the news. 'Oh hell! Has it?' she had responded when hearing of the result. 'Oh dear, oh dear. Dear, oh dear, oh dear.' One could almost hear china tea cups fall and smash in kitchens across Hampstead.

'I'd woken Bob Inglis [a fellow journalist] from deep sleep with the news that *The Lord of the Rings* had been voted, by the readers of Waterstone's and Channel 4 viewers, the best book of the century,' she went on breathlessly. 'Inglis's reaction was echoed up and down the country wherever one or two literati gathered together.'[5]

Ignoring the pretension and self-aggrandisement behind these comments, as Professor Tom Shippey points out: 'She meant surely, "two or three *literati*", unless the literati talk only to themselves (a thought that does occur); and the term *literati* is itself interesting. It clearly does not mean "the lettered, the literate", because obviously that group includes the devotees of *The Lord of the Rings*, the group being complained about (they couldn't be devotees if they couldn't read). In Jeffreys' usage, *literati* must mean "those who know about literature". And those who know, of course, know what they are supposed to know. The opinion is entirely self-enclosed.'[6]

Of course, Jeffreys was not alone in her dismay. During the

following days, disbelief turned to outrage amongst many journalists and writers. Some attempted ridicule (again); the novelist
Howard Jacobson sniffed, 'Tolkien – that's for children, isn't it?
Or the adult-slow. It just shows the folly of these polls, the folly
of teaching people to read. Close all the libraries. Use the money
for something else.'[7]

Such comments are, of course, laughable, but we must put
them into context. The views of Jeffreys, Jacobson and others
appeared in a piece in which the opinions of a large and diverse
group of personalities from the Arts were canvassed. The con-
tributors knew their sound-bite would be read by a large number
of people and that theirs would be alongside the views expressed
by their contemporaries. It was perhaps inevitable that such
people would try to show off.

Elsewhere, feminists and others looking for any stick with
which to beat Tolkien persisted in calling *The Lord of the Rings* a
book for 'adolescent boys'. Again, this is quite inaccurate because,
more than many books written in recent decades, *The Lord of the
Rings* is read by men and women, boys and girls without any
apparent gender skew in the statistics. Support for this has come
from the writer Andrew Nikolds, who recalled his experiences of
first being introduced to Tolkien's books during the 1970s.
'You'd walk up the escalator [on the Northern Line in London]
that had all these girls standing on the right-hand side,' he said,
'all with a copy of *The Lord of the Rings* bent open at a page.'[8]

After the shock came the suspicion. On a radio programme,
the critic Mark Lawson implied that there had been some vote-
rigging going on, a suggestion leapt upon by desperate
anti-Tolkien observers. It was the fault of the internet and
'Tolkien's anorak-clad troops'.[9]

And so, in an attempt to prove their point, the 'literati' of the

Daily Telegraph decided to organise their own poll in which their readers were asked to vote for their favourite book and their favourite author. *The Lord of the Rings* was voted favourite book and Tolkien, their favourite author. This only added salt to the wounds and cries of foul play were still heard, but now more muted. Two months later, the Folio Society carried out its own poll amongst its 50,000 members; no outsiders were allowed to vote. Ten thousand members responded. Tolkien's *The Lord of the Rings* garnered 3,270 votes, Jane Austen's *Pride and Prejudice* was second with 3,212 votes and *David Copperfield* appeared third, with 3,070 votes.

By this point, most critics had been forced into an embarrassed silence, but the hardy Germaine Greer still seethed. 'Ever since I arrived at Cambridge as a student in 1964 and encountered a tribe of full-grown women wearing puffed sleeves, clutching teddies and babbling excitedly about the doings of hobbits, it has been my nightmare that Tolkien would turn out to be the most influential writer of the twentieth century. The bad dream has materialised. At the head of the list, in pride of place as the book of the century, stands *The Lord of the Rings*. Novels don't come more fictional than that. Most novels are set in a recognisable place at a recognisable time; Tolkien invents the era, the place and a race of fictitious beings to inhabit it.'[10]

So, why does Tolkien attract so much criticism from people who consider themselves knowledgeable about literature? What is the hidden agenda? What is the subtext?

Perhaps the greatest puzzle is this: what is wrong with a writer creating a fantasy world complete with 'the era, the place and a race of fictitious beings to inhabit it'? Who made up the rules? Why shouldn't fiction deal with such things? Indeed, surely one of the roles of the novelist is to take the reader into a different reality, or else the work is no longer fiction. Even the most mundane fiction, if it is fiction at all, describes an alternative reality. Who has set down a rule which says that a novelist is allowed a certain level of fantasy, but only so much?

Tolkien's writing was never fashionable within the literary fraternity. His contemporaries, writers like Edmund Wilson (who reads him now?), found favour by writing books that dealt supposedly with deep-rooted human emotion; these authors wanted to make it clear they were addressing 'real issues', investigating the human condition and helping readers better to understand life. As a consequence, what a Germaine Greer or a Mark Lawson would consider great literature – not for the 'adult slow' – are books that deal with what they consider important – moral values, what it is to be a human being, and perhaps, on occasion, such relative ephemera as political or religious debate. And indeed, many, many wonderful books that deal with these ideas have been written, but according to the rules of the modern literary critic, there are only a certain, very limited number of prescribed ways in which these subjects may be dealt with. And, what many of these critics fail to recognise is that Tolkien did deal with them throughout *The Lord of the Rings* and *The Silmarillion*. It is simply that he did not deal with them in the way some critics liked.

At the beginning of the twenty-first century, literature finds itself at something of a watershed. For several decades now, style has become increasingly dominant over content. Go to any bookshop and you will find the shelves groaning under the weight of plot-less novels, in which the way a thing is said is made out to be far more important than the thing itself. Almost without exception, these writers could not begin to marshal the talents required to write a book with the power of *The Lord of the Rings*, and indeed, the current dominance of plot-less novels peopled by caricatures or nonentities comes from the fact that few darlings of the literary establishment possess what should be the first prerequisite of a novelist – the ability to tell a good story well. Perhaps, then, the hidden agenda is insecurity on the part of the so-called *literati*.

Today, well-written fantasy literature is gradually infiltrating the literary world. The jaded figures who were once doyens of the literary establishment are slipping into obscurity, left behind by the natural process of evolution, forgotten. The massive commercial success and well-deserved critical acclaim for J.K. Rowling, Philip Pullman, Iain Banks and other modern story-tellers has made a long overdue impact upon the attitudes of many critics. Some of these writers have crossed genres by writing children's fiction with adult aspects, an approach not so different, in their idiosyncratic way, to that of Tolkien half a century ago. J.K. Rowling was recently considered as a contender for many mainstream adult literary awards and Philip Pullman's work was recently awarded the Whitbread book of the year award.

The most bitter critics of *The Lord of the Rings* are those who have, through insecurity, tried to make it go away. *The Oxford Companion to English Literature* compiled by Margaret Drabble affords Tolkien only twelve lines to Joyce's seventy-six; but these efforts have proved entirely wasteful. Apart from being the best-loved author of the twentieth century, Tolkien has become a hugely influential figure within the literary world.

Today, the fantasy genre is perhaps the biggest-selling and most widely read of all literary forms and most fantasy authors would admit to owing a great debt to Tolkien for bringing it into such stark relief. Beyond this, the world of Middle-earth has acted as an inspiration for many modern computer games and the entire industry that has grown up around *Dungeons and*

Dragons has its roots in Tolkien's mythical world. For many young people, indulging in role-playing and computer games is a way of extending their involvement in Middle-earth long after the book has been read and reread.

And Tolkien's influence has spread beyond conventional fantasy. It is not difficult to see the spirit of Tolkien in the Harry Potter books, even if his settings and plots are far removed from adventures at Hogwarts. In the cinema and on TV, Tolkien's influence may be seen in *Star Wars*, *Star Trek* and *Babylon 5*. Indeed, *Star Wars* is in many ways 'The Lord of the Rings in space', with Gandalf replaced by Obi-Wan Kenobi, Frodo played by Luke Skywalker, the chief of the Nazgûl substituted by Darth Vader and Sauron represented by the Evil Emperor.

Beyond this, Tolkien's world has become the subject of a growing number of learned books dealing with every aspect of Tolkien's creation and dissecting meaning and nuance in his writing. Undergraduate dissertations and PhD theses have been written about Middle-earth and there are university lecture courses on *The Lord of the Rings*. Putting the words 'Tolkien' or 'The Lord of the Rings' into a search engine brings up some half million sites. After starting as a slow-burning success, an estimated 100 million copies of *The Lord of the Rings* and close to 60 million copies of *The Hobbit* have been sold around the world, a figure that between the two titles increases by around 3 million a year. Each of the books has been translated into thirty languages, including Serbo-Croat, Icelandic, Hebrew and Russian.[11] The word 'hobbit' may be found in *The Oxford English Dictionary*, and a first edition of *The Hobbit* in pristine condition was recently sold at Sotherby's for a staggering £43,000.

Tolkien's work also influences people in tangential ways. Professor Tom Shippey, who holds Tolkien's old chair at Oxford

University, has said that Tolkien had 'turned me into an observer. Tolkien turns people into birdwatchers, tree-spotters, hedgerow-grubbers.'[12] And, as I have mentioned, I know at least one person who studied Icelandic to degree level after being inspired by Tolkien and his work.

Amidst this growing enthusiasm, Christopher Tolkien has worked hard to cast further light on the details of Middle-earth. After his father's death he took on the enormous task of trying to catalogue and eventually to edit the vast collection of notes, fragments, half-finished stories and completed tales that had formed untidy piles and over-flowed from filing cabinets in the author's study.

Tolkien had produced three distinct versions of *The Silmarillion*: the 'Sketch', 'The Quenta' (or 'brief History of the Noldoli' written about 1930) and the most detailed of the three, the 'Quenta Silmarillion', which Tolkien had given to George Unwin late in 1937, after the publication of *The Hobbit*. The 'Quenta Silmarillion' was the author's primary working manuscript and was heavily annotated and revised.

Christopher Tolkien's first task was to produce a self-consistent and self-contained version of *The Silmarillion* from this vast collection of papers. It was something Tolkien could never bring himself to do and it needed the finesse of someone close to the originator of the mythology, who understood Middle-earth almost as well as its creator, but who was sufficiently detached to be capable of bringing the work to a publishable form.

The Silmarillion, long-awaited by Tolkien fans around the world, appeared in 1977. It is a beautiful, complex, sometimes difficult book. For Tolkien's admirers and those who were mystified and confused by the details of the tale that had unfolded in *The Lord of the Rings*, *The Silmarillion* provided many answers and placed much in context. After finishing *The Silmarillion*, Christopher Tolkien went on to edit *Unfinished Tales of Númenor and Middle-earth* which revealed more, and between 1983 and 1996, twelve volumes of edited Tolkien material, taken from the vast archive of notes, have appeared which extend the mythology still further; this collection is called *The History of Middle-earth*.

On 19 December 2001, Tolkien's legions of fans across the globe were finally rewarded with the long-awaited release of the first 'Lord of the Rings' films, *The Fellowship of the Ring*. For more than a year before the release of the film, websites had been reporting every minute detail of the production process, and rumours and gossip had been circulating amongst the fans. Some websites even had clocks counting down the days and the hours until the first screening.

Tolkien has long been of interest to Hollywood film-makers. The first approach came from a group of producers who in 1957 had written a synopsis for a possible film script. The synopsis proposed by Forrest J. Ackerman, Morton Grady Zimmerman and Al Brodax was passed on to Tolkien who predictably hated almost everything about it. He wrote a two-thousand-word deconstruction of the proposal (which was almost as long as the proposal itself) in which he picked over the most minute details of what had been written. However, on this occasion, he had every good reason to; it was an appalling travesty of a treatment in which the story was turned into something childish and patronising. After a brief exchange of letters it became clear to the American film-makers that they would probably not get far with their ideas and so it was dropped.

Much later, the film rights for *The Lord of the Rings* were obtained by United Artists and it is claimed that the director John Boorman was paid a seven-figure sum for writing a script in which the three volumes were condensed into a single feature-length film. United Artists did not like the script and Boorman went on to make a string of other movies, including *Excalibur* and *Deliverance*. Perhaps one of the strangest stories linking Tolkien with Hollywood emerged a few years ago when it was revealed that at some point during the mid-1960s, The Beatles contemplated making a cartoon film of *The Lord of the Rings* with the voices of the Fab Four used for the lead characters.

In 1978, the director Ralph Bakshi produced a version of *The Lord of the Rings* using a technique called 'rotoscoping' which involved a blending of human action and animation years before computer graphics made such effects almost commonplace. The film was slated by the critics not least for the fact that it stopped abruptly part-way through the telling of the story. Bakshi's film was intended as the first part of the entire saga, but after it was received with such little enthusiasm by both critics and Tolkien fans alike, plans for future filming were scrapped.

The modern version of *The Lord of the Rings* is in an entirely different league and long before its release it was expected to become the biggest box-office hit in cinema history, outstripping *Star Wars*, *E.T.* and other blockbusters. Directed and co-scripted by New Zealander Peter Jackson, it is as much a labour of love as a commercial enterprise.

Jackson, a devoted Tolkien fan, began to take seriously the idea of filming *The Lord of the Rings* in 1994. He approached Miramax, who by this time owned the rights. The executives there had no clear understanding of Tolkien's work and were convinced that the only way to make the film was to condense the story into one movie. Jackson refused to accept this and saw the potential to create a series of films in the vein of *Star Wars* or the Indiana Jones movies. So, Miramax gave Jackson two weeks to find backers to produce the films in the way he visualised them. He found New Line Cinema (part of AOL/Warner) and conjured the funds to produce three films on an epic scale.

All the filming was done in New Zealand, which offers the perfect variety of intense landscape needed to reproduce Middle-earth before the camera. Jackson has lived and breathed *The Lord of the Rings* since the proposal stage in 1994 and at the time of writing, crews are still working on parts II and III of the trilogy of films, due for screening in December 2002 and 2003.

The filming of *The Fellowship of the Ring* alone took 274 days using a crew of over 2,000 people and some 300 sets. The budget has been estimated conservatively at $200 million. The cast includes veteran actors, Ian McKellen (Gandalf), Ian Holm (Bilbo) and Christopher Lee (Saruman) along with younger stars Cate Blanchett as Galadriel, Liv Tyler as Arwen and Hugo Weaver (Elrond). The hobbits are played by relative newcomers Elijah Wood (Frodo), Sean Astin (Sam), Billy Boyd (Pippin) and Dominic Monaghan (Merry).

Some fans were initially anxious that the film-makers would take liberties with the original book, and there were indeed some discontented individuals who were sceptical. Richard Crawshaw of the Tolkien Society claimed that, 'Tolkien himself never thought a film could be made of the book. We feel that no movie could ever capture the full depth and flavour of the book.' But Peter Jackson, who worked sixteen hours a day on the film for over five years, obviously felt differently to stalwarts of the Tolkien Society. 'It has taken all the years since Tolkien wrote his book for film-making technology to catch up with his imagination,' he declared in May 2001.[13] The producer of the film, Barrie Osborne, said, 'We took a lot of care to capture Tolkien. We took a lot of care to be faithful to what the fans expect.'[14]

Those who saw advance clips and trailers of the movie bore out what the film-makers claimed. According to a writer who was on the set and followed the making of the film from an early stage, 'the spirit of Tolkien is there. The film is dark, threatening.'[15] And Jackson himself wanted to place his personal stamp upon it. 'I want to make the kind of movie Tolkien himself would have enjoyed,' Jackson said before the release of the film. 'But to do it with integrity, for me, means making a Peter Jackson movie – my own very personal version of a passionate, classic British work.'[16]

Months before the release of the film the hype and the excitement began to grow rapidly. During 2000, the earliest teaser trailer for the film was downloaded 1.7 million times and when an official movie website was created in the summer of 2001, it received 62 million hits during its first week. A 90-second trailer was also screened at some cinemas showing the film *Pearl Harbor* and, according to Tolkien's publishers, each time the clip was shown sales of *The Lord of the Rings* leapt. Leading up to the release of the film, newspaper reports in the US and the UK told of huge increases in sales of Tolkien's titles. Six months before release, 250,000 copies of a special film-tie-in edition of *The Lord of the Rings* had been sold in the US alone and the thirteen-hour ten-CD audio version of the book retailing at $70 rocketed up the audio book chart. A representative of Tolkien's US paperback publisher Ballantine reported, 'Sales are going through the roof.'[17] There are also indications that the legions of Harry Potter fans, mostly children aged 7–14, are now discovering Tolkien for the first time.

Naturally, these reactions were immensely encouraging and when the film was screened around the world at the end of December 2001, all the excitement and the hype, as well as the claims of the movie-makers, proved justified. *The Lord of the Rings: The Fellowship of the Ring* broke all box-office records, delighted the critics and the paying public alike and was quickly perceived as an honourable and accurate portrayal of Tolkien's masterpiece, a film that appealed to both fans and newcomers.

The following March the film was nominated for thirteen Oscars (one short of the record set by *All About Eve* in 1950 and *Titanic* in 1997) and on the night it took four statues (all in technical categories). Reviews of the film were almost universally filled with praise. Eleanor Ringel Gillespie, film critic for the *Atlanta Journal and Constitution*, declared: 'The miracle that Jackson has managed is that you can know every nook and cranny of Middle-earth by heart or never have gotten any closer than your Burger-King Frodo goblet to be entranced by this movie.'[18]

The often hard-to-please Cosmo Landesman of the *Sunday Times* declared: '*The Lord of the Rings* ends not with a bang but a quiet cliffhanger. This film is so terrific that after almost three hours in the cinema you leave for home longing for more.'[19] And John Anderson in *Newsday* said of the film: 'Certainly the most rousing and ambitious adventure film of many years and bodes well for the future of the Tolkien fan.'[20]

It also bodes well for the finances of the Tolkien estate. Over Christmas 2001 and into the New Year, *The Lord of the Rings* in movie-adaptation format and the original trilogy, along with *The Hobbit*, took up the top positions in bestseller lists around the world. The rights to the film were sold long ago and little from the film and the merchandising will go to Tolkien's descendants, but during the next few years annual sales of *The Lord of the Rings* and Tolkien's other works are expected to increase enormously and the profit-sharing deal set up by Rayner Unwin in 1952 still operates so that the Tolkien estate earns far more from each book sold than they would under the more usual royalty system.

And yet, ironically, if they watch it at all, the Tolkien family are certain to dislike the film more than anyone. Tolkien himself was always distrustful of Hollywood and did not approve of anyone attempting to meddle with his work. Tolkien's literary executor, Christopher Tolkien, has no links at all with the film or its producers, and according to sources close to the Tolkien family, the author's children concur with their father's view and the view of many readers who believe that a film of the book should not be made. They feel that the books tell the whole story and do not need to be reinterpreted by anyone else.

In many ways, *The Lord of the Rings* is almost entirely unique. It has out-sold every other fictional work, it has provoked more controversy than almost any other book of the twentieth century, and almost fifty years after its first appearance, a film version is bringing it to the attention of many millions more, an entire new generation of potential readers who have yet to discover Middle-earth and its peoples. But what is it about this most famous of fantasy stories that draws new generations to it? What is it that appeals to the often tarnished tastes of twenty-first century readers just as it did to those picking it up in any of the other five decades since its first publication?

In stark contrast to what the critics say, with *The Lord of the Rings*, Tolkien succeeded in creating not just a fantasy world with prerequisite battle scenes, strange beings and high adventure, he also mined human emotions and explored character to a degree comparable to any modern literary author. Unfortunately, the critics of Tolkien's work often miss these deeper levels within the story of Middle-earth.

Tolkien explored the theme of friendship and loyalty. Using the device of the Ring itself, he considered the concept of addiction. Any being, human, hobbit, elf or even istari is influenced by the power exerted by the Ring and each individual reacts to it in their own way and this not only drives the story on but offers character insights.

Tolkien's characters are often described as being either impossibly good or unrealistically, irredeemably evil, but there are two faults with this view. The first is that even the good characters have weaknesses – the hobbits break rules, elves and dwarves harbour deep resentments toward one another. Furthermore, the good individuals are capable of imagining being evil – for example, in Lothlorien, Galadriel considers what she could do with the Ring. The evil characters cannot imagine anyone not being seduced by the power of the Ring and Sauron lives in fear of some great Lord, Gandalf or Aragorn perhaps, taking it and challenging Mordor openly. Sauron, the ultimate evil, cannot conceive that any living thing would throw away the chance of power and destroy the Ring, that great object of addiction. The second fault with the argument that Tolkien's characters are mere extremes is highlighted by the presence of two key figures – Boromir, a corruptible man who is essentially good and redeems himself with his final actions, and Gollum, surely one of the most intriguing and pitiful personalities in all literature, eaten away by his own addiction to the Ring.

Tolkien then was not only successfully able to create a mythology and an alternative reality that inexplicably so upset Germaine Greer and other critics, he was able to do much more. He created believable, multifaceted characters, he explored an array of emotional and spiritual dilemmas and was master of an art missing in so much twenty-first century fiction – the ability to control a complex plot and to tell a gripping story.

Beyond this, Tolkien's work strikes a chord with many people because it offers security. Middle-earth is a world that is recognisable but alien and it offers temporal grandeur, tradition, heritage, vast, elegant sweeps of time over which important things are preserved. Middle-earth is a world in which the past is as important as the present and valued more than any thoughts for the future.

Another charge against Tolkien is the idea that his work is pure escapism. *The Lord of the Rings* is immensely enjoyable, and so as a highly successful form of entertainment it aids escapism if that is required, but it also operates at a much deeper level than that. Part of Tolkien's great success as an author comes from the fact that he instinctively understood the concept of Jungian archetypes.

Early in the twentieth century Jung posited the idea of the 'collective unconscious' and suggested that we have in our sub-conscious minds a set of primitive images common to all human beings, whatever their age or cultural background. Jung referred to these archetypes as primordial images, 'the most ancient and the most universal thought-form of humanity. They are as much feelings as thoughts.' He considered them to be more than mere inherited ideas and instead defined them as 'potential forms' waiting to be animated and brought to consciousness.[21]

All great artists, whatever their field, have the ability to manipulate emotions by understanding archetypes. Steven Spielberg does this, as does George Lucas. Painters such as Picasso instinctively understood the power of the archetype, The Beatles could do the same. Many of those who know the best way to tune into archetypes do not realise what they are doing, and if they did they would probably lose their power to inspire. Tolkien had little time for psychology and was scornful of those who believed in the power of psychotherapy, but that did not matter because he did not need to intellectualise his innate power in order to animate the archetypes within us all.

Because of this ability, Tolkien was able to infuse his work with extraordinary power. And, it is because of this power that readers have become so totally absorbed by the author's creation. For the Tolkien fan, there is never enough. The true devotee always wants more – more detail, more information. Tolkien could have written ten million words about Middle-earth, he could have covered ten million pages and it still would not have been enough to satisfy entirely. Yet, it is a testament to the man's genius that with a mere thousand pages, his writing continues to captivate the minds of millions and to offer his readers a entirely believable and absorbing alternative reality unmatched in the history of literature.

Chapter Notes

Chapter I: Childhood

1 The School Certificate was an early form of school examination comparable to the modern GCSE taken by sixteen-year-olds in Britain.

2 It's easy to imagine that this experience planted the seed for the idea of Shelob (the deadly giant spider that lived on the borders of Mordor), but it's more likely that as this tale seeped into Tolkien family legend, it was always there as a backdrop in the author's mind so that when Tolkien came to write the appropriate scene in *The Lord of the Rings* he visualised a spider rather than, say, a rat or a snake.

3 One exception to this was the delight Tolkien expressed for the musical arrangements Donald Swann created for a selection of his poems, *The Road Goes Ever On*, in 1967.

4 'Middle English' refers to language and literature from the period 1100–1500. Any literature composed or language spoken between 700 and 1100 is termed 'Old English' and anything written after 1500 is considered 'Modern English'.

Chapter 2: Two Women

1   From a letter to Michael Tolkien, 18 March 1941. *The Letters of J.R.R. Tolkien*, edited by Humphrey Carpenter with the assistance of Christopher Tolkien, London, George Allen and Unwin, 1981, p. 340.

2   From a letter to Michael Tolkien, 1 November 1963. Ibid, p. 401.

3   From a letter to Amy Ronald, 16 November 1969. Indeed, Tolkien once referred to Father Francis Morgan as 'my second father' (letter to Michael Tolkien, 24 January 1972, *Letters*, p. 416). Father Francis was born in January 1857, just a few weeks before Tolkien's real father.

4   Tolkien suffered from a speech impediment, a slurring of his words that seemed to become worse as he grew older, and he often blamed this on his rugby injury.

Chapter 3: Oxford

1   Charles Moseley, *J.R.R. Tolkien*, Northcote House Publishers, Plymouth, 1997, p. 16.

Chapter 4: Marriage and War

1   There were some air-raids on British cities during the First World War. On the night of 19–20 January 1915, bombing attacks on London by Zeppelin dirigible airships under the control of the German navy caused more anger than panic. There were eighteen more such raids in 1915. The largest killed fifty-nine people in London on 13 October.

2   Wilfred Owen, *Dulce Et Decorum Est*. Oxford English Faculty, Oxford University, Facsimile S, f316r.

3   In view of this, it is perhaps telling that in his autobiography, C.S. Lewis devoted three entire chapters to his unpleasant experiences at public school but only part of one to his own time in the trenches. 'It is too cut off from the rest of my experience,' he wrote, '. . . and often seems to have happened to someone else.' (C.S. Lewis, *Surprised by Joy: The Shape of My Early Life*, Geoffrey Bles, London, 1955, Chapter 12.)

4   According to some accounts, the bells were ringing on 11
    November 1918, in Shrewsbury to celebrate the Armistice when
    the telegram arrived at the Owen home informing Wilfred's par-
    ents of their son's death.

Chapter 5: Fantastic Worlds

1   The *Prose Edda* is a creation myth and the central document of the
    ancient Icelandic religion, equivalent to the Christian *Old Testament*.
    Beowulf dates from around 700 AD and the author is unknown. In
    the poem, the hero, Beowulf, rescues the Danes from a monster,
    Grendel. Half a century later he is slain while saving his own tribe,
    the Geats, from a fire dragon. Believed to have derived from Norse
    folklore, it was written shortly after the introduction of Christianity
    to the Nordic peoples and the poem combines many pagan and
    Christian elements. Perhaps even closer to Tolkien's creation is the
    Kalevala, based upon an oral tradition thought to have roots at least
    2,000 years old. The modern version comes to us thanks to the
    endeavours of a Finnish doctor named Elias Lönnrot who dedi-
    cated many years of his life to composing the *Kalevala* from oral
    poems. He published the first written edition in 1835.
2   E.M. Forster, *Howards End*, Penguin, London, 1989, p. 262.
3   This aspect of Middle-earth is considered in more detail in
    Chapter 12.
4   William Morris, *The Wood Beyond the World*, Dover Press, New York,
    1972.
5   Earendel (Tolkien later changed the spelling to Eärendil), it tran-
    spires, is part-man, part-elven. It is later explained in *The Silmarillion*
    that he is the son of Tuor of the Edain (the ancestors of the
    Númenoreans) and of Idril, who was daughter of Turgon, King of
    the High-Elven of Gondolin.

Chapter 6: Climbing the Ladder

1   For a highly entertaining account of how the dictionary started
    and the human story behind it read *The Surgeon of Crowthorne*, by
    Simon Winchester, Penguin, London, 1998.

Chapter 7: A Don's Life

1   Desmond Albrow, *Catholic Herald*, 31 January 1997.

2   J.R.R. Tolkien, *Letters From Father Christmas*, George Allen and Unwin, 1976, London, p. 154.

3   'The Adventures of Tom Bombadil' first appeared in *The Oxford Magazine*, Vol. LII No. 13, February 1937, pp. 464–5, Oxford Oxonian Press.

4   *Beowulf*, line 2561.

Chapter 8: A Man's World

1   C.S. Lewis, Diary entry for 11 May 1926, The Lewis Papers, the Wade Collection, Wheaton College, Wheaton, Illinois, USA.

2   The sign outside the pub depicts the baby Ganymede being carried away by Jove's eagle and it is believed that this acted as the inspiration for Tolkien's illustration of Bilbo in the eagle's erie used in *The Hobbit*.

3   Tolkien considered Dorothy Sayers a competent enough writer but thought some of her work 'vulgar'.

4   C.S. Lewis, 'Williams and Arthuriad' (part of Williams and Lewis, *Arthurian Torso*), Oxford University Press, Oxford, 1948, p. 1.

5   Unpublished letter to Arthur Greeves, 11 January 1944, quoted in Clyde Kilby, *Tolkien and the Silmarillion*, Harold Shaw Publishers, USA, 1976, p. 73.

6   Ibid, p. 67.

7   Nigel Reynolds, *Daily Telegraph*, 20 January 1997.

8   *Letters of C.S. Lewis*, edited by W.H. Lewis, Geoffrey Bles, London, 1966, p. 287.

9   Letter to Sheldon Vanauken, 17 April 1951, from the 'Memoirs of the Lewis Family', the Wade Collection.

10 Humphrey Carpenter, *The Inklings: C.S. Lewis, J.R.R. Tolkien, Charles Williams and their Friends*, George Allen and Unwin, 1978, p. 52

11 Roger Lancelyn Green and Walter Hooper, *C.S. Lewis: A Biography*, Collins, London, 1974, p. 241.

12 This book is now in the Wade Collection, Wheaton College, Wheaton, Illinois, USA. It is interesting to note however that

Lewis's character, Wormwood, the apprentice devil of *The Screwtape Letters*, predates Tolkien's Wormtongue, Saruman's spy in *The Lord of the Rings*.

13 From an unpublished memoir of Lewis by Peter Bayley, quoted in Carpenter, *The Inklings*, p. 120.

14 *Letters of C.S. Lewis*, edited by W.H. Lewis, Geoffrey Bles, London, 1966, pp. 196–7.

15 Charles Williams, *Divorce*, Oxford University Press, 1920.

16 C.S. Lewis with A.O. Barfield, W.H. Lewis, Gervase Mathew, Dorothy Sayers and J.R.R. Tolkien, *Essays Presented to Charles Williams*, Oxford University Press, Oxford, 1947, p. x.

17 Henry S. Resnick, *Niekas*, Volume 18, Number 43.

18 From a letter to Michael Tolkien, 1963, *Letters*, p. 341.

Chapter 9: To *The Hobbit*

1 C.S. Lewis to Arthur Greeves, 4 February 1933, the Wade Collection.

2 *J.R.R Tolkien, Scholar and Storyteller: Essays in Memoriam* (edited by Mary Salu and Robert T. Farrell), Cornell University Press, Ithaca and London, 1979, p. 34.

3 Quoted in Humphrey Carpenter, *J.R.R. Tolkien: A Biography*, HarperCollins, London, 1977, p. 184.

4 Tolkien to Charles Furth, George Allen and Unwin, 17 January 1937, *Letters*, p. 15.

5 Even so, there remain forty-five cases in which the author directly addresses the reader.

6 Tolkien to Stanley Unwin, 15 October 1937, *Letters*, p. 24.

7 Ibid.

8 *The Times*, 8 October 1937.

9 *Times Literary Supplement*, 2 October 1937.

10 C.S. Lewis, *Of This and Other Worlds*, p. 111, Geoffrey Bles, London, 1967.

11 C.S. Lewis, 'On Stories', in *Essays Presented to Charles Williams*, 1947, p. 104.

12 Tolkien to Charles Furth, 13 May 1937, *Letters*, p. 17.

Chapter 10: The War and the Ring

1   The reader at George Allen and Unwin considered the book not quite good enough for publication but thought that Lewis would one day come up with a novel that was better and worthy of publication. He was wrong over the first point but spot on with the second. *Out of the Silent Planet* is now considered a science fiction classic and has sold in vast numbers around the world since it was first published by the Bodley Head in 1938.

2   Tolkien to Unwin, 16 December 1937, *Letters*, p. 26.

3   During the seventeen years between Tolkien beginning *The Lord of the Rings* and the publication of the first volume, *The Fellowship of the Ring* in 1954, Lewis published no fewer than twenty titles including eight full-length novels.

4   Joseph Pearce, *Tolkien. Man and Myth: A Literary Life*, HarperCollins, London, 1998, p. 70.

5   Clyde Kilby, *Tolkien and The Silmarillion*, Harold Shaw Publishers, USA, 1976, p. 17.

6   J.R.R. Tolkien to Michael Tolkien, 9 June 1941, *Letters*, p. 55.

7   Of course, the timing could not have been worse and the deal fell through. However, *The Hobbit* was eventually translated into German and published in 1957.

8   423 copies of the book in sheets were destroyed.

9   First published in *The Dublin Review* (432), January 1945.

10 J.R.R. Tolkien to Christopher Tolkien, 9 October 1945, quoted in *The Inklings*, p. 205.

Chapter 11: Entangled

1   W.H. Lewis's diary 12 November 1949, housed in the Wade Collection, Wheaton College, Wheaton, Illinois.

2   Tolkien to Sir Stanley Unwin, 24 February 1950, *Letters*, p. 136.

3   Tolkien despised the artwork produced for the cover of this book and protested about it vigorously. After much argument the artist, a young woman, Milein Cosman, was replaced with another illustrator named Pauline Baynes whose work was much more to Tolkien's liking.

4   Although nothing was said, it is quite possible that in the back of
    his mind Rayner Unwin also thought that by publishing *The Lord of
    the Rings* in three separate volumes he could halt the second and third
    volumes if *The Fellowship of the Ring* did even worse than they feared.
5   C.S. Lewis, Bodleian Library, Oxford, MS. Eng lett. C.220/5, fol.77.

Chapter 12: The World of Middle-earth

1   C.S. Lewis, *Time & Tide*, 14 August 1954.
2   *Manchester Guardian*, 20 August 1954.
3   Howard Spring, *Country Life*, 26 August 1954.
4   A.E. Cherryman, *Truth*, 6 August 1954.
5   *Oxford Times*, 13 August 1954.
6   Bernard Levin, *Truth*, 16 October 1955.
7   Peter Green, *Daily Telegraph*, 27 August 1954.
8   Edwin Muir, *Observer*, 22 August 1954.
9   W.H. Auden, *The New York Times Review of Books*, 10 October 1954.
10 Quoted in Pearce, *Tolkien. Man and Myth*, p. 129.
11 C.S. Lewis. *Time and Tide*, 22 October 1954.
12 Edwin Muir, *Observer*, 27 November 1955.
13 Edmund Wilson, *The Nation*, 14 April 1956.
14 Henry S. Resnick, *Niekas*, Volume 19, Number 43.
15 'The Man Who Understands Hobbits', Charlotte and Dennis
    Plimmer, *Daily Telegraph Magazine*, London, 22 March 1968. The
    letter, to a fan, was recently sold at auction in London for £4,800.
16 Kilby, *Tolkien and The Silmarillion*, p. 51. The hills referred to here are
    almost certainly the Chilterns.
17 Ibid, p. 52.
18 See Michael White, *Super Science*, Earthlight, Simon and Schuster,
    London, 1999, Chapter 12.
19 It is also interesting that Tolkien decided to name Númenorean
    kings using words that have a distinct Egyptian ring to them.
20 Some observers have even suggested that the Elven way-bread,
    Lembas, represents the Holy Sacrament.
21 For two other reasons, 25 March is a significant date in the
    Christian tradition. It is the *felix culpa*, the date of the Fall of

Adam and Eve and it is also the date of the Annunciation and the conception of Christ — precisely nine months before his birth on 25 December.

22 'The Quest Hero', Neil D. Isaacs and Rose A. Zimbardo (editors), *Tolkien and the Critics: Essays on Tolkien's 'The Lord of the Rings'*, University of Notre Dame Press, Notre Dame, 1968, p. 53.

23 Kilby, *Tolkien and The Silmarillion*, p. 59.

24 Quoted in Pearce, *Tolkien. Man and Myth*, p. 194.

25 *A Film Portrait of J.R.R. Tolkien*, Visual Corporation Ltd, 1992.

26 Ibid.

27 In Alida Becker (editor), *The Tolkien Scrapbook*, Running Press, Philadelphia, 1978, p. 26.

28 Paul H. Kocher, *Master of Middle Earth: The Fiction of J.R.R. Tolkien*, Houghton Mifflin, Boston, 1972, p. 26.

29 In Becker (editor), *The Tolkien Scrapbook*, p. 86.

30 *Independent*, London, 20 January 1997.

31 Tom Shippey, *J.R.R. Tolkien: Author of the Century*, HarperCollins, London, 2000, p. 170.

32 This is a particularly odd position to adopt bearing in mind that Tolkien had published his short story *Leaf By Niggle* which is clearly deliberately allegorical in nature.

33 Kilby, *Tolkien and The Silmarillion*, p. 31.

34 The most obvious examples of this are the many points of similarity to be found between *The Lord of the Rings* and Macdonald's *The Princess and the Curdie*. This is particularly poignant in the scene in *The Lord of the Rings* in which King Théoden is revitalised by Gandalf after Wormtongue has sent his monarch into a stupor. In *The Princess and the Curdie*, the king of Gwyntystorm is similarly restored to health.

35 It's interesting to note that in his book, *The Great Divorce*, published in 1946, Lewis quoted Macdonald as an epigraph.

36 Letter to Christopher Tolkien, 28 July 1944, *Letters*, p. 88.

37 *Mythprint*, the newsletter of the Mythopoeic Society, Altadena, USA, September 1973.

Chapter 13: The Final Years

1 Equivalent to about £35,000 today.

2 *Times Literary Supplement*, 3 September 1973.

3 There was one occasion when his displeasure was perfectly justified. A Ballantine paperback edition of *The Hobbit* published in
1965 in the United States carried artwork from an artist who, it
transpired, had not had time to read the book. The cover illustration consisted of a lion, two emus and a tree with bulbous fruit.
When a furious Tolkien queried what the artist was trying to
convey and in particular what the tree with the bulbous fruit might
be, he was told it was a Christmas tree.

4 Kilby, *Tolkien and The Silmarillion*, p. 16.

5 'The Man Who Understands Hobbits', Charlotte and Denis
Plimmer, *Daily Telegraph* magazine, London, 22 March 1968.

6 Kilby, *Tolkien and The Silmarillion*, p. 13.

7 In Mary Salu and Robert T. Farrell (editors), *J.R.R. Tolkien, Scholar
and Storyteller: Essays in Memoriam*, Cornell University Press, Ithaca
and London, 1979, pp. 33–4.

8 *The New Yorker*, 15 January 1966.

Chapter 14: The Legend Lives On

1 In Robert Giddings (editor), *J.R.R. Tolkien: This Far Land*, Vision and
Barnes and Noble, London, 1983, pp. 82–3.

2 'Dissension among the Judges', Philip Toynbee, *Observer*, 6 August
1961.

3 Walter Scheps, 'The Fairy-tale Morality of *The Lord of the Rings*', in
Jarad Lobdell (editor), *A Tolkien Compass*, Open Court, La Salle,
1975, pp. 43–56.

4 Michael Moorcock, *Wizardry and Wild Romance*, Victor Gollancz,
London, 1987, p. 125. John Goldthwaite, *The Natural History of
Make-Believe*, OUP, Oxford, 1996.

5 Susan Jeffreys, *Sunday Times*, 26 January 1997.

6 Professor Tom Shippey, *J.R.R. Tolkien: Author of the Century*,
HarperCollins, London, 2000. p. xxi.

7 *Sunday Times*, 26 January 1997.

8   *Sunday Times*, 26 January 1997.
9   Humphrey Carpenter (Tolkien's first biographer), *Independent*, 20 January 1997.
10 Germaine Greer, *W* magazine, Winter/Spring 1997.
11 The Danish edition published in 1977 was illustrated by Queen Margrethe II of Denmark.
12 Professor Tom Shippey, *A Film Portrait of J.R.R. Tolkien*, Visual Corporation Ltd, 1992.
13 'Hobbits go to Hollywood', Richard Brooks, *Sunday Times*, 13 May 2001.
14 'News from Middle-earth', *Starlog*, August 2001, p. 30.
15 Interview with the author.
16 'One Ring to Rule Them All', Gary Gillatt, *Dreamwatch*, August 2001, pp. 44–9.
17 'Hobbits take Revenge on America,' Tony Allen-Mills, *Sunday Times*, 1 July 2001.
18 Eleanor Ringel Gillespie, *Atlanta Journal and Constitution*, 18 December 2001.
19 Cosmos Landesman, *Sunday Times*, 'Culture', pp. 4–5, 16 December 2001.
20 John Anderson, *Newsday*, 19 December 2001.
21 C.G. Jung, *The Basic Writings* (edited by Violet de Laszo), Bollingen Series, Princeton University Press, Princeton, NJ, 1969.

A Chronology

1891	Tolkien's parents Mabel and Arthur marry in Cape Town.
1892	3 January. Ronald Tolkien born in Bloemfontein.
1894	17 February. Ronald's brother Hilary born in Bloemfontein.
1896	Tolkien's father dies in Bloemfontein (15 February) while Ronald, Hilary and Mabel are in England.
1896	Summer. Family move to Sarehole.
1900	Mabel Tolkien received into the Catholic Church. Family return to live in central Birmingham. Tolkien enters King Edward's School.
1901	22 January. Queen Victoria dies.
1901	Family move to King's Heath district of Birmingham.
1902	Family move to Oliver Road in the Edgbaston district of Birmingham. The boys leave King Edward's School and enrol at St Philip's Grammar School.
1903	Tolkien is awarded a scholarship for King Edward's and returns there in the autumn.

1904	November. Tolkien's mother dies from diabetes aged thirty-four.
1905	The brothers move to Aunt Beatrice's house.
1908	The brothers move to the Faulkners' house.
1909	Spring. Tolkien begins his romance with Edith Bratt. Autumn. Tolkien fails in his attempt to pass Oxbridge Entrance examination. Enforced separation from Edith.
1910	Autumn. Tolkien succeeds in his second attempt to pass the Oxbridge Entrance examination and is offered an Exhibition to Exeter College, Oxford.
1911	Summer. Visits Switzerland. October. Begins studies at Oxford.
1913	January. Reunited with Edith. Summer. After obtaining a Second Class for his Honour Moderations, Tolkien changes course to read English Language and Literature.
1914	January. Edith is received into the Catholic Church. The same month the couple become engaged to be married. 4 August. Britain declares war on Germany. October. Ronald returns to a near-empty University to resume his studies.
1915	Summer. Awarded First Class degree.
1916	22 March. Ronald and Edith are married in Warwick. 4 June. Ronald embarks for France with the British Army. 1 July. Battle of the Somme begins. 14 July. Tolkien first sees action at the front line. November. Shipped home with trench fever.
1917	16 November. First son John born.
1918	11 November. First World War ends. Later that month, Tolkien moves to Oxford with his family to begin working on *The New English Dictionary*.

1919	Tolkien begins giving private tuition to students. Family moves to Alfred Street.
1920	Tolkien accepts the position of Reader in English Language at Leeds University. October. Tolkien's second son Michael born. Christmas. First Father Christmas letter.
1922	Tolkien works with E.V. Gordon on an edition of *Sir Gawain and the Green Knight*
1924	October. Tolkien appointed Professor of English Language at Leeds University. November. Third son Christopher born.
1925	October. Tolkien is appointed Rawlinson and Bosworth Professor of Anglo-Saxon at Oxford University.
1925	Spring. Tolkien forms the Coalbiters. Summer. Becomes friends with C.S. Lewis.
1926	January. Family move into 22 Northmoor Road, Oxford. May. The General Strike.
1929	Tolkien's daughter Priscilla born.
1930	Tolkien family move from 22 to 20 Northmoor Road.
1930/1	Tolkien thought to have begun *The Hobbit*.
1933	The Inklings begin to meet.
1935	11 June. Tolkien's guardian Father Francis Morgan dies aged seventy-eight.
1937	September. *The Hobbit* is published in Britain. Late December. Tolkien begins to write *The Lord of the Rings*.
1938	Spring. *The Hobbit* published in America by Houghton Mifflin. Tolkien wins the *New York Herald Tribune* award.
1939	3 September. Britain declares war on Germany.
1942	C.S. Lewis's *The Screwtape Letters* is published.
1943	Tolkien writes *Leaf By Niggle*.

1945	7 May. The war in Europe ends.
	Fellow Inkling Charles Williams dies suddenly.
	Summer. Tolkien appointed Merton Professor of English Language and Literature at Oxford.
1947	March. The Tolkien family move to 3 Manor Road.
1949	Autumn. Tolkien completes *The Lord of the Rings*.
	Farmer Giles of Ham is published.
	December. Tolkien meets Milton Waldman of Collins publishing house.
1950	C.S. Lewis's *The Lion, the Witch and the Wardrobe* is published.
	The Tolkien family move to 99 Holywell Street.
	Wrangles over the manuscript of *The Lord of the Rings* begins.
1952	Autumn. George Allen and Unwin acquire *The Lord of the Rings*.
1953	Edith and Ronald move to 76 Sandfield Road, Headington.
1954	August. *The Fellowship of the Ring* is published.
	November. *The Two Towers* is published.
1955	October. *The Return of the King* is published.
1957	The original manuscripts of *The Hobbit* and *The Lord of the Rings* are sold to an American university.
1959	Tolkien retires from his professorship.
1962	Publication of *The Adventures of Tom Bombadil*.
1963	22 November. C.S. Lewis dies – the same day as President Kennedy and writer Aldous Huxley.
1965	August. Pirate edition of *The Lord of the Rings* is published in America by Ace Books. Late that year, Ballantine publish an official edition.
1966	Settlement reached with Ace Books and Tolkien is paid all royalties. Publicity generated by this makes *The Lord of the Rings* an international bestseller.

March. Edith and Ronald celebrate their Golden Wedding Anniversary in the gardens of Merton College.

1967   *Smith of Wootton Major* published.

1968   Edith and Ronald move to 19 Lakeside Road, Poole.

1971   29 November. Edith dies.

1972   March. Tolkien moves to a flat in Merton Street, Oxford. Spring. Awarded C.B.E. (Commander of the Order of the British Empire).
June. Made Honorary Doctor of Letters at Oxford University.

1973   2 September. Tolkien dies in Bournemouth.

1976   *The Father Christmas Letters* published.

1977   *The Silmarillion* published.

1979   *Pictures by J.R.R. Tolkien* published.

1982   *Mr Bliss* published.

1983–1996   *The History of Middle-earth* published in twelve volumes (edited by Christopher Tolkien).

1984   *Roverandom* published.

2001   Summer. *The Hobbit* and *The Lord of the Rings* appear in *The New York Times* bestseller list.
December. The first part of *The Lord of the Rings* film – *The Fellowship of the Ring* – released globally. (Parts II and III scheduled for 2002 and 2003 release).

2002   July. A first edition of *The Hobbit* sold at Sotherby's for just over £43,000.

Selective Bibliography

The non-academic published works of J.R.R. Tolkien.

The Hobbit: or There and Back Again, George Allen and Unwin, London, 1937.

Leaf By Niggle, First published in the *The Dublin Review*, January 1945. (Published, along with *On Fairy-Stories*, as *Tree and Leaf*, George Allen and Unwin, London, 1964.)

Farmer Giles of Ham, George Allen and Unwin, London, 1949.

The Fellowship of the Ring: being the First Part of The Lord of the Rings, George Allen and Unwin, London, 1954.

The Two Towers: being the Second Part of The Lord of the Rings, George Allen and Unwin, London, 1954.

The Return of the King: being the Third Part of The Lord of the Rings, George Allen and Unwin, London, 1955.

The Adventures of Tom Bombadil and other verses from the Red Book, George Allen and Unwin, London, 1962.

Poems 'Once Upon a Time' and 'The Dragon's Visit' in *Winter's Tales for Children: I*, edited by Caroline Hillier, Macmillan, London, 1965.

Smith of Wootton Major, George Allen and Unwin, London, 1967.

The Road Goes Ever On: A Song Cycle. Poems by J.R.R. Tolkien set to music by Donald Swann, George Allen and Unwin, London, 1967.

The Father Christmas Letters, edited by Baillie Tolkien, George Allen and Unwin, London, 1976.

The Silmarillion, edited by Christopher Tolkien, George Allen and Unwin, London, 1977.

Pictures by J.R.R Tolkien, foreword and notes by Christopher Tolkien, George Allen and Unwin, London, 1979.

Unfinished Tales of Númenor and Middle-earth, edited by Christopher Tolkien, George Allen and Unwin, London, 1980.

Mr Bliss, George Allen and Unwin, London, 1982.

The Monsters and the Critics and Other Essays, edited by Christopher Tolkien, George Allen and Unwin, London, 1983.

The History of Middle-earth. Twelve volumes, all edited by Christopher Tolkien.

I.   *The Book of Lost Tales, Part One*, George Allen and Unwin, London, 1983.

II.   *The Book of Lost Tales, Part Two*, George Allen and Unwin, London, 1984.

III.   *The Lays of Beleriand*, George Allen and Unwin, London, 1985.

IV.   *The Shaping of Middle-earth: The Quenta, the Ambarkanta, and the Annals*, George Allen and Unwin, London, 1986.

V.   *The Lost Road and other Writings*, Unwin Hyman, London, 1987.

VI.   *The Return of the Shadow*, Unwin Hyman, London, 1988.

VII.   *The Treason of Isengard*, Unwin Hyman, London, 1989.

VIII.   *The War of the Ring*, Unwin Hyman, London, 1990.

IX.   *Sauron Defeated: The End of the Third Age, the Notion Club Papers and the Drowning of Anadune*, HarperCollins, London, 1992.

X.   *Morgoth's Ring: The Later Silmarillion, Part One*, HarperCollins, London, 1993.

XI.   *The War of the Jewels: The Later Silmarillion, Part Two*, HarperCollins, London, 1994.

XII.   *The Peoples of Middle-earth*, HarperCollins, London, 1996.

Books about J.R.R Tolkien and Middle-earth.

Anderson, Douglas A. (editor), *The Annotated Hobbit*, Unwin and Hyman, London, 1988.

Becker, Alida (editor), *The Tolkien Scrapbook*, Running Press, Philadelphia, USA, 1978.

Blackwelder, Richard A., *A Tolkien Thesaurus*, Garland, New York and London, 1990.

Bodleian Library, *J.R.R. Tolkien: Life and Legend. An Exhibition to Commemorate the Centenary of the Birth of J.R.R. Tolkien*, The Bodleian Library, Oxford, 1992.

Carpenter, Humphrey, *J.R.R. Tolkien: A Biography*, George Allen and Unwin, London, 1977.

Carpenter, Humphrey, *The Inklings: C.S. Lewis, J.R.R. Tolkien, Charles Williams and their Friends*, George Allen and Unwin, London, 1978.

Carpenter, Humphrey (editor, with the assistance of Christopher Tolkien), *The Letters of J.R.R. Tolkien*, George Allen and Unwin, London, 1981.

Carter, Lin, *Tolkien: A Look Behind The Lord of the Rings*, Ballantine Books, New York, USA, 1969.

Cunningham, Valentine, *British Writers of the Thirties*, OUP, Oxford, 1988.

Curry, Patrick, *Defending Middle-Earth, Tolkien: Myth and Modernity*, HarperCollins, London, 1997.

Flieger, Verlyn, *Splintered Light: Logos and Language in Tolkien's World*, William B. Eerdmans, Grand Rapids, Michigan, USA, 1983.

Foster, Robert, *The Complete Guide to Middle-earth: From The Hobbit to The Silmarillion*, Ballantine Books, New York, 1978.

George, Clark and Timmons, Dan (editors), *J.R.R. Tolkien and his Literary Resonances: Views of Middle-earth*, Greenwood Press, London, 2000.

Giddings, Robert (editor), *J.R.R. Tolkien: This Far Land*, Vision and Barnes and Noble, London, 1983.

Hammond, Wayne, *J.R.R Tolkien, Artist and Illustrator*, HarperCollins, London, 1995.

Helms, Randel, *Tolkien's World*, Thames and Hudson, London, 1974.

Isaacs, Neil D. and Zimbardo, Rose A. (editors), *Tolkien and the Critics: Essays on J.R.R. Tolkien's The Lord of the Rings*, University of Notre Dame Press, Notre Dame and London, 1968.

Johnson, Judith A. (editor), *J.R.R. Tolkien: Six Decades of Criticism*, Greenwood, London, 1986.

Kilby, Clyde, *Tolkien and The Silmarillion*, Harold Shaw Publishers, USA, 1976.

Kocher, Paul H., *Master of Middle-earth: The Fiction of J.R.R. Tolkien*, Houghton Mifflin, Boston, USA, 1972.

Lobdell, Jarad (editor), *Guide to the Names in The Lord of the Rings, A Tolkien Compass*, Open Court, La Salle, Illinois, USA, 1975.

Moseley, Charles, *J.R.R. Tolkien*, Northcote House Publishers, Plymouth, England, 1997.

Pearce, Joseph, *Tolkien. Man and Myth: A Literary Life*, HarperCollins, London, 1998.

Rosebury, Brian, *Tolkien: A Critical Assessment*, St Martin's Press, London, 1992.

Salu, Mary and Farrell, Robert T. (editors), *J.R.R. Tolkien, Scholar and Storyteller: Essays in Memoriam*, Cornell University Press, Ithaca, USA and London, 1979.

Shippey, Tom, *The Road to Middle-earth*, George Allen and Unwin, London, 1982.

Shippey, Tom, *J.R.R. Tolkien: Author of the Century*, HarperCollins, London, 2000.

Tyler, J.E.A *The Tolkien Companion*, Pan, London, 1977.

Wynn Fonstad, Karen, *The Atlas of Middle-earth*, HarperCollins, London,1994.

Other References.

Gibb, Jocelyn (editor, with contributions by Owen Barfield and others), *Light on C.S. Lewis*, Geoffrey Bles, London, 1965.

Green, Roger Lancelyn and Hooper, Walter, *C.S. Lewis: A Biography*, Collins, London, 1974.

Hooper, Walter (editor), *Of Other Worlds: Essays and Stories*, Geoffrey Bles, London, 1966.

Hooper, Walter, *C.S. Lewis: A Companion and Guide*, HarperCollins, London, 1996.

Lewis, C.S., *The Pilgrim's Regress: An Allegorical Apology for Christianity, Reason and Romanticism*, J.M. Dent, London, 1933.

Lewis, C.S., *The Allegory of Love: A Study in Medieval Tradition*, Clarendon Press, Oxford, 1936.

Lewis, C.S., *Out of the Silent Planet*, The Bodley Head, London, 1938.

Lewis, C.S., *The Screwtape Letters*, Geoffrey Bles, London, 1942.

Lewis, C.S., *Perelandra* (Also known as *Voyage to Venus*), The Bodley Head, London, 1943.

Lewis, C.S., *That Hideous Strength*, The Bodley Head, London, 1945.

Lewis, C.S., *The Great Divorce*, Geoffrey Bles, London,1946.

Lewis, C.S., *The Lion the Witch and the Wardrobe*, Geoffrey Bles, London, 1950.

Lewis, W.H. (edited and with an introduction by), *Letters of C.S Lewis*, Geoffrey Bles, London, 1966.

Williams, Charles, *All Hallows' Eve*, Faber and Faber, London,1945.

Websites.

Typing in TOLKIEN or LORD OF THE RINGS generates something in the region of half a million websites. Here are a sample of some of the more useful and entertaining ones.

The Tolkien Society may be found at http://www.tolkiensociety.org They are the original and official 'fan-club' and possess a great resource of Tolkien material.

You may also find the **Hypertextualized Tolkien FAQ** useful at http://www.daimi.au.dk/~bouvin/tolkienfaq.html

The Tolkien Network may be found at http://www.tolkien.nu and there are many others that link with this. There are also thousands of sites dedicated to every aspect of the film. These include: http://www.theonering.net, http://www.lordoftheringsmovie.com and http://thelordoftherings.com

Miscellaneous.

Anyone interested in Tolkien's life in Oxford and finding themselves in the city during the summer should afford themselves of the Inklings' Tour. This takes 90 minutes and starts each Wednesday at 11 a.m. outside Blackwell's Bookstore in Broad Street, Oxford.

Index

As the whole book is about JRR Tolkien, only personal items have been entered under his name. JRR is used as a sub-heading under his wife Edith's entry.